The Occupation of Justice

SUNY series in Israeli Studies

THE OCCUPATION OF JUSTICE

*The Supreme Court of Israel
and the Occupied Territories*

DAVID KRETZMER

STATE UNIVERSITY OF NEW YORK PRESS

Published by
STATE UNIVERSITY OF NEW YORK PRESS
ALBANY

© 2002 State University of New York

For information, address
State University of New York Press,
90 State Street, Suite 700, Albany, NY 12207

Production, Kelli Williams
Marketing, Patrick Durocher

Library of Congress Cataloging-in-Publication Data

Kretzmer, David, 1963–
    The occupation of justice : the Supreme Court of Israel and the Occupied Territories /
David Kretzmer.
        p. cm. — (SUNY series in Israeli studies)
    Includes bibliographical references and index.
    ISBN 0-7914-5337-5 (alk. paper) — ISBN 0-7914-5338-3 (pbk. : alk. paper)
      1. Israel. Bet ha-mishpaò ha-gavoha le-tsedeò. 2. Courts of last resort—Israel. 3.
Political questions and judicial power—Israel. 4. Civil rights—Israel. 5.
Jurisdiction—Israel. 6. Military government—West Bank. 7. Military government—Gaza
Strip. I. Title. II. Series.

KMK3466 .K74 2002
347.5694'035—dc21
                                                                                      2002017628

10 9 8 7 6 5 4 3 2 1

In memory of Marcia,
1943–1993

CONTENTS

PART III

PREFACE

The idea of a general study on the jurisprudence of the Supreme Court of Israel relating to the Occupied Territories first came to me ten years ago, at a time when Israel still maintained full control over the West Bank and Gaza. The Court was inundated at the time with petitions challenging measures adopted by the military authorities in their attempt to contain the Palestinian uprising, known as the *Intifada*. Much has changed since then. Israel and the PLO signed the Oslo Declaration of Principles and subsequent agreements. Parts of the Occupied Territories were transferred to the control of the Palestinian Authority. Negotiations have been continuing in an attempt to find a settlement to the long-standing conflict between Israel and the Palestinians, which will bring an end to occupation of the West Bank and Gaza. In September 2000 violence erupted and developed into a second uprising, now known as the *al-Aqsa Intifada*. At the time of writing both this *Intifada* and negotiations between the parties continue.

Following the Declaration of Principles and subsequent agreements, the transferal of powers to the Palestinian Authority, and the commitment of the parties to negotiate a final agreement, many people imagined (somewhat naively, it would seem) that the end of the occupation was in sight. Events since September 2000 have shown that this assessment was premature. So was the assumption that the Court's jurisprudence on the Occupied Territories would soon become an interesting, but completed, chapter in the Court's history. It now appears that this chapter will remain open for some time, although political and military developments will lead to changes in the type of cases brought before the Court.

Since the beginning of the *al-Aqsa Intifada* numerous petitions have been submitted to the Supreme Court challenging actions of the military on the West Bank and in Gaza. The Court has yet to rule on many of these petitions. Thus the study does not include judgments delivered after the beginning of the *al-Aqsa Intifada*.

In preparing this book I received help, advice and encouragement from many research assistants, friends and colleagues. I cannot possibly mention them all. I would, however, like to express my thanks and appreciation to a few people. Ruth Gavison encouraged me throughout the long project. Her friendship and support over the years have meant more than she can imagine. The innumerable discussions with her on the topics discussed here played a major role in helping me to crystallize my thoughts. Pnina Lahav, a friend of many years, offered me essential advice and warm encouragement at various stages. Her comments were, as always, insightful and thought-provoking. Special thanks to Dana Alexander, Ilan Saban, Orit Kamir, Maya Steinitz, Meryl Weissmann, and Or Tamir for their help and comments. I am also grateful to the Ford Foundation, who provided support for the research, and to the former director of their Middle East Program, Steve Riskin, who gave me the initial push. Nita Shechet and Sally Oren helped in editing the final text. Their work was much appreciated.

Finally, a special word of thanks to my mother, Yoel, Hava, Yonatan Yaakov, Vered, and Guy for their patience and love.

Jerusalem
February 2001

INTRODUCTION

The Supreme Court of Israel began reviewing actions of military authorities in the West Bank and Gaza soon after the Israel Defense Forces (IDF) occupied them in the 1967 Six-Day War. In subsequent years this review became a central feature of Israel's legal and political control over these territories. The Court has handed down hundreds of decisions covering a wide scope of actions in the Occupied Territories, ranging from establishment of civilian settlements, changes in local law, and building of highways to deportations, house demolitions, and administrative detention.

The Supreme Court's decisions relating to the Occupied Territories constitute a unique body of jurisprudence on the international law of belligerent occupation. However, it is not only the doctrinal side of this jurisprudence that is of interest. Entry into the arena of occupation created the potential of dissonance between the Court's regular jurisprudence and its jurisprudence of occupation. It also raised questions about judicial decision-making in a highly charged conflict situation, and the way courts handle the inherent tension between security arguments and individual rights in such a situation.

Judicial review has frequently been mentioned in response to criticism of government actions in the Occupied Territories. In a book published by the Israel Section of the International Commission of Jurists in 1981, the writers state that "the ability of residents of the administered areas to petition the Israeli High Court of Justice does more than anything else to guarantee the maintenance of the rule of law."[1]

Writing twelve years later, lawyers in the Military Advocate-General's Unit of the IDF declared:

This judicial review by Israel's highest Court has not only provided a form of redress for the grievances of Area inhabitants and a safeguard for their rights; it has also provided a powerful symbol and reminder to the officials of the Military Government and Civil Administration of the supremacy of law and legal institutions and of the omnipresence of the Rule of Law wherever Israeli officials' writ may run.[2]

The perception of judicial review as a guarantee of the rule of law rests, first and foremost, on the enormous prestige the Supreme Court enjoys both in Israel and among members of the legal and judicial professions in other countries. It is bolstered by the lack of precedent for review by domestic courts over acts of military authorities in occupied territory. Cases in which the Court has interfered in decisions of the authorities, such as the *Elon Moreh*, *Jerusalem Electricity Corporation*, *ACRI*, and *Morcous* cases,[3] are also cited as evidence of legal constraints placed on authorities through the mechanism of judicial review.[4]

At times members of the defense and military establishment and some right-wing politicians have displayed an antagonistic attitude to the Court that reinforces the "rule of law perception." They have claimed that judicial review hampers the effectiveness of measures adopted to maintain order, thereby impairing the military's efforts to control the local population. Perhaps the bluntest expression of this view was presented by the late prime minister and minister of defense, Yitzchak Rabin, in explaining why he had agreed to hand over control of Gaza to the PLO. Rabin stated: "I hope that we will find a partner which will be responsible in Gaza for the internal Palestinian problems. It will deal with Gaza without the problems of the High Court of Justice, without the problems of *B'Tselem* and without the problems of all kinds of sensitive souls and all kinds of mothers and fathers."[5]

Actually, the Court has interfered infrequently in decisions of the military. The negative attitude of critics stems mainly from the notion that mere accountability of the military to an outside body undermines its authority, that delays caused by judicial review reduce the deterrent effect of some measures (such as deportations and house demolitions), and that pressure by judges or even the threat of judicial review have often forced authorities to back down from proposed action.

From a radically different perspective, it may be argued that the main function of the Court has been to legitimize government actions in the Territories. By clothing acts of military authorities in a cloak of legality, the Court justifies and rationalizes these acts. Even if this has not produced legitimization in the eyes of residents of the Occupied Territories themselves, it has done so both for the Israeli public, in whose name the military authorities are acting, and for foreign observers sympathetic to Israel's basic position. The main evidence in support of this view is that in almost all of its judgments relating to the Occupied Territories, especially those dealing with questions of principle, the Court has decided in favor of the authorities, often on the basis of dubious legal arguments. It is indeed true that in a few cases the Court has decided against the authorities. However, these "landmark cases" serve only to enhance the legitimizing function of the court by reinforcing the "image of the court as an impartial body which boldly challenge[s] the government in pursuit of justice."[6]

It has long been accepted that judicial review of governmental action "has two prime functions—that of imprinting governmental action with the stamp of legitimacy, and that of checking the political branches of government."[7] Judicial review by the Supreme Court over actions of authorities in the Occupied Territories has fulfilled both of these functions. It remains to inquire which function has been dominant.

The jurisprudence of the Court, on which this book focuses, cannot alone provide a full answer to this question, since the Court may have a restraining influence on the authorities even when not passing judgment against them. In many cases the authorities have stepped down from a proposed action following remarks made by the judges during the hearing or acted on a recommendation in the judgment. Thus, for example, in one early case, which related to the refusal of the authorities to allow use of the name "Palestine Bank," the negative reaction of the judges during the preliminary hearing prompted the authorities to withdraw their objection to use of the name.[8] In another case, the authorities implemented the Court's recommendation to establish a court of appeal against decisions of the military courts, even though the Court had rejected the argument that the authorities were legally obliged to establish such a court.[9] More important, many cases relating to the Occupied Territories are settled out of court, in what I shall term the "Court's shadow." There is a significant disparity between the chances of residents of the Occupied Territories succeeding in obtaining a favorable judicial decision and their chances of obtaining an out-of-court remedy.[10] I shall return to the implications of this disparity when discussing the function of review in the concluding chapter.

The Supreme Court's approach in decisions relating to the Occupied Territories must be examined in light of two factors:

1. the political background of the occupation of the West Bank and Gaza, and the way that occupation was, and still is, perceived by the vast majority of Israelis;
2. the nature of the Supreme Court of Israel, its position in the Israeli political system and its general record in matters relating to judicial review of governmental action.

THE OCCUPATION: BACKGROUND

Origins

The 1967 War was a watershed event in the history of the State of Israel. In the course of this war the Jewish state occupied territories previously held by the surrounding Arab states: Egypt, Jordan, and Syria. In order to apprehend the political environment in which the Supreme Court of Israel operated when it first entertained petitions relating to the West Bank and Gaza, it is important to understand the background to the occupation of these territories by Israel.[11]

On 15 May 1967 Egypt reinforced its infantry and armored forces in Sinai on Israel's southern border. The following day, Egyptian President Gemal Abdul Nasser demanded of United Nations Secretary-General, U Thant, that the UN withdraw its Emergency Force placed on the Israel-Egypt border in the wake of Israel's withdrawal from Sinai, which it had captured during the 1956 Sinai Campaign. On the same day two Egyptian armored divisions were sent into Sinai as reinforcement for the 70,000 Egyptian soldiers and members of the Palestinian Liberation Army already there. A few days later, Egypt imposed a blockade on the passage of Israeli ships through the Straits of Tiran, and on 30 May it signed a defense pact with Jordan. All these steps were accompanied by constant declarations by Nasser and the Arab press about the pending war that would lead to Israel's destruction.

Israeli intelligence assessments had not foreseen imminent war, and the Egyptian moves took Israel's political leaders by surprise. The general consensus among Israel's political leadership was that diplomatic steps should be taken to find a political solution to the crisis. As the crisis deepened, especially after the blockade of the Straits of Tiran, there was a growing fear among almost all the political parties represented in the *Knesset* and the general public that Israel's very existence was threatened and that if a political solution were not found, military force would have to be used to meet the threat.

During the period between 15 May and the outbreak of war on 5 June (known in Israel as the waiting period), the government strengthened the armed forces by calling up the reserves while seeking a political solution to the crisis, first and foremost by international action to lift the blockade on Israeli shipping. At the same time, public pressure mounted to broaden the government by incorporating members of the main opposition bloc, GAHAL, as well as by appointing General Moshe Dayan minister of defense, a position then held by Prime Minister Levi Eshkol.[12]

The diplomatic talks bore little fruit. Despite international resolutions in favor of free shipping and a specific guarantee given by the

United States to Israel regarding freedom of shipping in the Straits of Tiran and the Suez Canal, the United States, Britain, and France were not prepared to take effective measures to lift the blockade or reduce the threat to Israel, while the USSR was openly hostile to Israel and supportive of the Arab countries. The government decision of 4 June 1967 to take military action to meet the threat on the Egyptian border enjoyed wide public and political support. In the *Knesset* debate that took place on the day the war started, all parties supported the government's policy, with the sole exception of the pro-Moscow New Communist List.

With the benefit of hindsight it is now possible to analyze wider historical factors that led to the 1967 crisis.[13] It may be questioned whether President Nasser really intended going to war. Yet there can be little doubt that at the time the military leadership, the main political parties, and virtually the entire Jewish public in Israel perceived the situation as one that imposed an existential threat to the State of Israel. Its borders, set by Armistice Agreements signed in 1949 with the surrounding countries, left the country vulnerable to attack. Israel is minute in size (at some points the distance between the Armistice Line with Jordan and the Mediterranean Sea was less than 10 kilometers), and there was a genuine fear that if it did not act, it would be attacked simultaneously on a number of fronts, which could lead to a catastrophe.[14]

The initial aim of military action in 1967 was the removal of the threat to the State of Israel that had been posed by massing Egyptian forces in Sinai, removal of the UN Emergency Force, and the blockade on Israeli shipping in the Straits of Tiran. After the start of war, further aims developed that had neither been part of the original plan of action, nor defined in advance by the Cabinet. In the days preceding the war a message was sent to King Hussein of Jordan, promising that if Jordan refrained from military action against Israel in the event of hostilities between Israel and Egypt, Israel would not attack Jordan. Nevertheless, after Israel's preemptive strike against Egyptian forces in Sinai, Jordanian artillery began firing on West Jerusalem. Another urgent message was sent to King Hussein calling on him to cease fire, but the artillery fire continued. After Jordanian forces occupied Government House, headquarters of the UN in the Middle East located on a hill in the southern part of Jerusalem, the order was given to mount a counterattack, and full-scale war ensued on the eastern front. Although there had been no initial plan to capture the whole of Jerusalem and the West Bank, once war started it had a dynamic of its own. Within two days, Israeli forces had taken the Old City of Jerusalem and occupied the whole of the West Bank. At the same time, Israeli forces in the south took the Gaza Strip and the whole of the Sinai Peninsula. Thus began the occupation.

The political leadership of Israel was not prepared, institutionally or psychologically, for deciding on the future of the territories occupied during the war. Nevertheless, decisions had to be made. No sooner had the fighting subsided than discussions began in a number of political forums on policy toward the Occupied Territories. The initial attitude was first and foremost a function of the tremendous feeling of relief that swept the public and the political leadership after the war. Decision-makers were determined that the country should never again be placed in such a vulnerable situation. The territories occupied during the course of the war were regarded primarily as a lever with which to improve, if not resolve, Israel's pressing security needs.

When domestic political discussions commenced, it became apparent that there was virtually total consensus that all territories taken should be retained until peace agreements with neighboring countries were negotiated. Divergent views within the Cabinet emerged regarding the future status of the West Bank and Gaza. While occupying the West Bank had not been an initial war aim, circles that believed the Jewish state should have control over the whole of the historical Land of Israel west of the Jordan River had always existed. They now regarded what had happened as an historic opportunity to realize their aims. Within a short time, voices were heard claiming that the Territories had not been occupied, but that parts of the homeland had been liberated from foreign occupation.

Less than two weeks after the war ended, the Cabinet Committee on Security began deliberations on government policy toward the Territories, followed by discussions in the full Cabinet. These discussions culminated in a formal resolution on those matters on which it was possible to reach consensus in the National Unity Government. According to this resolution, which remained secret, Israel would be prepared to offer peace treaties to Egypt and Syria, based on the international border between those countries and Palestine at the time of the British Mandate. While Gaza, which had been under Egyptian military rule since 1948, would remain in Israeli hands, no mention was made of the future of the West Bank.

On one question relating to the West Bank there was wide consensus: the future of Jerusalem. Within days of the capture of the Old City, the Cabinet decided on immediate action to annex the eastern part of the City, including the Old City.[15] At the government's initiative the *Knesset* enacted an amendment to the Law and Government Ordinance. This amendment stated that the law, jurisdiction, and administration of the state would apply to any part of the Land of Israel designated by the government. The government subsequently published a decree in the Official Gazette applying the state's law, jurisdiction, and administration in East Jerusalem.[16]

Divergence of opinion among Cabinet members regarding the future of the West Bank was not tempered by time. Some favored negotiating an agreement with local representatives of Palestinian residents; others thought that an agreement should be sought with Jordan. A further school of thought maintained that Israel should retain permanent control over all parts of the Land of Israel and that the law, jurisdiction, and administration of the state should eventually be applied throughout the whole of the West Bank and in Gaza. Prime Minister Eshkol was not a charismatic or strong leader, and he was unable to create a decision-making body that could set government policy on this matter. The result was a decision not to decide. Policy thus came to be determined by events and steps taken by those entrusted with the day-to-day administration of the Occupied Territories. This initial lack of decision was facilitated by the position of the Arab states at the Khartoum Conference in August 1967 that there would be no recognition of Israel, no direct negotiations, and no peace treaty.

The Israeli perception of the background to the occupation of the West Bank and Gaza had a decisive influence on the way the vast majority of Jews in Israel perceived the occupation itself. Most Israeli Jews shared the conviction that the pre-1967 borders made Israel's security highly vulnerable, and that territories captured in a war of self-defense should not be surrendered without reduction of that vulnerability by a political settlement.

Over the years some of the government's policies in the Occupied Territories (especially the establishment of civilian settlements) became highly controversial in Israel and attracted harsh international criticism. However, controversy over specific policies did not have a major impact on the fundamental attitude of most Jewish Israelis to the continuation of the occupation. It was still regarded as axiomatic that Israeli control should be maintained over the Territories until such time as a political settlement would be reached. Although there was a divergence of opinion on the way to promote such a political settlement, Israelis who believed in unilateral withdrawal were only to be found on the fringes of the political arena.

Stages

There have been several distinct stages in the occupation that began in 1967. Changes in the political and security situation affected both the willingness of Palestinian residents to petition the Supreme Court of Israel and the type of cases that reached the Supreme Court.[17]

During the first period of occupation, from 1967 until the early 1970s, Israel established and reinforced its control over the Territories.

Palestinian residents were allowed to manage their own affairs, but all forms of opposition to Israeli rule were crushed. In the immediate aftermath of the war there was some armed resistance against Israeli forces and Israeli targets by Palestinian groups such as *Fatah*. Palestinians considered to have supported or assisted such groups were punished by deportations, house demolitions, and other punitive measures.

By the early 1970s armed opposition against Israel within the Territories had largely been contained. While there were strong forces within the Israeli political system that favored maintaining permanent control over the West Bank and Gaza, the Labor Party, the leading party in the government, still regarded the occupation as a temporary situation that would eventually end with a political settlement under which Israel would relinquish control over most of the areas, especially those that were densely populated by Palestinians. Some Israeli settlements were established on the West Bank, especially in the Jordan valley and in the area surrounding Jerusalem. With the exception of Kiryat Arba, a settlement established on the outskirts of Hebron, the government did not allow establishment of settlements in the vicinity of Palestinian towns on the West Bank.

During the first decade of occupation some attempts were made to challenge actions of the military before the Supreme Court of Israel, and some important decisions were handed down. However, petitions to the Court by residents of the Occupied Territories were few and far between. There were probably a number of reasons for this: reluctance on the part of Palestinians to grant legitimacy to Israeli institutions, lack of familiarity with the Israeli system, and lack of involvement of Israeli political forces and lawyers who could both encourage Palestinians to seek redress in Israeli courts and provide the necessary legal assistance.

A radical change in government policy came about after the 1977 elections in Israel, in which Menachem Begin, leader of the right-wing Herut party, came to power. The Herut party was committed to retaining Israeli control, and eventually extending Israeli sovereignty over the West Bank and Gaza. In order to make separation of the Occupied Territories from Israel politically unfeasible, Mr. Begin's government actively promoted establishment of civilian settlements in all parts of the Occupied Territories.

In the period soon after the Begin government came to power, petitioning the Supreme Court in an effort to curb government actions in the Territories began to gain wide acceptance. The success of the petitioners in the famous *Elon Moreh* case may well have been a factor that spurred lawyers representing Palestinians to turn to the Court in attempts to challenge other government actions, such as house demolitions. Other factors were probably the involvement both of foreign NGO's committed to protecting Palestinian rights and of Israeli political groups opposed to the settlement policy of the Begin government, and the growth in Israel of NGOs committed to using the legal system to protect human rights.

The beginning of the *Intifada* (the Palestinian uprising) in December 1987 was the start of a new stage in the occupation. The military authorities responded to the *Intifada* with harsh measures, which included wide-scale administrative detentions, demolition of houses, curfews, and closure of Palestinian institutions. During this period, hundreds of petitions were submitted to the Supreme Court, generally challenging the legality of security measures. Many of these petitions were submitted by Israeli lawyers, both Jewish and Arab, opposed to the occupation, or by lawyers of Israeli human-rights NGOs.

The *Intifada* led to a change in attitudes toward continued control over the Territories among part of the Israeli public, especially the political and professional elites. Realization that the occupation was exacting an unacceptable moral and political price from the country prompted the political leadership to seek a political settlement that would free it from the yolk of occupation. The result was the Oslo Declaration of Principles and subsequent agreements. Under these agreements between Israel and the PLO, Israel relinquished effective control over most of Gaza and the towns in the West Bank to the Palestinian Authority. The majority of Palestinians in Gaza and the West Bank are no longer under direct control of Israeli authorities, although Israel's actions and policies still have an enormous impact on their lives. Israeli settlements remain in the Territories. Israel retains control over large areas of the West Bank and imposes severe restrictions on movement of Palestinians. It also retains indirect control over many facets of life within the areas controlled by the Palestinian Authority.[18]

Petitions submitted to the Supreme Court since the Oslo agreements have related largely to questions of residence and family unification, interrogations by the security authorities, building access roads to settlements, administrative detention, and house demolitions.[19]

THE SUPREME COURT—A PROFILE

Composition

The Supreme Court, the highest judicial tribunal in Israel, is composed of fourteen justices who sit in benches of three or more. From the Court's establishment in 1948 until the middle to late 1970s, all the justices had been educated outside Israel, generally in central Europe. With two notable exceptions, the leading justices of the generation still on the bench in the 1960s and 1970s had come to the Supreme Court after serving on lower courts.[20] They had not held public office before appointment to the bench, nor had they been involved in setting government policies in matters that were later to come before them in their judicial capacities.

Since the middle-to-late 1970s, justices of the older generation have gradually retired and been replaced by justices whose background and judicial outlook are quite different. In the first place, most justices of the new generation received their education in pre-independence Palestine or post-independence Israel. While the majority of justices were appointed after serving in lower courts, the dominant justices in recent years had no previous judicial experience before being appointed. More saliently, the two most dominant judges were appointed after serving in government office. The president of the Court from 1984 until 1995, Justice Meir Shamgar, was appointed in 1975 after serving for seven years as attorney-general, before which he had served as Military Advocate-General, a post he held at the time of the Six-Day War in 1967. In the latter capacity he had been responsible for establishing the legal framework for Israeli military rule over the territories that were taken by the IDF in the course of that war. The current president of the Court, Justice Aharon Barak, was dean of the Faculty of Law at the Hebrew University of Jerusalem when he was appointed to succeed Meir Shamgar as attorney-general. After a three-year term in that post he was appointed to the Supreme Court in 1978. He succeeded Justice Shamgar as president of the Court in 1995.

Functions

The Supreme Court fulfills two major functions. It serves as a court of appeal against decisions of the district courts, and it acts as a High Court of Justice. It is mainly in the latter role that the Court has achieved prominence in the Israeli political system, and it is in this role that it exercises review over actions of the authorities in the Occupied Territories.

The notion of a "High Court of Justice" is a remnant of the British Mandatory period of rule over the country. Under British Mandatory legislation the Supreme Court was given the jurisdiction to issue prerogative writs against government agencies, similar to those issued by the High Court of Justice in England.[21] When the independent State of Israel was founded, most British Mandatory legislation was left intact, including the legislation relating to the composition and jurisdiction of the courts. Thus it was that the Supreme Court retained its dual function as the final court of appeal and as a court of first, and last, instance in petitions to the "High Court of Justice." An Israeli statute, the Courts Law, 1957, which replaced the British Mandatory legislation, maintained the existing structure.

Over the years factors connected to the colonial nature of the British regime in Palestine, or to terminology connected with the English legal system, later changed and became associated with constitutional principles in the independent State of Israel. First, direct access to the highest court in the land in petitions for review of governmental action has become a fundamental feature of the constitutional system. Despite the Supreme Court's heavy load, this system has been retained, although in recent years review over certain defined matters has been transferred to the district courts. Second, while the term "court of justice" means no more than a court of law and has no connection to substantive notions of justice, the term was translated into Hebrew as *"beit mishpat latzedek,"* which means a law court of justice. Similarly, the English term "administration of justice," which refers to administration of bodies associated with application of law (i.e. courts and tribunals), became, in Hebrew, connected with remedies necessary for the sake of justice.[22]

The jurisdiction of the Court, as a High Court of Justice, is at present defined in section 15 of the Basic Law: Judiciary. Under section 15(c) of this law, the Court has the power to deal "with matters in which it sees need to grant a remedy for the sake of justice and which are not within the jurisdiction of another court or tribunal." According to section 15(d)(2) the Court has the power "to grant orders to state authorities, local authorities, their officials and other bodies and persons fulfilling public functions under law, to do an act or to refrain from doing an act in lawfully performing their duties." Jurisdiction over "bodies and persons fulfilling public functions under law" has provided the legal basis for expansion by the Court of its review in various spheres.[23]

Judicial Independence

A special Judges' Selection Committee selects all judges in Israel, including justices of the Supreme Court. This committee is composed of two Cabinet ministers (the minister of justice and one other minister, appointed by the Cabinet), two *Knesset* members elected by the *Knesset*, two members of the Israel Bar, the president of the Supreme Court, and two other justices of that court elected by their peers. The philosophy behind the composition of the committee is that, while it should be representative of the Israeli public (hence the inclusion of four politicians), professional nonpoliticians should be in the majority.

All judges are appointed to serve until the mandatory retirement age of seventy. They may not be removed from their posts unless a disciplinary court of their peers convicts them of a disciplinary offence or the

Selection Committee, by a majority of at least seven of its nine members, decides to remove them from their post. Judges' salaries are set by parliamentary committee decision. No decision may be made to reduce judges' salaries alone.

These strong institutional arrangements for protection of judicial independence place serious constraints on attempts to appoint judges who will take a pro-government position, to pressure judges to toe a political line, or to decide cases in a manner convenient for the government. In the absence of a formal constitution, the *Knesset* does indeed have power to amend the provisions that protect judicial independence. However, as the institutional arrangements reflect the ethos of the Israeli political system, it is highly unlikely that an overt move would be made to violate judicial independence. On the other hand, the jurisdiction of the Court is also defined in a *Knesset* statute, and it is not inconceivable that the *Knesset* could react to an over-activist court by redefining its jurisdiction.[24] It is precisely a threat of this nature that was raised in some quarters following the *Elon Moreh* case, the controversial decision in which the Court ruled that requisition of land for a Jewish settlement in the Occupied Territories had been illegal and that the land should be returned to its Arab owners.[25] Similar suggestions were raised as a reaction to the perception that review of deportation orders was holding up deportations. In summary, the chance of the government reacting to decisions of the Supreme Court that it finds politically unacceptable by initiating legislation to curb the institutional independence of the judiciary is negligible; the chance of it initiating legislation that would alter the Court's jurisdiction cannot be ruled out.

Public Opinion

A fairly recent study confirms that the Supreme Court enjoys a high degree of legitimacy, expressed in public support that cuts across different sections of the population.[26] This firm public standing of the Court is retained even when its decisions do not reflect social or political consensus. Alongside the state comptroller, the Supreme Court is the civilian state institution that enjoys the widest public support. Its prestige is almost equal to that of the IDF.

Although support for the Court as an institution is high, the degree of public support for specific decisions is a function of the subject matter of those decisions. As the authors of the previously mentioned study have put it:

> the more the declared matter of the High Court decision involves imposing civilian supervision over the security authorities, the more the support for the Court diminishes and reservation increases. This is

especially the case when the declared matter involves imposing civilian judicial review over the activities of the security authorities and the army in the territories.[27]

A small majority of the public supports access to the Supreme Court by Palestinians who claim to be the victims of injustice. There appears to be a strong correlation between support for the jurisdiction of the Court in this sphere and the political attitudes of people on the question of the Arab-Israel conflict. Those who define themselves as doves are more likely to support the right of Palestinians to petition the Court than those who define themselves as hawks. While most decisions of the Court enjoy fairly wide public support, no more than half the public supports decisions in which the Court has interfered with the actions of the military authorities in the Occupied Territories.

The public image of the Court is one of a body that is politically neutral. The Court is seen as an institution that adheres strictly to principles of procedural justice, examining every argument placed before it solely on its merits, without discrimination.

Judicial Activism

Our concern in this study is with the decisions of the Supreme Court relating to the Occupied Territories. Nevertheless, an understanding of the unique role that the Court has played, and continues to play, in the constitutional and political system of Israel will help contextualize the discussion of the Court's decisions relating to the Occupied Territories.

Israel does not have a formal constitution. Nor does it have a general bill of rights.[28] However, the Supreme Court, mainly in its capacity as a High Court of Justice, has forged what may be termed a judicial bill of rights. This "judicial bill of rights" has become a central element of the country's constitutional system.

The judicial bill of rights rests on the theory that basic rights of the individual are an essential feature of every democratic regime. As Israel's Declaration of Independence and its constitutional structure both reveal a fundamental commitment to democratic rule, certain basic rights must be recognized as accepted principles of the legal system. Even before any of these rights were defined in Basic Laws, the Court looked to accepted standards in other democratic countries and in international documents to define which rights were to be recognized. Over the years, the Court has referred to a long list of recognized rights that includes freedom of speech, the right to equality, freedom of association, the right to bodily integrity, and freedom of religion.

Until the enactment of two Basic Laws on human rights in 1992, the Court refused to accept the argument that a statutory provision of the

Knesset, or even a provision in British Mandatory legislation that remained in force, could be struck down because it was in conflict with a recognized individual right, such as freedom of religion. There was no judicial review of *Knesset* legislation.[29]

The absence of judicial review of *Knesset* legislation did not mean that the recognition of individual rights had no real significance. The concept of individual rights has played a central role in interpreting statutes and controlling administrative discretion and delegated legislation. Over the years the Court has interfered in a wide range of administrative decisions relating to statutory discretion in diverse matters such as licensing of the press, permits for public processions, censorship of plays and films, appointment and election of representatives in public bodies, and leasing of municipal premises. It has adopted interpretations of statutes that made them more compatible with fundamental rights and invalidated delegated legislation that placed restrictions on individual rights without clear statutory authority.

The development of a "rights-minded" jurisprudence has not meant that all the Court's decisions fit into a "rights-minded" pattern. In some areas of judicial decision-making the Court's decisions have been decidedly "executive-minded," although even in these areas there has been some change in rhetoric over the years that has tempered the executive-mindedness of decisions. The main area in which the influence of rights-minded jurisprudence has been limited is that of security powers. I shall return to this issue in chapters 7–10.

Some of the older generation of justices played a leading role in developing a jurisprudence protective of individual rights against governmental power. However, even these judges generally shared a fairly narrow view of their judicial role. This view stressed a clear division of powers between the legislative, executive, and judicial branches of government. The Court shied away from political questions unless dealing with such questions was essential to determine the legality of governmental action that deprived an individual of his or her rights or liberties.

With Justices Shamgar and Barak playing the leading role, the judges who have dominated the Court since the late 1970s adopted what would appear to be a more activist approach. The main expression of this activist approach has been a willingness to relax rules of standing and review governmental decisions that have no direct impact on the rights or liberties of specific individuals.[30] In the last few years the Court has also handed down a number of courageous decisions, supportive of human rights. Foremost among these are decisions forbidding the security services from using any form of physical force in interrogation of terrorist suspects,[31] denying the authorities the power to use the law on administrative detention to hold detainees as "bargaining chips,"[32] and deeming unlawful restrictions on Arabs purchasing houses in a communal settlement established on state land by the Jewish Agency.[33]

Opening its doors to general petitions regarding the legality of governmental action has placed the Court at the center of political life in the country. It has become common practice for politicians, public interest groups, and private individuals to submit petitions challenging controversial government decisions. The Court's readiness to entertain such petitions, intervention in highly sensitive issues of state and religion on which the public is widely divided, assumption of judicial review over parliamentary legislation under the Basic Laws enacted in 1992, and decisions in some of the cases mentioned have in recent years turned the Court into a controversial body. Retired justices of the older generation, academics, and politicians (especially those from the religious political parties) have criticized what they perceive to be the Court's unwarranted judicial activism. Proposals to change the composition of the Court so as to include representatives of wider sections of the population, especially in review of parliamentary legislation, have been raised in political and academic circles.

A number of the leading members of the older generation of justices were brought up or educated in central Europe and witnessed the collapse of the Weimar Republic and the rise of Nazism. Their interpretation of these events substantially influenced their attitudes in cases involving elements perceived as subversive. Thus, in a 1964 case that involved the refusal by the registrar of voluntary associations to register the Arab nationalistic movement *El-Ard* on the grounds that it was subversive, Justice Witkon mentioned the experience of the Weimar Republic that had collapsed, in his view, because it had not taken a strong stand against its internal enemies.[34] A year later, in the *Yeredor* case, the Court affirmed the decision of the Central Elections Committee to disqualify a list connected with the *El-Ard* movement from participating in the elections. Justice Sussman referred to the remark of Justice Witkon and the need to learn a lesson from the Weimar Republic.[35]

While justices of the younger generation have questioned the relevance of the Weimar experience in judicial decision-making, their perception of the nature of the State of Israel and its ideological foundations does not differ from that of their predecessors. Central to that perception is the notion of Israel as the state of the Jewish people. Although the Court has dismissed claims of a contradiction between this notion and the democratic principle,[36] particularistic elements involved in the Zionist ideology of a Jewish state or state of the Jewish people are entrenched in its jurisprudence. The interests of the Jewish collective are seen as synonymous with the public good, or the interests of the state itself. These judges cannot be neutral in a case involving any act perceived as challenging these interests.[37]

This book is divided into three parts. Part I addresses the basis for the Court's jurisdiction over actions carried out by Israel's military forces in areas not part of the country's territory and in which its legal system does not apply, the substantive norms applied by the Court, and the Court's attitude to the application and interpretation of international law. In Part II, I discuss the Court's decisions relating to two major political issues: establishment of Israeli settlements in the Occupied Territories and the status of the Palestinian residents of those territories. Part III is devoted to the manner in which the Court has handled petitions challenging security measures against Palestinian residents. In the final chapter I draw some general conclusions.

PART I

CHAPTER ONE

JURISDICTION, JUSTICIABILITY, AND SUBSTANTIVE NORMS

JURISDICTION

Over the years Israeli governments pursued policies aimed at integration of the Occupied Territories with Israel while refraining from formally annexing the West Bank and Gaza or applying the Israeli legal system in those areas. In theory, at least, the applicable law in those parts of the West Bank and Gaza that are still under IDF control is the law that prevailed when the IDF entered the area, subject only to changes introduced by military order.[1]

The Supreme Court of Israel is not an international forum. It stands at the pinnacle of the judicial branch of Israel's institutions of government; its jurisdiction and powers are defined in the laws of the State of Israel. It is not self-evident that the Court's power of review extends to actions carried out by the military in areas that are not part of Israeli sovereign territory and in which the Israeli legal system does not apply. There is precedent for the view that military commanders in occupied territory are not subject to the jurisdiction of the courts in their home country.[2]

When residents of the Occupied Territories first petitioned the Supreme Court, sitting as a High Court of Justice, the government's legal advisors had to decide whether to contest the Court's jurisdiction over such petitions. Meir Shamgar, attorney-general in the formative years of the Court's jurisdiction over the Territories, decided on a policy that was to guide government counsel in years to come: the authorities would ask the Court to rule on the merits of the petition without entering into the question of jurisdiction.[3] The reasons for this policy were probably varied. Mr. Shamgar has written that his basic idea was to ensure some form of external control over the actions of the military so as to prevent arbitrariness and maintain the rule of law.[4] This would be in line with the prevailing philosophy of the Court that "in areas in which the Court does not intervene the principle of rule of law is flawed."[5] It is fair to assume, however, that a further reason could well have been the notion that petitions to the Supreme Court of Israel by residents of the Occupied Territories would imply the recognition of Israel by the petitioners, as well as political legitimization of Israeli rule over the Territories.[6]

In the first reported decision dealing with the legality of actions taken by the military authorities in the Occupied Territories, the *Christian Society* case,[7] the jurisdiction question was not even mentioned by the Court. This was somewhat surprising, as the question of jurisdiction is an issue that a court will raise on its own initiative. From the Court's remarks in later cases, however, it seems that the authorities had in fact declared that they did not contest the Court's jurisdiction.[8] In the *Electricity Corporation* case, decided shortly after the *Christian Society* case, the Court simply stated that as in "previous matters that have come before this court (recently, for example, H.C.337/71 [the *Christian Society* case—D.K.]) counsel for the first two respondents (the minister of defense and the commander of the area) did not contest the jurisdiction of this court, to entertain petitions relating to the activities of an Israeli military commander in the area of his military rule."[9]

Resting jurisdiction solely on the respondent's failure to contest the issue was not a path the Court was eager to follow, for it implied that if at some future stage the authorities were to contest the issue, they could undermine the status of the Court's previous decisions. Thus, it was only a matter of time before the Court chose to discuss the jurisdiction question. In the *Rafiah Approach* case, Justice Landau mentioned that the authorities had once again refrained from contesting the Court's jurisdiction. He explained that the Court would therefore assume

> without ruling on the matter, that the jurisdiction exists on the personal level against functionaries in the military government who belong to the executive branch of the state, as "persons fulfilling public duties according to law," and who are subject to the review of this court under section 7 (b) (2) of the Courts Law, 1957.[10]

As judicial review of IDF acts in the Territories became a permanent feature of Israeli legal and political life, the legal basis for this jurisdiction suggested by Justice Landau lost its tentative nature and was adopted as the authoritative view of the Court.[11] Since the military commander and those acting on his behalf are public servants, who fulfill a public duty under law, they are subject to the statutory jurisdiction of the Supreme Court, acting as a High Court of Justice.

Resting the Court's jurisdiction over acts of the military in the Occupied Territories on interpretation of an Israeli statute has important implications. The jurisdiction is not dependent on the consent of the parties or on theories of natural or international law. Hence, the military authorities could not avoid judicial review by withdrawing their consent to the Court's jurisdiction. On the other hand, even though legislative power in the Occupied Territories is concentrated in the hands of military commanders, the *Knesset*, Israel's legislature, could redefine the Court's jurisdiction so as to exclude or limit review over decisions relating to the Territories.

JUSTICIABILITY

Jurisdiction is a necessary, but not always sufficient, condition for a court to decide a case on its merits. In countries following the Anglo-American system of law, courts have developed the doctrine of justiciability, under which a court may decline to exercise its jurisdiction in certain cases. As opposed to jurisdiction, which is determined by *external* constraints on the power of courts imposed by a constitution or legislation, justiciability involves an *internal* constraint placed by courts on their own decision-making power. It is a constraint employed by the courts to protect themselves from encroaching on the territory of other branches of government.

A number of features of petitions relating to the Occupied Territories could have made the justiciability doctrine relevant. The centrality of the Occupied Territories in the Israel-Arab conflict and the fact that West Bank residents are usually citizens of Jordan (which was in a formal state of war with Israel until 1994) could mean that governmental actions are "acts of state," one of the classic grounds of nonjusticiability in the English legal system.[12]

Second, some of the petitions challenged government policies that were highly controversial on both the domestic and international levels. Such petitions could arguably have been covered by the "political question doctrine," recognized in the United States as grounds for nonjusticiability.[13]

Third, when the occupation began, most Palestinian residents of the West Bank were citizens of Jordan, at the time a country in a formal state of war with Israel. It could have been argued that they lacked standing to challenge government actions before the courts of Israel.

"Act of State" Doctrine

Accepting the argument that all acts of the military in the Occupied Territories are covered by the "act of state" doctrine would have prevented substantive judicial review over those acts, thereby frustrating the policy of accepting the Court's jurisdiction. Hence the authorities never raised this argument in relation to the West Bank or Gaza.[14] Nevertheless, it is one of the theses of this study that even though the formal doctrine of "act of state" has never been considered as grounds for dismissing a petition, perception of acts by the authorities as acts of state is one of the factors explaining the Court's reticence in intervening. This perception remained hidden until Justice Cheshin articulated it in a house demolition case.[15]

Political-Question Doctrine

The political-question doctrine has been most relevant in cases relating to establishment of civilian settlements in the Occupied Territories, since the government's settlement policy has been highly controversial in Israel itself and has met a great deal of opposition on the international level, even by states usually supportive of Israel, such as the United States.[16] Most cases dealing with civilian settlements were brought by Palestinian landowners who contested the legality of the taking and use of their land for this purpose. In these cases the Court distinguished between an individual's claim that his or her property was taken illegally and the legality of establishing civilian settlements in the Occupied Territories. The political sensitivity of the latter question could make it nonjusticiable, but this did not affect the justiciability of individual property rights.

The *Beth El* case was heard while intensive peace negotiations were going on between Israel and Egypt. Nevertheless, Justice Witkon stated that he was not at all impressed with the argument that the "question before the Court is not justiciable as it is one that will be dealt with in peace negotiations and the Court does not deal with political questions that are in the government's sphere."[17] He explained: "On the assumption—that was not proved in this case—that a person's property has been damaged or taken illegally, it is difficult to believe that the Court will refuse a remedy to that person, because his right is likely to be the subject of political negotiations."[18]

Hence the Court was prepared to examine whether the individual's land had been requisitioned for security reasons, and within the framework of this argument to examine whether the authorities' grounds for establishing that settlement were indeed security grounds. On the other hand, it was not prepared to consider the argument that under article 49, paragraph 6, of Geneva Convention IV, establishing any civilian settlements in occupied territory is illegal. The main reason given was that the Geneva Convention is not enforceable in Israel's domestic courts.[19] However, one of the judges, Justice Landau, remarked that he had decided not to deal with the said argument more readily since he was aware that the issue of civilian settlements in occupied territory was internationally controversial and likely to be on the agenda of fateful international negotiations being conducted by the government. He added:

> It is better if matters, which by their very nature pertain to the international political plane, should be dealt with only on that plane. In other words, even although I agree that the petitioners' complaint is generally justiciable in court, since property rights of the individual are involved, this particular aspect of the matter should be regarded as non-justiciable upon application of an individual to this Court.[20]

In the *Elon Moreh* case, counsel for the authorities tried to persuade the Court that as the general question of civilian settlement was nonjusticiable, the Court should refrain from dealing with a petition that challenged a government decision to requisition uncultivated land for such settlement. The Court rejected the argument. Justice Landau conceded that the Court's decision would be highly controversial; it would meet with acclaim by those who supported the Court's conclusion and total and emotional rejection by those who did not. However, because the argument was that the authorities had acted illegally in taking the land of a specific individual, the Court had no choice but to examine the argument on its merits. Justice Landau explained that since private property rights were involved, an argument based on the "relativity" of the right was unacceptable. A military government wishing to affect property rights of an individual must show that it is acting within its legal powers, "and cannot exempt itself from judicial review by pleading non-justiciability."[21]

This stance of the Court on the justiciability of individual complaints, as opposed to general issues of policy, is not confined to questions of land rights. On the eve of the outbreak of hostilities in the Gulf in 1991, the military authorities had distributed gas masks to Israeli residents of the West Bank but not to Palestinians residing there. In an action brought by a Palestinian resident of the West Bank, the Court refused to accept that the political nature of the decision could make an argument of discrimination nonjusticiable.[22]

The distinction between a general issue of policy and expropriation of individual rights became relevant in a petition submitted in 1991 by the *Peace Now* movement challenging the legality of the Likud government's settlement policy.[23] The petitioners did not refer to any particular

settlement, but asked for an order to stop all settlement activities not
grounded in essential security considerations. The Court dismissed the
petition on the preliminary issue of justiciability without hearing argument on the merits of the case. Justice Shamgar, president of the Court,
held that a number of factors made the petition nonjusticiable: it called
for intervention in policy matters in the domain of another branch of
government, there was no concrete dispute, and the predominant nature
of the issue was political. He added that, even if the issue was a mixed
legal-political one, it was nonjusticiable because its dominant nature
was political.[24] Justice Goldberg went further and stressed that even if
the Court could decide the issue on legal grounds, it should not do so.
He explained that "a judicial determination, which does not pertain to
the rights of an individual, must give way to the political process, which
is so important and meaningful."[25] Any decision of the Court on the
merits could be seen as direct interference with the peace process; the
case was therefore one of those rare cases that a court must refuse to
hear so as not to undermine public trust in the law. Justice Goldberg
ended his opinion with the following words: "The petitioners have the
right to place a 'legal mine' on the Court's threshold, but the Court does
not have to step on a mine that may destroy its foundations, which are
the public trust in it."[26]

Standing

There is some support for the idea that the standing of aliens to challenge the legality of government action before domestic courts is
restricted. In *Johnson* v. *Eisentrager,*[27] German prisoners held by the
American military authorities in Europe attempted to bring a habeas
corpus action before courts in the United States. In response, the U.S.
Supreme Court distinguished between the standing of resident and nonresident aliens. The former are deemed within the jurisdiction of the
Court and have limited standing to sue in domestic courts, though they
will be precluded from use of the courts to accomplish a purpose that
might hamper the war effort or aid the enemy. In contrast, nonresident
aliens do not have access to the courts and may not bring action against
the authorities during hostilities or a war. On the basis of this analysis,
the Court held that as nonresident aliens who were not within its territorial jurisdiction, the German prisoners lacked standing to sue for
habeas corpus. Relying on the approach in *Johnson* v. *Eisentrager,* the
authorities could conceivably have argued that residents of the Occupied
Territories are nonresident enemy aliens who may not bring suit before
the Israel Supreme Court. Obviously such an argument would have been
incompatible with the policy decision to accept jurisdiction of that

court. As part of the policy not to challenge the jurisdiction of the Supreme Court, the authorities therefore also decided not to challenge the standing of residents in the Occupied Territories to bring suit.[28] The Court has never mentioned this issue.

SUBSTANTIVE LAW

Once the obstacles of jurisdiction, standing, and justiciability had been resolved, the Court was forced to decide what substantive law was pertinent. When the IDF entered the Territories in 1967, the military commanders published proclamations stating that the prevailing law would remain in force, subject to changes made by military order or proclamation. The norms of the local legal system were therefore clearly relevant. However, three other questions arose.

1. Is international law relevant in proceedings before a domestic court? If so, would the government raise the arguments that it had raised in the domestic and international political arenas, namely, that the West Bank and Gaza should not be regarded as occupied territory, and that the law of belligerent occupation was therefore not relevant to the specific situation there?

2. The Court's jurisdiction rests on the notion that the military authorities "perform public functions under law." Does this mean not only that these authorities are subject to the Court's jurisdiction as a High Court of Justice, but that they are also subject to the substantive rules and principles of Israeli administrative law that apply to all branches of government?

3. What is the status of the military orders, which, under the above proclamations, can amend local law? Are such orders subject to judicial review?

The first question will be discussed in the next chapter. The rest of this chapter will be devoted to a discussion of the second and third questions.

Rules of Israeli Administrative Law

The Supreme Court adheres to the theory that governmental powers are to be exercised by authorized governmental authorities and not by the Court itself. Sitting as a High Court of Justice, rather than a court of appeal, the Court's function is to examine the *legality*, rather than *correctness*, of government decisions. In carrying out this function the Court has created a body of law that has been described as Israel's common law.[29] This body of law rests on three principles: (1) no administrative authority may perform an act, especially if that act affects the liberties of the individual, unless specifically empowered by law to do so; (2) in exercising their powers, administrative authorities are bound by rules of procedural fairness, such as the duty to afford a hearing to a person likely to be adversely affected by an administrative decision; and (3) administrative discretion must be exercised reasonably, without discrimination, for a proper purpose and on the basis of relevant considerations.

In the initial cases relating to the Occupied Territories petitioners based their arguments either on international law or on the local law. The Court addressed only the first principle—the existence of legal power to perform the challenged act—and failed to examine whether that act was compatible with the other principles of Israeli administrative law.[30] The change came in the *Al-Taliya* case.[31] After mentioning the duty and powers under international law of the military authorities to maintain public order, Justice Shamgar added: "The exercise of powers by the respondents will be examined according to the criteria which this court applies when it reviews the act or omission of any other arm of the executive branch, while taking into account, of course, the duties of the respondents that flow from the nature of their task, as explained above."[32]

This dictum expresses the *theory* of the Court regarding the applicability of Israeli administrative law presented in many cases since the *Al-Taliya* decision. The theory is that all the rules of administrative law that apply to governmental authorities acting in Israel apply to the military acting in the Occupied Territories.[33] However, these rules must be applied in the light of the special status of the military authorities in the Occupied Territories, *as perceived by the Court.*[34]

The Court has been fairly receptive to arguments of procedural fairness, especially those invoking the hearing requirement. It has been more reticent in rigorously applying the rules restraining use of administrative discretion. Nevertheless, in a few cases by applying these rules the Court has intervened in decisions of the military authorities.[35] In some cases in which the principles of administrative law should clearly have been relevant, the Court has simply ignored them.[36] In many other cases, especially those dealing with demolition or sealing of houses, the Court has mentioned the test of reasonableness but failed to apply the test in the way the Court itself has claimed that it should be applied, namely, to examine the balance between the various considerations taken into account by the administrative body.[37]

In summarizing this brief discussion of the Court's attitude to application of administrative law to decisions of the military commander, it should be noted that this law has provided the Court with a potent weapon with which to challenge decisions of the authorities that meet standards of local and international law. Extending grounds of judicial review beyond the rules of belligerent occupation has allowed the Court to argue that in protecting the rights of residents in the Territories it has gone much further than required by international law.[38] Furthermore, because administrative law may be regarded as an internal constraint, whereas international law may be seen as an external constraint, the political implications of overturning an act of the military on the grounds of Israeli administrative law are less threatening than overruling the same act on grounds of international law. This may explain why, when alternative grounds exist for overruling an act, the Court has sometimes seemed to place greater emphasis on administrative law.

Military Orders

Under the rules of international law, when an army occupies enemy territory all governmental power, including legislative power, is concentrated in the hands of the military commander. This principle was expressed in Proclamations issued by the commanders of the Israel Defense Forces when they took control of the West Bank and Gaza in June 1967. Section 3 of the Proclamation on Law and Administration stated: "Any power of government, legislation, appointment, or administration with respect to the Region or its inhabitants shall henceforth be vested in me alone and shall be exercised only by me or by a person appointed by me to that end or acting on my behalf."[39]

Military commanders have used their legislative powers extensively, promulgating military orders in a wide range of areas, including security and fiscal matters, administrative affairs, education, and the status of civilian settlements. Exercise of these legislative powers raised a number of fundamental legal questions. These relate to the limitations placed by international law on legislative powers of an occupying power. When may a military commander introduce changes into the local law? May the commander promulgate legislation that has long-term effects or produces fundamental changes in the occupied territory? The attitude of the Supreme Court on these questions will be discussed in chapter 4. The question examined here relates to the scope of judicial review over legislative acts of the military commander.

The question of judicial review over military legislation in the Occupied Territories must be discussed in light of the Israeli constitutional system that, following the British model, long regarded primary legislation as beyond the pale of judicial review. The issue the Court had to contend with is whether the legislation of the military commander should be regarded as parallel to primary legislation and thus immune from review, or as parallel to subordinate or delegated legislation, hence subject to review under the rules of administrative law previously reviewed.

The Court first expressly discussed this question in the *Rafiah Approach* case. Counsel for the government argued that legislation of the military commander should have the same status in the Court's eyes as primary legislation of the *Knesset*. Justice Witkon articulated the case against judicial review of military legislation, namely that in exercising legislative power the military commander was acting as the sovereign legislator in the Occupied Territories. As opposed to an administrative authority, whose power to promulgate subordinate legislation must rest on a mandate granted by the sovereign legislative body, the military commander is not dependent on such a mandate. Justice Witkon's conclusion was that military legislation should be regarded by the Court as primary legislation that is not subject to judicial review, either under the standards of Israeli administrative law or those of international law.

Justice Witkon's view received no support. Indeed, in the *Rafiah Approach* case itself the other justices on the bench adopted a different approach. Justice Kister suggested that while a military commander in occupied territory is in effect the source of his own power, in all his actions he is subject to orders from his superiors. In every "enlightened country" he is also bound to comply with the rules of international law that limits his authority.[40]

Justice Kister's view soon became the accepted approach of the Court. In the *VAT* case,[41] the issue concerned military orders that imposed value added tax (VAT) in the Occupied Territories. The Court did not doubt its power to review these orders so as to decide whether the military commander had exceeded the legislative powers of a belligerent occupant under international law. However, it added a gloss: because the military commander is part of the Israeli administration, all his acts, including his legislative acts, are subject to review under Israeli administrative law.[42]

Since the *VAT* case, it has become the accepted practice of the Supreme Court that legislative acts of the military commanders are subject to review both under the rules of Israeli administrative law and the rules of public international law.[43] The Court regards the position of the military commander as a member of the Israeli public administration as the decisive factor that subjects all his actions to judicial review under Israeli administrative law. The Court strongly presented this view in the *Hamas Deportation* case, when it stated: "Security legislation may not effect changes in general, well-established norms of administrative law, which our law regards as principles of natural justice."[44]

While in exercising their powers the military authorities are bound by the rules of administrative law, the Court has held that the source of those powers lies in public international law. In the *Ja'amait Ascan* case, after reviewing the precedents on this question, the Court said: "This review reveals that from the legal point of view the source of the authority and power of the military commander in an area subject to belligerent occupation lies in the rules of public international law that deal with *occupatio bellica*, and that are part of the laws of war."[45]

Given the Court's view that the military commander derives authority and powers from the rules of public international law dealing with belligerent occupation, it would seem that each and every act of the military should be examined to see whether it complies with these rules. In reviewing the jurisprudence of the Court, it becomes apparent that the Court has not consistently carried out such an examination. On the contrary, in many cases it has done its utmost to avoid resort to standards of international law. Moreover, as we shall see in the following chapters, even when the Court has been prepared to look to international law, the way it has applied and interpreted it has often prevented it from serving as a meaningful constraint on the powers of the military.

CHAPTER TWO

APPLICATION OF INTERNATIONAL LAW

Application of the international law of belligerent occupation in petitions relating to the Occupied Territories raises several related but discrete questions. First, are the rules of international law enforceable in Israel's domestic courts? Second, assuming a positive answer, is the legal regime on the West Bank and in Gaza indeed one of belligerent occupation? If so, do all norms of international law relating to belligerent occupation apply in the specific context of the West Bank and Gaza? Before analyzing the attitude of the Court on these questions, each requires explanation.

DOMESTIC ENFORCEMENT AND APPLICABILITY ISSUES

Enforcement of International Law in Domestic Courts

Legal systems differ in their approach to the enforcement of international law in their domestic courts. The approach of English law is based on a distinction between two sources of international law. Norms of customary international law are regarded as part and parcel of the common law of the realm, and as such they are applied in domestic courts unless inconsistent with an act of parliament. Norms of conventional law (i.e., norms deriving from international treaties) do not automatically become part of the domestic law of the land. Courts do not enforce them unless they have been incorporated in domestic law by an act of parliament.[1] The Supreme Court of Israel adopted this approach to international law long before occupation of the West Bank and Gaza.[2]

Is the distinction between customary and conventional law relevant in petitions relating to the Occupied Territories? If so, what is the status of the various norms of the international law of belligerent occupation? Two documents describe, or prescribe, the international law of belligerent occupation: the Regulations annexed to the Hague Convention (IV) Respecting the Laws and Customs of War on Land, 1907 (the Hague Regulations) and the Geneva Convention Relative to the Protection of Civilian Persons in Time of War, 1949 (Geneva Convention IV). Are the norms in both these instruments part of conventional law, or do they have the status of customary international law?

Applicability of the International Law of Belligerent Occupation

On the day the IDF took over the West Bank, the military commander issued a proclamation that he had assumed all governmental powers in the area, and that the prevailing law would remain in force subject to any orders that he would promulgate.[3] Attached to this proclamation was the Security Provisions Order that contained detailed provisions for IDF rule in the occupied areas. This order included provisions relating to establishment of military courts and the procedure before them, definition of security offenses, powers of arrest and search by soldiers, and granting of security powers to the military commanders, such as the power to impose a curfew or to close an area. It also included the following provision:

> [A] military tribunal and the administration of a military tribunal shall observe the provisions of the Geneva Convention of August 12, 1949 Relative to the Protection of Civilian Persons in Time of War with respect to legal proceedings, and in the case of conflict between this Order and the said Convention, the provisions of the Convention shall prevail.[4]

The order that included this provision had been prepared long in advance in a special contingency file of legislation to be applied if the IDF were to occupy enemy territory.[5] The provision was based on the assumption that under international law any territory outside the existing boundaries of the state taken in the course of war with neighboring countries would be regarded as occupied territory to which Geneva Convention IV would apply. As it could be argued that conventional international law was not automatically applicable in the military courts, the Convention was incorporated in the military legislation.

Not long after the 1967 War ended, it became clear that the perception of the territories taken by the IDF in that war as "occupied territories" was incompatible with the political stance of many Israeli politicians, especially those who within a short time were referring to "liberated" territories.[6] This was most probably the reason why the above provision was revoked soon after the war.[7] An order enacted by the military commander of the area in August 1967 simply replaced the section in which this provision appeared with another provision that had absolutely nothing to do with the Geneva Convention.[8] In this way the formal legislative adoption of the Geneva Convention as the supreme norm of military law in the Territories was repealed.

The departure of the military authorities from the legislative adoption of Geneva Convention IV (apparently in response to emerging political attitudes toward the Territories) was soon supported by legal argument. In 1968 Professor Y. Blum published an article that dealt with the legal status of Israel on the West Bank.[9] Blum's main argument was that as the annexation of the West Bank by Jordan in 1950 had not received international recognition, it was not the sovereign territory of another state when taken by Israel in 1967. It was therefore doubtful whether Israel should be regarded as an occupying power. He suggested that in such a situation Israel was not bound by those parts of the law of belligerent occupation whose object is to protect the sovereign rights of the previous regime, though it was obligated to abide with the humanitarian aspects of belligerent occupation law.

The government had always preferred to refer to the Territories as "administered," rather than occupied. It now openly contested application of the Geneva Convention to the situation in the West Bank and in Gaza. Adopting Blum's distinction between the whole corpus of belligerent occupation law and those parts regarded as humanitarian law, the official position of the government became that while Geneva Convention IV did not formally apply, the IDF would abide by its *humanitarian* provisions.[10]

The official legal argument against the Convention's application to the situation on the West Bank and in Gaza is based on a highly formalistic interpretation of article 2 that has been articulated by Meir Shamgar.[11] Article 2 of the Convention, which deals with its application, states:

> In addition to the provisions which shall be implemented in peace-time, the present Convention shall apply to all cases of declared war or of any other armed conflict which may arise between two or more of the High Contracting Parties, even if the state of war is not recognized by one of them.
>
> The Convention shall also apply to all cases of partial or total occupation of the territory of a High Contracting Party, even if the said occupation meets with no armed resistance.

The government's argument is based on the second paragraph of article 2. The claim is that as neither the West Bank nor Gaza was the territory of a "High Contracting Party" when occupied by Israel in

1967, the Convention does not formally apply to their occupation. This point was made by Israel Foreign Minister Moshe Dayan in a speech before the 32nd session of the UN General Assembly in 1977,[12] and guided the legal stand of Israel's representatives in international bodies.[13]

The government's legal argument was rejected by the ICRC,[14] leading Israeli academics,[15] and foreign experts in international law.[16] The drafting history of article 2 reveals that the second paragraph was introduced to ensure application of the Convention in cases of occupation that did not result from armed conflict.[17] This was thought necessary as a result of the Nazi occupation of Denmark, which did not initially meet with armed resistance.[18] The second paragraph is irrelevant in cases of occupation arising from armed conflict, as these are covered by the first paragraph.[19] According to this paragraph, the Convention applies to the occupation of territory deriving from the 1967 armed conflict between Israel, Egypt, and Jordan, which are all parties to the Convention. Second, the ICRC has argued, the Geneva Convention is not concerned with the sovereignty of parties to a conflict. The Convention applies to all cases in which territory is occupied in the course of an armed conflict, irrespective of the status of that territory.[20] Even if the relevant paragraph is the second paragraph in article 2, the term "territory of a High Contracting Party" employed in that paragraph refers to any territory controlled by the High Contracting Party that was occupied in the course of armed conflict. Finally, it has been argued that there is a "custom of viewing the laws of war, including the laws on occupations, as formally applicable even in cases which differ in some respect from the conditions of application as spelt out in the Hague and Geneva Conventions."[21]

Despite its argument that the Geneva Convention does not formally apply to the occupation of the West Bank and Gaza, the government repeatedly declared its willingness to abide by the humanitarian provisions of the Convention.[22] Furthermore, while in the international arena government spokesmen often objected to the notion that the West Bank and Gaza should be termed occupied territories, the government never formally contested the applicability of the Hague Regulations to these areas.[23]

Distinction between Enforcement and Applicability Issues

Despite the conceptual distinction between the domestic enforcement and applicability issues, they are at times confused. In the present context, the main source of confusion is the difference between the Hague Regulations and Geneva Convention IV. As we shall see, the Supreme Court has held that the Hague Regulations are domestically enforceable, while those provisions of the Geneva Convention that have been relied on in cases presented before the Court are not. The official stand of the Government of Israel is that the Geneva Convention does not apply to the situation on the West Bank and Gaza. It has not taken a similar clear stand on applicability of the Hague Regulations.

COURT'S DECISIONS ON ENFORCEMENT
AND APPLICABILITY QUESTIONS

In *Christian Society for the Holy Places* v. *Minister of Defense*,[24] the petitioner claimed that the military commander had exceeded the legislative powers of an occupying power under the Hague Regulations and Geneva Convention IV. Although this argument raised all the questions previously described, the only question to which the Court referred was the issue of domestic enforceability. Without distinguishing between the Hague and Geneva Conventions, it expressed doubts whether it could enforce conventions "that are a commitment between the signatory nations and are part of international law that binds the states in their mutual relations."[25] Counsel for the minister of defense declared that "it was not his intention to put this issue before the Court, as the commander of the area acts in accordance with the conventions, and his defense rests on the argument that he adhered to the conventions."[26] The Court therefore stated that it would reserve its doubts and refrain from deciding whether the conventions could be enforced in the domestic courts.

In the first few years of the occupation it became standard practice for the authorities to adopt the approach they had taken in the *Christian Society* case.[27] Nevertheless in the *Rafiah Approach* case the judges were bothered both by the question of the applicable law and the legitimacy of a court skirting this question. In what may have been an attempt to show that ruling on the position under international law was not solely a function of the authorities' consent, Justice Landau saw fit to remark:

> While our courts derive their jurisdiction from the laws of the state and not from international law . . . it is a well-accepted rule, following the English rule, that a court in Israel "will interpret a local statute, if its contents do not demand otherwise, according to the rules of public international law." . . . One may argue that it surely follows that the court will judge the validity of an administrative act in the areas of military government according to public international law, when there is no Israeli statute that applies and there is therefore no possibility of a clash between international law and the national Israeli law.[28]

Justice Landau's wording is revealing. He refers to "the areas of military government" rather than "the occupied territories," but does not tell us what international law applies in "areas of military government"

that are not regarded as occupied. In truth, the international law to which
he was referring was the law of belligerent occupation. He does not
explain why this law should be relevant in territory that is not occupied.

Government counsel had once again declared that the military
commander believed he had acted in accordance with the Hague and
Geneva Conventions, and had asked the Court to rule on the legality
of his actions under these conventions. As a result, despite his
remarks on the legitimacy of resorting to rules of international law,
Justice Landau did not rule on the applicability of international law
in general, nor of the Hague and Geneva Conventions in particular.
In fact he stressed that these questions are "all still open questions
before this court."[29]

Unlike Justice Landau, Justice Witkon was not prepared to accept
the authorities' consent as sufficient basis for a judicial decision. As he
regarded both the Hague and Geneva Conventions as part of conventional international law, Justice Witkon did not consider them enforceable in a domestic court. He took a skeptical attitude to the government
practice of agreeing to the Court's ruling according to international conventions as he feared that without an undertaking that this agreement
would be granted in all cases, litigation before the Court became a "sort
of arbitration."[30]

In applying the rule that conventional international law is not
enforceable in Israel's domestic courts, Justice Witkon followed the
approach taken in the *Christian Society* case, lumping together the
Hague Regulations and Geneva Convention as conventional law.[31] In
response to this decision, Professor Y. Dinstein published an article in
which he explained that a distinction should be drawn between the
Hague and Geneva Conventions.[32] Dinstein showed that the Regulations
attached to the Hague Convention are universally regarded as reflecting
customary law and they should therefore be regarded as part of the
domestic law of Israel.

In the *Beth El* case,[33] Justice Witkon accepted Dinstein's argument
and conceded his mistake in failing to distinguish between the Hague
Regulations and Geneva Convention. The former are part of customary
law enforceable in domestic courts. This meant that he was confronted
with the question relating to Israel's status of Israel in the Occupied Territories. He showed little hesitation in expressing his view on this issue,
stating that the situation in the territories taken in the 1967 War is "one
of belligerency, *and the status of the respondents in respect of the occupied territory is that of an occupying power.*"[34]

Justice Witkon's only reservation related to the enforcement of *conventional* law in domestic tribunals. He was prepared to examine the
petitioners' arguments relating to breach of the Hague Regulations, but

Ayyub v. Minister of Defense [1978]

solidly refused even to consider the argument that establishment of civilian settlements in the Occupied Territories violates article 49 of Geneva Convention IV. Justice Witkon was convinced that even if certain articles in the Geneva Convention are mere statements of customary law, "provisions of the Geneva Convention regarding the transfer of population from or to occupied territory do not come under already existing law. They are intended to enlarge, and not merely clarify or elaborate the duties of the occupying power."[35]

Justice Landau was once again not prepared to commit himself on the formal applicability of the law of belligerent occupation to the situation then pertaining on the West Bank. He began his examination of the situation under international law by noting the government's reservation that it was "not going into the legal question of the actual applicability of the rules of international law in the area occupied by the IDF since 1967,"[36] and added:

> These words hint at the Israeli argument based on the fact that at the time of the IDF's entry into Judea and Samaria that territory was not occupied by a sovereign power whose occupation thereof enjoyed international recognition. We have not been asked to deal with this question in this petition, and that reservation thus belongs to the group of reservations mentioned by me in the [*Rafiah Approach* case], which remain open in this court.[37]

It should be noted that Justice Landau did not limit his remarks on the applicability question to the Geneva Convention. He referred to the very applicability of the rules of international law, undoubtedly meaning those rules relating to belligerent occupation. Despite this doubt about the applicability of the "rules of international law" to the position on the West Bank, Justice Landau was prepared to rule on the assumption that these rules applied. But he was not prepared to ignore the domestic enforceability question and to rule on the legality of acts according to conventional law. The petitioners' main argument against the legality of Israeli civilian settlements in the Occupied Territories was based on the final paragraph in article 49 of Geneva Convention IV that forbids transfer of part of an occupying power's civilian population to occupied territory. Having established that the drafters of the Convention did not regard this paragraph as an expression of existing law, Justice Landau refused to discuss the government's argument that the provision does not apply to voluntary transfer of nationals of the occupying power to occupied territory.

The *Elon Moreh* case[38] concerned the legality of a requisition order for private land taken for a civilian settlement. The settlers, who joined the action as respondents, were not bound by the attorney-general's

decision to skirt the applicable-law question. They argued that the
landowners' arguments based on the international law of occupation were

> totally irrelevant, since the dispute is internal between the Jewish peo-
> ple returning to its land and the Arab residents of the land of Israel and
> what is involved is neither "conquered territory" nor "occupied terri-
> tory" but the very heart of the Land of Israel, our right to which is
> beyond doubt; and secondly since in historical fact Judea and Samaria
> were part of the British Mandate and conquered by force of arms by
> our eastern neighbor—a conquest and annexation which were never
> recognized by anyone (other than England and Pakistan).[39]

This argument combined the political-ideological stance of the government (that the Territories should not be regarded as occupied) with
Blum's legal argument that the law of belligerent occupation does not
apply unless the territory taken in war is the sovereign territory of
another state. It seemed that the Court was at last being forced to confront these arguments and to rule whether the legal regime on the West
Bank was indeed one of belligerent occupation.

In replying to the settlers Justice Landau referred to the "important
argument which Israel has voiced in the international arena" regarding
the status of these areas.[40] Nevertheless, he refused to deal with the arguments on the merits, explaining that "the scope of the hearing of this
petition is delimited primarily by the requisition order issued by the
regional commander, and the immediate source of the order is, according to all views, the powers that international law vests in the military
commander of territory captured by his forces in war."[41]

It seems to me that by exercising the powers granted to a belligerent occupant under international law to restrict private rights the
authorities necessarily accepted that the applicable legal regime was
one of belligerent occupation. By allowing the government to reserve
its opinion on the applicability of the law of belligerent occupation,
while concomitantly exercising the powers of a belligerent occupant,
Justice Landau joined the government's attempt to enjoy the best of
both worlds.

Justice Witkon once again took a different line. In response to the
settlers' argument that the West Bank is not occupied territory, he stated
that had serious doubt arisen about the status of the area, the Court
would have been obliged to refer to the Foreign Ministry for an official
certificate defining its status.[42] Justice Witkon himself entertained little
doubt about its status, and stated quite plainly: "It is a mistake to think
(as I read recently in a newspaper) that the Geneva Convention does not
apply to Judea and Samaria. It applies even though it is not 'justiciable'
in this court."[43] This is the only judicial statement in which an explicit

stand has been taken rejecting the government argument about the applicability of the Geneva Convention.[44]

In the *Elon Moreh* case (discussed in chapter 5) the Court unanimously held that under the rules of customary international law the requisition order for private land issued by the military commander was invalid. At the end of his judgment Justice Landau stated that a military government is not permitted to create facts that are designed to persist after the end of its rule in the area, the fate of which has not yet been determined.[45] This was a clear statement that the IDF's acts in the Territories are subject to the limitations placed on the acts of a belligerent occupant by customary international law.

In challenging the status of the West Bank as occupied territory, the Elon Moreh settlers argued that in fact Israeli law applied.[46] The Court rejected the argument.[47] In another case decided shortly afterwards it pointed out that one must not confuse

> the question of sovereignty in Judea and Samaria according to international law and the rights and duty of the military commander to maintain public order in the area, in order to preserve his control of the area and to institute a regime based on the rule of law, for the good of the residents there. This right and this duty, which are based on the rules of customary international law, are expressed in article 43 of the Hague Regulations.[48]

From this dictum it is clear that although the Court still wanted to reserve judgment on the question of Jordanian sovereignty over the West Bank, it no longer entertained doubts that the legal regime is one of belligerent occupation regulated by the Hague Regulations. As these regulations reflect customary international law, they bind the military authorities on the West Bank until such time as the *Knesset* passes a law that states otherwise (or the status of the Territories is changed by international agreement).

Later decisions no longer contain the caveat that appears in Justice Landau's opinions in the *Beth-El* and *Elon Moreh* cases. The Court simply applied customary international law as a matter of course.[49] Eventually Justice Barak provided an unequivocal ruling that the legal regime on the West Bank and in Gaza is based on the law of belligerent occupation. He described the normative basis for examining the legality of IDF acts in the Occupied Territories in the following way:

> In the Six Day War "East" Jerusalem and Judea and Samaria were taken by the IDF. In "East" Jerusalem the "law, jurisdiction and administration of the State" were applied (see section 1 of the Government and Law Order (No.1), 5727–1967). The approach to Judea and Samaria was different. The law, jurisdiction and administration of

Israel were not applied in Judea and Samaria. . . . Judea and Samaria are held by Israel by way of military occupation or belligerent occupation. In the area a military government was established at the head of which is the military commander. The powers and authority of the military commander are derived from the rules of public international law that deal with belligerent occupation.[50]

The final development in the Supreme Court's approach to the application of the law of belligerent occupation to the situation in the Occupied Territories was provided in two deportation cases heard after the Peace Agreement between Israel and Egypt.[51] In these cases it was argued that once peace had been established between Israel and Egypt the law of belligerent occupation no longer applied in Gaza (which had been taken from Egypt in 1967). In both cases the Court rejected the argument and held that, as the peace agreement did not apply to Gaza and the military government remained intact, Gaza was still subject to the international law of belligerent occupation. In the one case Justice Elon added that under the Camp David Accords the fate of Gaza and of the West Bank were linked and the status of these two territories was the same. He added: "And as all are agreed that Judea and Samaria are subject to belligerent occupation, despite the Camp David Accords, the same law must apply to the status of the Gaza Strip."[52]

GOVERNMENT'S COMMITMENT TO RESPECT HUMANITARIAN LAW

The applicability of the Hague Regulations to the situation on the West Bank and Gaza and their enforceability as customary international law in Israeli Courts have gained judicial recognition. However, the Court time and again rejected the claim that Geneva Convention IV, or specific articles therein, have become part of customary international law that may be enforced by domestic courts.[53] In light of this attitude, the Court never ruled on the argument regarding applicability of the Convention to the specific situation pertaining on the West Bank and Gaza before parts of these areas were transferred to the full or partial control of the Palestinian Authority.[54]

Several attempts were made to show that the domestic courts should enforce the Geneva Convention even if it is only conventional law.[55] The most persuasive of these rests on the notion that the rationale for non-application of conventional law in the domestic courts does not apply in the case of occupied territory. As such territory is ruled directly by the executive branch of government, which wields executive, legislative and judicial power, enforcing treaties made by that branch of government would in no way undermine the legislative supremacy of parliament.

Although this view enjoys considerable support among English legal scholars[56] the Supreme Court rejected it in two leading cases.[57]

While the Government of Israel adopted the stand that Geneva Convention IV does not apply to occupation of the West Bank and Gaza, it stated that it would adhere to the Convention's humanitarian provisions. In the *Kawasme II* case, Justice Landau regarded this commitment as a "political decision, that does not touch on the legal sphere which concerns this court."[58] In subsequent cases, two judges opined that the government's declared commitment may have some legal force, either as a binding administrative directive[59] or as a binding governmental undertaking.[60] The implications are that the government's declared commitment to abide by humanitarian law may be enforced, though only if the Court is of the view that justice requires its enforcement in a specific case. In the *Ketziot* case, which dealt both with holding of administrative detainees in a detention center outside the Territories and conditions in that center, Justice Bach distinguished between these two issues. Although he accepted that holding administrative detainees in Israel was incompatible with the Convention, he held that the humanitarian aspect of the Convention provision that had been violated was not dominant and did not demand judicial enforcement. On the other hand, he held that the overcrowded conditions in the prison were incompatible with article 85 of the Convention and, because the rules regarding overcrowding were clearly of a humanitarian nature, "in this matter the government must be obligated to abide by its declared policy according to which it intends to abide by the humanitarian provisions of the international treaties."[61]

In relying on the government's commitment to respect the humanitarian provisions of the Geneva Convention rather than on the international obligations undertaken by the State of Israel when it ratified the Convention, the judges confused two issues. The government's commitment was made to mitigate its position that the Convention does not formally apply to the West Bank and Gaza. However, the problem the judges who relied on the said commitment wished to address was not the applicability, but the domestic enforcement problem. It is hard to see why the government's declaration that the State of Israel would respect the humanitarian provisions of the Convention should have a stronger standing in domestic law than the formal legal commitment made by its ratification of the Convention. As already intimated, the policy behind non-enforcement of international treaties that have not been incorporated by parliamentary legislation should not apply to occupied territories, in which law-making power is in the hands of the executive branch of government rather than parliament.[62]

Despite its steadfast position that Geneva Convention IV is not enforceable in Israel's domestic courts, in a number of cases the Supreme

Court has examined the compatibility of government actions with the Convention's provisions. In early cases, such as the *Rafiah Approach* and the *Electricity Co. (No.1)* cases, it did so after the authorities expressly agreed to review of their actions according to the Geneva Convention. In later cases, the Court expressed its opinion on the Convention even though the authorities raised the non-enforceability argument or did not expressly agree to waive it.[63] In the next chapter I shall discuss how the Court interpreted the Convention's provisions.

CHAPTER THREE

INTERPRETING GENEVA CONVENTION IV

The Supreme Court has refused to regard Geneva Convention IV as part of customary international law enforceable in domestic courts. Thus, even assuming the Convention's applicability to the occupation of the West Bank and Gaza, the Court need never have expressed an opinion on the interpretation of the Convention's substantive provisions or on arguments that certain IDF actions are incompatible with those provisions. Nevertheless, the Court expressed its opinion on such arguments on more than one occasion. In the earliest cases the Court followed this path after government counsel had expressly stated that as the authorities were convinced that they had acted in accordance with the provisions of the Convention, they agreed to review of their acts according to its strictures.[1] In later cases, especially those dealing with deportations, the authorities no longer took this stand. Instead they argued that as conventional law the provisions of the Convention are not enforceable in domestic courts.[2] Although the Court accepted this argument, it nevertheless took a stand on the substantive argument.

While the Court has interpreted some provisions of Geneva Convention IV, it has steadfastly refused to examine whether establishment of civilian settlements in the Occupied Territories is compatible with the final paragraph in article 49, which prohibits an occupying power from deporting or transferring parts of its own civilian population into the occupied territory. In both the *Beth El* and *Elon Moreh* cases,[3] petitioners challenged the legality of settlements. It will be recalled that in the former case Justice Landau suggested that the general argument against the legality of settlements should be regarded as "non-justiciable upon application of an individual to this court."[4] Nevertheless, in the *Elon Moreh* case, the state attorney explicitly asked the Court "to confirm to the authorities that from the point of view of the Geneva Convention there is nothing wrong in transferring land to settlers for their settlement needs."[5] The Court refused to do so. Justice Witkon stated that the question is not an easy one, with no answer in international jurisprudence. His conclusion that the petitioners should prevail on other grounds, both according to domestic law and customary international law, meant that the matter did not call for a decision. He saw fit to stress, however, that his failure to rule on the issue should not be interpreted as agreement with the attitude of either of the parties.[6] In other words, while he was in no way intimating that government settlement policy was incompatible with the Geneva Convention, he was not prepared to provide the government with the legal legitimization for this policy that it sought from the Court.

The Court's attitude on the settlement issue contrasts starkly with its attitude on the legality of deportations under the first paragraph of article 49. On this issue the Court has expressed its opinion more than once. In doing so it has opted for an interpretation of article 49 that has received some of the harshest criticism ever directed toward a decision of the Court by a leading Israeli academic.[7] One of the points made by this critic is that the Court need not have gone out of its way to give a convoluted interpretation to article 49 when it did not have to interpret the article at all.

Why did the Court abandon the approach adopted on the settlement issue? Why did the Court see fit to express its opinion on a provision of the Geneva Convention that it regards as unenforceable in an action by a private individual? The Court itself did not provide an answer to this question. One possible explanation lies in the change in the generation of judges that was discussed in the introductory chapter. Another possible explanation lies in the difference between deportation cases (in which the Court has been prepared to interpret article 49, paragraph 1, of the Geneva Convention), and settlement cases (in which the Court has refused to interpret paragraph 6 of the same article). The former decisions relate to basic rights of specific individuals and the Court may have been more reluctant to dismiss such cases on formal grounds than cases relating to general policies.[8] The problem with this explanation is that Justice Landau, who refused to interpret article 49 in the settlement cases, also refused to provide a definitive interpretation of that article in the single deportation case in which he wrote an opinion.[9]

Whatever the explanation for the willingness of the Court to interpret the Geneva Convention while sticking to its ruling that as conventional law it may not be enforced before domestic courts, the manner in which the Court has interpreted the Convention merits consideration.

DEPORTATIONS AND ARTICLE 49 OF THE CONVENTION

The primary context in which a discrete argument based solely on the Geneva Convention has been made concerns the legality of deportations. The Hague Regulations, which have gained recognition as expressions of customary law, contain no provision relating to deportations. On the other hand, Geneva Convention IV contains an express prohibition of deportations. In petitions relating to deportations petitioners attempted to persuade the Court that this prohibition should be enforced.

The Court refused to accept the argument that the prohibition on deportations reflects customary law,[10] or that it may be enforced under other theories relating to the domestic enforceability of the Geneva Convention.[11] Nevertheless, it has dealt in detail with the argument that deportations of the type carried out by the IDF are indeed prohibited by the Convention.

Article 49 of Geneva Convention IV states: "Individual or mass forcible transfers, as well as deportations of protected persons from occupied territory to the territory of the Occupying Power or to that of any other country, occupied or not, are prohibited, regardless of their motive."

The text of article 49 is pellucid. It refers to individual and mass transfers as well as to deportations. The prohibition is presented as an absolute prohibition that knows no exceptions. The words "regardless of their motive" would seem to imply that the prohibition applies even if the object of the deportation is to protect the security of the occupied area. The unqualified nature of the prohibition would seem to mean that deportations are outlawed whether or not accompanied by due process. Not surprisingly, therefore, it is the almost universal opinion of experts in international law that article 49 places an absolute prohibition on deportations of residents of occupied territories.[12] This view is supported in the official ICRC commentary on the Convention, written before the occupation of the West Bank and Gaza.[13]

The Supreme Court first addressed the argument that all deportations are prohibited under article 49 in *Awwad* v. *Commander of Judea and Samaria*.[14] For reasons that he failed to explain, Justice Sussman, president of the Court at the time, ignored the domestic enforceability and applicability questions and dealt with the argument on its merits, albeit in a somewhat casual manner.[15] He stated:

> I also did not find substance in the argument that use of regulation 112 is contrary to article 49 of the Fourth Geneva Convention of August 1949 Relative to the Protection of Civilian Persons in Time of War. The object of this treaty, as Dr. Pictet explains in the commentary he wrote

on the convention (at p. 10), is to protect the citizen against arbitrary
action of the occupying army, and the purpose of the above article 49
is to prevent acts, such as the horrendous acts that were committed by
the Germans in the Second World War, during which millions of citizens were expelled from their homes for various purposes, generally to
Germany so that they could be employed in enforced labor for the
enemy, as Jews and others were deported to concentration camps to be
tortured and annihilated.[16]

This reply of Justice Sussman to the argument that article 49 prohibits all deportations is totally inadequate. First, while he cites Pictet's
commentary on the Convention as authority for his view that the purpose
of the Convention was to prohibit arbitrary action by the occupying
power, Justice Sussman ignores Pictet's view, in the very same commentary, that the prohibition on deportations is absolute.[17] Second, assuming
that the purpose of the Convention was indeed the purpose cited by Justice Sussman, does this mean that the clear language of a provision in the
Convention can be ignored? Furthermore, if the only purpose of the Convention had been to outlaw arbitrary action, surely it would have been
sufficient to forbid all arbitrary action by an occupying power. Why was
it necessary to single out deportations? Finally, there is absolutely no contradiction between the assumed purpose of the Convention and a provision that prohibits all deportations "regardless of their motive." The
logic behind such absolute language could well have been to prevent any
exploitation of exceptions to the prohibition, on the theory that it is easier to police an absolute prohibition than one that allows for exceptions.

Justice Sussman attempted to strengthen his view on the meaning of
article 49 by stating that the said article does not derogate from the
occupying power's right to adopt measures necessary to protect its own
security. In doing so he totally ignored article 78 of the Convention,
which limits measures that may be taken for this very purpose.[18] Furthermore, the idea that forced transfer of people might be essential for
security reasons is conceded in article 49 itself. The second paragraph in
this article expressly licenses "total or partial evacuation of a given area
if the security of the population or imperative military reasons so
demand." Following Justice Sussman's reading of the Convention, this
paragraph is superfluous.[19]

Despite its inadequacy Justice Sussman's view was accepted as the
definitive interpretation of article 49. In the *Kawasme II* case the petitioners once again argued that all deportations of residents from occupied territory are outlawed by international law. The main question
addressed by the Court was whether *customary* international law recognizes a general prohibition on deportations. However, Justice Landau
(who had succeeded Justice Sussman as president of the Court) pre-

sented both Justice Sussman's view in the *Awwad* case and the petitioners' argument, which was based on the ICRC Commentary's statement
that the prohibition on deportations is absolute, the distinction between
the first two paragraphs of article 49 and the implications of article 78.
He also mentioned the petitioners' argument that a distinction must be
drawn between the reason for including the prohibition on deportations
and the clear language of article 49 (which applies not only to mass
deportations, but to individual deportations as well). In reply to these
arguments Justice Landau stated:

> As against this argument one may point out that deportation of indi-
> viduals was also carried out sometimes under Hitler's regime, in order
> to realize the same policy that led to mass deportations, and that none
> of the paragraphs in article 49 apply to deportation of persons who
> endanger the public peace—as this court ruled in H.C. 97/79 (the
> *Awwad* case—D.K.). In the words of J. Stone in his lecture "No Peace
> No Law in the Middle East" (Sidney,1969) 17:
>
> ". . . it seems reasonable to limit the sweeping literal words of Article
> 49 to situations at least remotely similar to those contemplated by the
> draftsman, namely the Nazi War II practices of large-scale transfers of
> population, whether by mass transfer or transfer of many individuals,
> to more hostile or dangerous environments, for torture, extermination
> or slave labor."[20]

The basis for Justice Landau's reply to the petitioners' arguments
was Justice Sussman's view, which Justice Landau attempted to bolster
by citing *part* of a quote from a lecture by Professor Julius Stone. I shall
return to Stone's lecture in my discussion of the *Afu* case. For the
moment, it should be noted that after suggesting the reply to the petitioners' argument, Justice Landau stated explicitly that "*whatever the
correct interpretation to the first paragraph in article 49 may be*," the
Geneva Convention is not part of customary law and cannot be relied
on before the domestic courts of Israel. He declared that he would therefore refrain from ruling on the compatibility of the deportation orders
with article 49 of the Geneva Convention.

In *Na'azal* v. *IDF Commander in Judea and Samaria* [21] another
attempt was made to challenge the legality of deportations. In rejecting
the petition Justice Shamgar referred to the decisions in the *Awwad* and
Kawasme II cases. He also added an argument mentioned in an article
he had written while serving as attorney-general of the State of Israel.[22]
Article 49 refers to deportation of a person "from occupied territory to
the territory of the Occupying Power or to that of any other country,
occupied or not." Justice Shamgar argued that when a Jordanian citizen
is deported to Jordan, he is not deported to "any other country."[23]

It is difficult to understand the significance of the deportee's citizenship for this issue. There is no mention of this element in article 49.[24] Furthermore, it is abundantly clear that when article 49 speaks of deportation "from occupied territory to the territory of the Occupying Power or to that of any other country," the term "any other country" refers to any country *other than that of the Occupying Power*. Any other interpretation is not only inconsistent with a literal reading of article 49; it leads to a conclusion that is manifestly absurd, for it implies that when a state occupies *part* of the territory of another state it may deport all the citizens of that state to the non-occupied part of the state without violating article 49. This reading of article 49 hardly commends itself.

The Supreme Court returned to article 49 in the *Afu* case, which was heard by an enlarged bench of five justices, headed by the president of the Court, Justice Shamgar. The Court was unanimous in rejecting the argument that a domestic court could enforce the Geneva Convention. It could therefore have refrained from deciding whether all deportations are prohibited under article 49 of the Convention. Nevertheless, it transpired that the judges were divided on this question, which was discussed in some detail. The majority joined Justice Shamgar, who reiterated the Sussman approach and tried to shore it up by further argument. In a strong dissent Justice Bach accepted the argument that article 49 means what it says, namely that all deportations are prohibited.

Justice Shamgar began his judgment in the *Afu* case by presenting his perception of the principles of interpretation in Israeli domestic law and in international law. His basic approach to a legal text is that it should not be tied to semantics; rather, it should be interpreted so as to give effect to its purpose and achieve consistency between various provisions. Justice Shamgar also stated that in interpreting international treaties, the preferred interpretation is one that least restricts the sovereignty of the state party.

Having set out his general approach, Justice Shamgar proceeded to interpret article 49. His interpretation rests on two propositions. First, the literal meaning of a provision in a treaty should not be adopted automatically, even when this meaning seems perfectly clear and leads to a result both coherent and workable. It is incumbent upon a court to look to the purpose of the provision, which can be judged by the evil that the provision was supposed to remedy. Second, the sole purpose of including an express prohibition on deportations in the Geneva Convention was to outlaw deportations of the type carried out by the Nazis.

Both of these propositions are highly questionable. First, as was argued in the *Afu* case, the accepted principle in interpretation of treaties, as formulated in article 31 of the Treaty on Treaties,[25] is that a treaty should be interpreted according to the ordinary meaning of the terms of the treaty, in their context and in light of the treaty's object and purpose. Under article 32 of the Treaty recourse to the circumstances of the treaty's conclusion may be had only when relying on the ordinary meaning leaves the provision ambiguous or obscure, or leads to a manifestly absurd or unreasonable result.

Justice Shamgar was well aware of the rules of interpretation in the Treaty on Treaties. In support of his view that departs from a literal reading of article 49, he argued that reading this provision as an absolute prohibition on deportations would mean that terrorists and enemy agents who infiltrated the area could not be deported;[26] because this is an unreasonable reading of article 49, the literal reading should be rejected. Article 49 must therefore be confined to deportations of the Nazi type, which, he assumed, had provided the impetus for introduction of this article into the convention.

The dissenting judge, Justice Bach, presented the answer to this argument.[27] Article 49 only applies to "protected persons." *Residents* of occupied territory convicted of terrorism or espionage are indeed "protected persons" and they may not be deported. This can hardly be called absurd. However, persons who enter the occupied territory illegally are not "protected persons," and therefore article 49 does not apply to them.[28]

Justice Shamgar assumed that everyone in occupied territory is a protected person entitled to protection of the Convention. This assumption contradicts the view expressed in a previous decision in which the Court expressed doubt whether a former resident of the area who had returned under a visitor's permit could be regarded as a protected person.[29] The definition of "protected persons" refers to people who "find themselves" in occupied territory.[30] While aliens who happen to be in territory at the moment of occupation may indeed be included in this definition, it seems that people who enter occupied territory illegally do not "find themselves" in that territory and are therefore not protected persons. Even if there is some doubt over interpretation of the term "protected person," Justice Shamgar's theory of interpretation is interesting. His premise for rejecting the clear meaning of article 49 rests on a dubious interpretation of the term "protected person" in article 4 which had already been dismissed by the Court. No attempt was made to apply to article 4 the canons of interpretation used in interpreting article 49.

Justice Shamgar once again quoted the statement of Professor Julius Stone (supporting a restrictive interpretation of article 49), cited by Justice Landau in the *Kawasme II* case. He remarked that no explanation was given to the Court as to why it should adopt Pictet's interpretation rather than Stone's.[31]

There are a number of reasons why Pictet's view should have been preferred to Stone's. First, as Justice Shamgar himself mentioned twice in the *Arjov* case in which he *accepted* Pictet's interpretation of a provision in the Convention, Pictet's commentary is the *official* ICRC commentary on the Convention.[32] It was written before 1967, was not related to any specific conflict and is therefore obviously an objective view of the Convention. Stone's view was expressed in a lecture delivered 18 months after the Six-Day War in which Stone was obviously writing as an advocate for Israel rather than as an objective outsider concerned with the proper interpretation of the Geneva Convention.[33] Second, Stone was not making a general statement about article 49. He connected the view on article 49 to an interpretation he suggested of article 78, under which it would have been legal to expel Jordanian citizens to Jordan *rather than interning them*. Finally, Stone also based his view on the fallacy that the only situations contemplated by the draftsmen of article 49 were "the Nazi World War II practices of large-scale transfers of population." I shall briefly elaborate on these second and third points.

Stone realized that any departure from a plain interpretation of article 49 would face a serious obstacle. Article 78 of the Convention allows an occupying power to take safety measures if it considers this necessary for imperative reasons of security, but states that "it may, at the most, subject them to assigned residence or to internment." This would seem to imply that deportations, even for imperative reasons of security, are ruled out. Stone's solution to this dilemma was as follows:

> common sense suggests that in most of the cases deportation to Jordan would be a less severe measure than internment, within the license of Article 78. For the hostile activities in question have invariably been on behalf of Jordan, to which they were deported, and where they might expect to be welcome and even rewarded, sometimes by high public office.

Stone then proceeded to state: "*Insofar as Article 49 conflicts with this meaning of article 78* it seems reasonable to limit the sweeping literal words of Article 49 (emphasis added)."[34]

In other words, Stone was restricting his reading of article 49 to circumstances in which deportation is a less severe measure than internment. He opined that such were the circumstances "in most of the cases" of the twenty-three people deported to Jordan between the end of hostilities in 1967 and his November 1968 lecture. One must assume that even according to Stone's interpretation, in the cases in which deportation was not less severe than internment, the prohibition in article 49 would hold.

In the context of the Israel-Palestinian conflict the issue of deportations is an especially sensitive issue, which has connotations that extend far beyond the consequences for the individual involved.[35] Stone's view that deportation is less severe than internment is therefore obviously questionable (unless the deportee is offered the choice, a possibility mentioned by Stone himself). Be this as it may, what is apparent is that the Supreme Court adopted one part of Stone's view without mentioning his restriction. The words "Insofar as Article 49 conflicts with this meaning of article 78" were omitted from Justice Landau's quote from Stone, which was repeated by Justice Shamgar in the *Afu* case.

While Stone had only argued that deportations to *Jordan* were not unlawful, the deportations under review in the *Kawasme II* and *Afu* cases were deportations to Lebanon. Justice Shamgar made no attempt to examine whether Stone's view could stand in these circumstances. Nor did he explain how a narrow interpretation of article 49, which allows deportations on security grounds, can be deemed consistent with article 78, which limits security measures, "at the most," to internment.

As stated previously, Justice Bach dissented from the majority view on the interpretation of article 49. He held that even if the Nazi experience triggered the inclusion of article 49, the absolute nature of the prohibition on deportations was quite clear and was consistent with article 78 of the Convention. There was therefore no justification whatsoever for abandoning the ordinary meaning of article 49.[36]

The second proposition on which Justice Shamgar based his interpretation of article 49 rests on the Court's assumption in both the *Awwad* and *Kawasme II* cases, supported by Stone, that the impetus for including the prohibition on deportations in Geneva Convention IV was the experience with the Nazi deportations in World War II. The participants in the Conference that adopted the Geneva Convention, as well as subsequent commentators like Pictet, were indeed mindful of the Nazi deportations. This does not mean, however, that they regarded the prohibition on deportations in the Convention as a response to the Nazi deportations.[37]

The international tribunal at Nuremberg held that the Nazi deportations were a violation of *customary* international law.[38] There was therefore no real need to include a merely declaratory article in the Geneva Convention. More important, review of the drafting history of Geneva Convention IV undermines the assumption that the provision on deportations was introduced in response to the Nazi deportations.[39]

The original draft for a convention to protect civilians in wartime, prepared by a commission established by the ICRC, was submitted to the 15th International ICRC Conference, which met in Tokyo in 1934. The Conference adopted the draft as a useful basis for diplomatic negotiations.

These negotiations were suspended at the outbreak of the Second World War. However, the Committee of Government Experts, which prepared the initial drafts of the Geneva Conventions after the War, referred extensively to the Tokyo draft.[40]

Article 19 (b) of the Tokyo draft states: "Deportations outside the territory of the occupied State are forbidden, unless they are evacuations intended, on account of the extension of military operations, to ensure the security of the inhabitants."[41]

The Committee of Government Experts Report referred to this provision and stated: "The Commission thought that a clearer distinction should be drawn than in the Tokyo draft, between deportations and evacuations (removals)."[42]

The Committee therefore redrafted the provision on deportations.[43] Its draft was the basis for article 49 that was included in the final version of Geneva Convention IV. Thus article 49 is based on a provision outlawing deportations from occupied territory drafted *before* the Second World War. It was not a response to Nazi deportations. Possible responses to the Nazi experience were the explicit reference to "individual or mass forcible transfers," and the statement that the prohibition applies to such transfers and to deportations "regardless of their motive."

In light of scathing criticism of the decision in the *Afu* case,[44] attempts were made to persuade the Supreme Court to reconsider the majority view.[45] The Court refused to do so. Even Justice Bach, who dissented from the view taken by the majority on the interpretation of article 49, ruled that there was no point in reconsidering the issue, since an absolute prohibition on deportations is not part of customary law that will be enforced by the Court.[46]

HOLDING DETAINEES OUTSIDE OCCUPIED TERRITORY

Shortly after judgment was delivered in the *Afu* case the interpretation of article 49 became an issue again. The *Ketziot* case[47] concerned conditions of detention of administrative detainees in the Ketziot detention camp, set up in Israel shortly after the *Intifada* in the Territories began in December 1987. One of the petitioners' arguments was that under the terms of Geneva Convention IV the occupying power is forbidden from holding administrative detainees outside the occupied territory itself. Holding the detainees in Israel was therefore incompatible with the terms of the Convention.

The authorities responded with a number of counterarguments, including the familiar argument that the terms of the Geneva Convention are not enforceable before the domestic courts. They pointed out that the

Geneva Convention does not include an express prohibition against holding administrative detainees in the territory of the occupying power, and added that even if it did, an Israeli statute that specifically states otherwise was to be preferred to the terms of the Convention.[48]

The petitioners' argument was based on two main provisions of the Convention: article 49, which, as seen previously, outlaws forcible transfers and deportations of persons from occupied territory to the territory of the occupying power, and article 76, which stipulates: "Protected persons accused of offenses shall be detained in the occupied country and if convicted they shall serve their sentences therein."

Justice Shamgar accepted the argument that as conventional law, and especially conventional law inconsistent with a domestic statute, the terms of the Convention could not be enforced by a domestic court, even if the petitioners' arguments in respect to the Convention were well founded. He therefore only referred in passing to the substantive argument regarding the interpretation of the Convention. The interpretation he chose was interesting, however, for it combines the antitextual interpretation of article 49, adopted in the *Afu* case, with a purely textual and literal interpretation of article 76 of the Convention.

Justice Shamgar took the view that, as article 76 refers only to persons accused or convicted of offences, it does not apply to administrative detainees. The Convention contains detailed provisions regarding treatment of administrative detainees and since it does not expressly apply article 76 to such detainees, "one may argue that . . . the Convention does not see the first part of article 76 as belonging to those principles that apply to administrative detainees."[49] Justice Shamgar mentioned that he had not overlooked the view of Pictet who, in the ICRC Commentary to the Convention, states that article 78 dealing with administrative detention must be read together with article 49 which outlaws deportations and forcible transfers. He stated, however, that "Pictet's conclusion is not based on the express text of article 78, but rather on an interpretation built by him, which, with all due respect, I do not accept."[50]

Putting these two interpretations together, we get the following picture: article 49 should not be interpreted literally and therefore, despite what it says, it does not prohibit all deportations. Article 76 should be interpreted literally. If it says "accused and convicted persons," it should be applied to those categories of persons only, and should not be applied to administrative detainees who have not been formally accused or convicted. The fact that this interpretation renders a result that is somewhat anomalous is of no interest.

Justice Bach once again took a different view of the Convention. He accepted Pictet's view that when article 49 is considered together with article 76, the conclusion must be that detainees may only be held within the territory of the occupied country itself.[51] Justice Bach considered Justice Shamgar's reading of article 76 to be overliteral. The prohibition on transfer of accused and convicted persons out of occupied territory should apply with even greater force to detainees who have not been accused or convicted.[52]

ARTICLE 2 AND APPLICATION OF THE CONVENTION

The Supreme Court has never authoritatively ruled on the Convention's application on the West Bank and in Gaza. However, Justice Shamgar, who was a party to the decision in the *Awwad* case and wrote both the *Na'azal* decision and the majority opinions in the *Afu* and *Ketziot* cases, referred to this question at length in his nonjudicial capacity and in one of his judgments. It is revealing to examine which theory of interpretation he adopted in examining the question.

In his capacity as attorney-general and in an article written after elevation to the bench, Justice Shamgar presented the argument against the formal applicability of Geneva Convention IV to the situation in the West Bank and Gaza. This argument rests on a highly literal reading of the second paragraph in article 2 of the Convention. Had Justice Shamgar concentrated on the historical background of paragraph 2, he would surely have ruled that this paragraph is entirely irrelevant to the question of the Convention's application to those territories taken by Israel in the course of the 1967 armed conflict. The Conference of Government Experts convened by the ICRC to prepare the Geneva Conventions after the Second World War recommended that the Conventions be applicable to "any armed conflict, whether the latter is or is not recognized by the parties concerned" and also to "cases of occupation of territories in the absence of any state of war."[53] Following this recommendation, under the first paragraph of article 2 the Convention applies to any occupation arising out of an armed conflict. Under the second paragraph it also applies to cases of occupation that did not result from an armed conflict. This is fully explained in the ICRC Commentary.[54]

Despite the drafting history and the clear exposition in the ICRC Commentary, Justice Shamgar explained the view taken by the Israeli authorities since his term as attorney-general in the following way:

> According to the view taken by the Israeli authorities the wording of the paragraph does not support this restrictive interpretation, *whatever the primary intention of those who drafted the text.* On the contrary, the general context, the syntax of the sentence and the use of the word "even" in the last clause of the second paragraph contradict the

argument that the second paragraph adds to the Article only the specific situation mentioned in the last clause (starting with the word
"even"). Would the paragraph refer only to the situation where occupation is not met with resistance, the word "even" would have been
entirely superfluous. In other words, the text adopted accords a more
general meaning to the second paragraph than the one connected with
its final clause only, *whatever the meaning intended to be conferred on
it by its draftsmen.*[55]

It may be argued that Justice Shamgar wrote this passage in his nonjudicial capacity and that he was presenting the government view without necessarily subscribing to it. However, in a judicial decision in which
he made passing reference to the applicability question, Justice Shamgar
addressed the argument that article 2 should be interpreted in light of its
underlying intention. He had this to say about the argument: "Even if
we are prepared to make the drastic assumption that this was indeed the
intention, the question still arises whether adequate expression was
given to this intention in the text of the convention."[56]

The theory of interpretation adopted here is that even when the text
of a treaty is ambiguous one may not take into account the intention of
the drafters, unless it was given some expression in the text itself.

THE GENEVA CONVENTION: WHAT THEORY OF INTERPRETATION?

Two inconsistent theories of interpretation were adopted in interpreting
different provisions in the same convention. One is a highly formalistic
semantic theory that seeks to discover the meaning of a provision exclusively by examining its wording, ignoring its background and drafting
history. The other is an antiformalistic approach that ignores the clear
wording of the text and seeks its meaning in the assumed evil its authors
sought to prevent. As *theories* of interpretation, these are diametrically
opposed. In their manner of *application* to different provisions in the
Geneva Convention they have one thing in common: the result was that
most favorable to the authorities.

It may be argued that there is a justification for two different theories of interpretation: one that relates to substantive provisions, the other
to procedural issues, such as the Covenant's application. The decision in
the *Ketziot* case reveals, however, that a formalist literal approach may
be adopted even when interpreting a substantive provision.

In cases dealing with Israeli domestic law Justice Shamgar was a
leading proponent of the approach that, when two interpretations of a
statute are credible, the courts must opt for the one that furthers individual rights.[57] In interpreting the Geneva Convention he adopted a

diametrically opposed approach, namely that a treaty should be interpreted so as to be least restrictive of the sovereignty of states parties. This approach has been categorically rejected in interpretation of human rights treaties.[58] Its adoption in interpreting Geneva Convention IV, a treaty on humanitarian law, reveals a great deal about the Court's attitude in cases relating to the Occupied Territories.

CHAPTER FOUR

THE BENEVOLENT OCCUPANT

The law of belligerent occupation recognizes that military needs will be the major concern of every army of occupation. Nevertheless, because the occupying army has control over the occupied territory the occupying power has the duty to take over the first and most basic task of every government: maintaining law and order and facilitating everyday life. Furthermore, since political control over new territory must not be achieved by force but by international negotiation, the occupying power may not use the occupation as a means of changing the political status of the occupied territory. The latter principle is expressed in the restriction imposed by international law on the occupying state's power to change laws in occupied territory.

In the drafting stage of the Hague Regulations, these two obligations of an occupying power were dealt with in separate articles.[1] However, in the final version of the Regulations, they were both included in article 43 that states: "The authority of the legitimate power having in fact passed into the hands of the occupant, the latter shall take all the measures in his power to restore, and ensure, as far as possible, public order and safety, while respecting, unless absolutely prevented, the laws in force in the country."

Accepting that article 43 reflects customary international law, which is enforced in domestic courts, forced the Supreme Court to grapple both with the general questions of interpretation that this article poses, as well as those arising out of the specific political context. By forging a close connection between the two obligations included in article 43, the Court subjected the restrictions on the legislative power of the military

to the duties imposed on the occupant in the first part of article 43. The
duty to respect the laws in force unless the occupant is absolutely prevented from doing so were relaxed by the Court, and the occupying
power's duty "to restore, and ensure . . . public order and safety"
became the nexus of all questions regarding article 43. The first issue I
shall address therefore is the way the Court has interpreted the duty to
restore and ensure public order and safety.

DUTY TO RESTORE AND ENSURE PUBLIC ORDER AND SAFETY

The Notion of Civil Life

According to prevailing notions at the time the Hague Regulations were
drafted, the main task of government was to prevent disruptions to public order rather than to take responsibility for social and economic welfare.[2] By the time Israel took over the Occupied Territories in 1967, con-
ceptions of government had changed. This change is reflected in the
decisions of the Supreme Court that define the scope of the occupying
power's duty to restore and ensure public order and safety.

The first published decision dealing with the Occupied Territories,
the *Christian Society* case,[3] dealt with an amendment introduced by the
military government into the Jordanian Labor Law to facilitate mandatory arbitration of labor disputes.[4] The petitioner, a charitable organization that ran a hospital in Bethlehem, was involved in a dispute with the
hospital staff. In its petition to the Supreme Court the petitioner argued
that the amendment to the Jordanian law exceeded the powers of a belligerent occupant under article 43.

In addressing this argument Justice Sussman pointed out that the
English translation of article 43 does not do justice to the original French
text. The French text refers to the duty of the occupying power to restore
and ensure "l'ordre et la vie publique," which should be translated as
"public order and civil life" (rather than public order and safety).[5] This
implies that the occupant's duty is not confined to preventing breaches of
public order; it encompasses restoring and ensuring "the whole social,
commercial and economic life of the community."[6] The occupying power
must take account of changing circumstances and adopt measures,
including legislative measures, needed to ensure "civil life." As the matter was put in a later decision, ensuring public order and civil life involves
"exercising regular administration, with all the branches accepted in our
times in a well-ordered state, including security, health, education, welfare, as well as quality of life and transportation."[7]

All three judges in the *Christian Society* case agreed with the wide
view of "public order and civil life." However, they were divided on a

major question of principle: how is one to judge whether measures are indeed adopted in order to ensure civil life? Writing for the majority, Justice Sussman argued that all depends on the *motive* behind the measures: if it was to further the good of the local population, the measures would be regarded as necessary to ensure civil life. In rejecting this approach Justice Haim Cohn stressed the distinction between "restoring" and "ensuring" public order and civil life.[8] In his view, the term "restore" implies that the gauge of the legitimacy of measures taken to restore public order and civil life is the situation that existed before the occupation began. The occupying power may not introduce innovations, even if its motive is to further the welfare of the local population. Furthermore, the duty to *ensure* public order and civil life must be seen as connected with measures taken to *restore* them. After public order and civil life have been restored, the need may arise to take further measures to ensure that they will be maintained, "but these ensuring measures must not change the nature of public order and civil life that were restored."[9]

The views of Justice Sussman and Justice Cohn reflect radically different approaches to the status and role of a military government in occupied territory. Both views are problematic. Justice Sussman's "benevolent occupant" approach paves the way for far-reaching changes in occupied territory under the guise of measures taken for the good of the local population. As Professor Dinstein warned in a note written in response to the decision in the *Christian Society* case: "One should remember that the occupant's concern for the needs of the local population is not always genuine, and it is sometimes essential to protect this population from the bear's hug of the occupant."[10]

On the other hand, Justice Cohn's "maintenance" approach might be tenable in a short-lived occupation during which social and economic conditions in the occupied territory remain much as they were when the occupation began. It becomes untenable when the occupation continues for an extended period of time during which conditions in the occupied territory change fundamentally. Thus, even if Justice Cohn's approach had been adopted when the *Christian Society* case reached the Court a few years after the occupation began, it could not have survived the prolongation of the occupation in changing economic, social, and political circumstances.

The distinction between restoring and ensuring public order and civil life has been referred to in later decisions,[11] but the connection that Justice Cohn attempted to create between the legitimacy of measures taken to restore and ensure public order and civil life was categorically rejected by the Court. The "benevolent occupant" approach suggested by Justice Sussman became the accepted view of the Court. The application of this approach will be analyzed below.

Public Order

Stressing the duty to ensure "civil life" (a term taken as synonymous with the general welfare of the local population) has not led to abandonment of the issue of public order in its narrow sense. It has been accepted as axiomatic not only that the military commander has the power to take measures to protect the security of his troops, but that he has the duty to take measures aimed at protecting general security in the area.[12] The Court has held not only that severe security measures are permissible under article 43, but that they may be positively required as part of the occupying power's duty to ensure public order.

The notion of a duty under article 43 to adopt severe security measures was first raised in the *Awwad* case,[13] in which it was argued that deportation of persons on security grounds is a violation of article 49 of Geneva Convention IV. As discussed in the previous chapter, in the *Awwad* case Justice Sussman based his interpretation of article 49 on its assumed purpose. He saw fit to add, however, that "[I]t is obvious that the above convention does not detract from the duty of the occupying power to ensure preservation of public order in the occupied territory, which is imposed upon it in article 43 of the Hague Convention of 1907, nor from its right to take measures needed to protect its own security."[14]

Citing article 43 of the Hague Regulations in order to legitimize a measure that is inconsistent with the Geneva Convention perverts the very purpose of the Convention. Precisely because the Geneva Convention recognizes that the occupying power has the power to protect security, it lays down provisions whose object is to *limit* measures that may legitimately be taken in exercising this power. Besides ignoring article 78 of the Geneva Convention that makes this point quite clear, Justice Sussman also ignored the fact that article 43 of the Hague Regulations stipulates that the occupant shall take all measures *in its power* to restore public order. Any measure prohibited by international law is not in the occupant's power.

Use of article 43 to legitimize security measures adopted by the military authorities was not confined to the *Awwad* case. The Court relied on article 43 to justify restrictions on freedom of the press,[15] refusal to allow local elections,[16] and imposing a bond on parents to ensure good conduct of their minor children.[17]

Restrictions on the military's power to adopt measures they considered necessary to ensure public order was addressed by Justice Shamgar in the *VAT* case. Justice Shamgar stated that the military must strike a fair balance between military needs and humanitarian considerations and that "the military interest or military necessity of themselves do not allow severe violation of humanitarian rights."[18]

An attempt to strike such a balance was made by Justice Goldberg in the *Tamimi* case.[19] This case arose out of a demand by practicing lawyers on the West Bank to establish a bar association elected according to Jordanian law. The military commander's response to the demand was to promulgate a military order establishing a bar council whose members, rather than being elected, would be appointed by the head of the civil administration in the military government and would enjoy only some of the powers given to the bar association under Jordanian law. The petitioners challenged the validity of this order.

While the Court was reluctant to challenge the military commander's assessment that allowing an independent bar association could endanger public order, it held that the commander had not even considered trying to find an acceptable balance between his duty and power to protect security and the interest in professional independence, especially in the free profession of lawyers. It therefore ordered the commander to consider amending the military order so as to allow limited autonomy to the bar association.

In the discussion below of the way the Court has reviewed use of discretion in security cases, we shall see that while the Court has frequently mentioned the duty of the commander to balance security factors with other considerations, it has almost invariably refused to enter the balancing issue itself, and has bowed to the discretion of the military commander. The duty to balance has more often been part of the Court's rhetoric than of its actual decision-making. The *Tamimi* decision would appear to be one of the few exceptions, though one of dubious significance.[20] On the face of the decision itself the final result might indeed appear to be a victory for the petitioners. They received an absolute order against the military governor and were even awarded costs. In effect, however, the victory was a limited one. Notwithstanding the balancing act of the Court, the principle of professional independence was subordinated to the overriding interest of the military commander. The commander was merely ordered to allow some degree of input by the lawyers themselves.

LEGISLATIVE CHANGES

The principle of international law (articulated in article 43) that an occupying power must respect the laws in force in the occupied country was formally recognized in 1967. Upon capturing areas previously held by the enemy the military commanders issued proclamations that the prevailing law would remain in force, subject to such changes as would be made by military order.[21] Over the years, however, far-reaching changes were introduced into the laws that apply both in the West Bank and in Gaza.[22] Several attempts were made to challenge the validity of changes in the law by arguing that they were incompatible with the occupying power's duty to respect the laws in force in the country "unless absolutely prevented."

The first such attempt was made in the *Christian Society* case, previously mentioned. As we have seen, in that case Justice Sussman adopted a broad interpretation of the belligerent occupant's duty "to ensure public order and civil life." He then proceeded to posit a close connection between this duty and the scope of the military government's power to introduce changes into local law. Article 43 requires the occupying power to respect the laws in force in the occupied territory "unless absolutely prevented." Could it be said that legislative changes introduced in order to promote the social and economic welfare of the local population could not be absolutely prevented? Justice Sussman replied to this question in the following way:

> Reasonable interpretation of the words "absolutely prevented" in article 43 requires us to interpret the article in the light of the occupying power's duty towards the population in the occupied territory, and I have already shown, that this duty includes the duty to regulate social and economic affairs.[23]
>
> . . . whenever the laws in force in occupied territory do not enable the military government to fulfil its duty towards the residents of the territory, an "absolute prevention" prevails which authorizes it to change those laws.[24]

Applying this test, Justice Sussman reached the conclusion that the military governor was well within his powers in changing the Jordanian Labor Law to facilitate its implementation.

In his dissenting opinion, Justice Haim Cohn recognized that the military governor had acted in good faith in order to promote better labor relations. He also accepted that the Jordanian Labor Law was worthy of implementation and that regulating settlement of labor disputes was preferable to letting matters deteriorate to strikes and lockouts. However, as noted, his position was that an occupying power's duty under article 43 of the Hague Regulations is not to establish an ideal society, or even to promote those arrangements that appear best, but to restore and ensure those arrangements of civil life that prevailed before the occupation. Because the Jordanian Labor Law had not been implemented before the occupation, it was not within the military governor's power to amend the law to make its implementation possible.

Justice Cohn also anticipated an argument raised at a later stage, namely that one of the tests for the legitimacy of new arrangements instituted in occupied territory is whether such arrangements exist in the occupying power's country.[25] After pointing out that Israel has no law of mandatory labor arbitration, Justice Cohn added: "As long as 'public order and civil life' exist in Israel without mandatory arbitration and mandatory judicial resolution in labor disputes, the argument cannot stand that 'public order and civil life' in the Territories require such mandatory arbitration and mandatory judicial resolution."[26]

The majority view, which gauges the legislative powers of the occupying power according to the "benevolent occupant" approach, prevailed. The Court repeated the idea that being "absolutely prevented" from changing local law means only that the law may not be changed unless there is a need to change it, and that the need is to be judged by the duty to ensure public order and civil life.[27] In the *Tabeeb* case the Court reviewed various authorities on the international law of belligerent occupation and, relying mainly on the seminal article by E. H. Schwenk,[28] concluded that "[i]n fact, the 'prevented' mentioned in the last part of article 43 is not 'absolute' at all. The question is one of priorities and of the facility of achieving the goals set out in the first part of the article, namely 'ensuring civil life.'" [29]

Similarly, in the *VAT* case, the Court stated that the question was whether there was a need for legislative changes. It added:

> The *need* of which we are speaking may be a military need, on the one hand, and humanitarian considerations, on the other hand, and the absolute prevention may derive from legitimate interests of the military government in maintaining public order or from concern for the local population and ensuring its civil life. Of course, in all cases there must be a fair balance between the considerations, so that a military interest or military need of themselves do not permit severe violation of humanitarian rights.[30]

Subordinating limitations on law-changing power to the *duty* to ensure public order and civil life means first and foremost that those limitations are relaxed. Furthermore, it means that in certain circumstances the authorities are not only permitted to introduce legislative changes, but that they may have a positive obligation to do so.[31]

Authorities on the international law of belligerent occupation agree that the term "absolutely prevented" cannot be taken literally.[32] Some flexibility must be allowed in exercise of governmental functions in occupied territory, especially when the occupation is prolonged and conditions change. Nevertheless, the Court's interpretation has stripped the restrictions on legislative changes of any significant meaning. Article 43 might just as well have stated that the military commander must act in the best interests of the local population except where prevented from doing so by military necessity.

In the context of a case like the *Christian Society* case, application of the benevolent occupant approach to the question of legislative changes is appealing. But what characterized that case was that the changes introduced into the legislation were not part of the political agenda of the occupying power; their *sole* motive was to alleviate a local problem. Such cases are rare. There has generally been a strong connection between steps taken by the military and the *political* agenda of the Government of Israel, in whose name the military commanders are acting. I shall now examine how the Court has dealt with such cases.

BENEVOLENT OCCUPANT APPROACH

Welfare of the Local Population:
Two Models of Judicial Decision-Making

Two cases dealing with the supply of electricity on the West Bank illustrate the difficulties in applying the principles first laid down in the *Christian Society* case. The judgments in these two cases represent two models of judicial decision-making.

The *Electricity Co. (No. 1)* case[33] dealt with a decision by the military government relating to supply of electricity to the city of Hebron. Before 1967 residents of Hebron had received electrical power from generators run by the municipality. As needs grew, and especially after the Jewish settlement of Kiryat Arba had been built on the outskirts of Hebron, electricity supplied by generators became insufficient. To deal with the problem, the military commander promulgated two orders: one granting an official in his administration all the powers of the electricity council provided for under Jordanian law, the second granting the said official the power to deal with electricity, that is, to generate electricity, supply, and sell it. Armed with these powers and an order from the military commander to deal with electricity in the municipal area of Hebron, the appointed official authorized the Israel Electricity Company to generate electricity from a power station set up at military headquarters in the area and to supply and sell the electricity to the Hebron municipality. The Palestinian Electricity Company for the Jerusalem District, which had received a concession from the Jordanian government to supply electricity in other areas of the West Bank before 1967, attacked these arrangements. One of its arguments was that the orders promulgated by the commander effected changes in Jordanian law that were incompatible with article 43 of the Hague Regulations.

The Court dismissed the petition. It held that the military orders had been promulgated to enable the commander to ensure a steady and adequate supply of electricity. As concern with the economic welfare of the population in the area was one of the commander's duties under article 43, the commander had not violated this provision in acting to ensure the supply of electricity.[34]

In theory, the Court's decision in this case merely follows the "benevolent occupant" approach adopted by the majority in the *Christian Society* case. The military commander was acting to further the economic and social welfare of the local population and his acts could therefore be regarded as acts taken to ensure "civil life." However, as opposed to the *Christian Society* case, the military commander's decision in this case, which made the residents of Hebron dependent on an Israeli supplier of electricity, had obvious political implications. It could not honestly be said that the *sole* reason for the commander's decision was the benefit of the local population.[35] In fact it is by no means clear that concern for the welfare of the residents of Hebron was even the *dominant* factor in the commander's decision. Furthermore, if we examine consequences of a decision, rather than its motives, even if the decision was of immediate economic benefit to Hebron residents, making them dependent on an Israeli supplier was not necessarily in their political interest.[36]

On one significant point the Court in the *Electricity Co. (No.1)* case extended the principles laid down in the *Christian Society* case: it included the interests of Israeli settlers on the West Bank as a factor to be considered within the framework of article 43. The Court stated that "the residents of Kiryat Arba must be regarded as having been added to the local population and they are also entitled to a regular supply of electricity."[37]

Given the dubious legal status of the civilian settlements (discussed in chapter 5), regarding settlers as part of the local population for the purposes of article 43 is highly problematical.[38] Its implications are far-reaching. Article 43 attempts to resolve the potential conflict between the governmental duties of an occupant bound to ensure civil life in the occupied territory and the nonsovereign and temporary nature of occupation by limiting the power to change laws to those cases in which changes absolutely cannot be prevented. By broadening the meaning of civil life to include all the interests of the local population and allowing changes in local law to promote those interests, the Court had already weakened the restraining influence of article 43. If the test is the interests of the local population and the Israeli settlers in the area become part of that population, the potential for changing the law becomes almost unlimited.[39]

The second electricity case, *Electricity Co. (No. 2)*[40] also dealt with supply of electricity on the West Bank, but the approach taken by the Court contrasts starkly with that in the first case. The issue before the

Court was a consequence of a political decision to end the concession of the Jerusalem Electricity Company to supply electricity to East Jerusalem and parts of the West Bank.[41] Under the terms of the concession that had been granted to the company before 1967 by the Jordanian government, the government could purchase the plant from the concession owner after a stipulated period. When that period was about to end, the Government of Israel decided to purchase the Company's plant and to grant the concession to supply electricity to the Israel Electricity Company. To implement this decision, two acquisition orders were sent to the Jerusalem Company. The first, relating to the company's plant in Jerusalem, was sent by the Israeli minister of energy; the second, relating to the plant on the West Bank, was sent by the military commander of the area. In the latter order, the military commander informed the company that he was purchasing the plant "because it is required in order to ensure essential services in the area."

The company challenged the validity of both acquisition orders. It argued that the order issued by the military commander violated article 43 since the military commander has to preserve the status quo and is not authorized to introduce drastic changes. Furthermore the real motive of the commander had not been to improve the supply of electricity, but to tie local residents to the Israel Electricity Company for political reasons.

As the notice sent by the military order had not required a change in legislation, Justice Kahan assumed that article 43 was not directly applicable to the issue before the Court.[42] Nevertheless, influenced by the connection between the two parts of article 43 created in the previous decisions, he held that "the first part of article 43 can guide us as to the actions of the area commander in occupied territory and as to the limitations that customary international law places on use of his powers."[43]

While in the *Christian Society* and *Electricity Co. (No.1)* cases, the policy behind the Court's decisions had been to widen the scope of the governmental powers under article 43, Justice Kahan emphasized the restrictions on those powers inherent in the underlying philosophy of article 43. He stressed that the main feature of a regime of belligerent occupation is its temporary nature, even when the occupation lasts for an extended period. Justice Kahan added:

> From the provision about respect for the existing law one learns, that in the absence of special reasons the military commander must not, generally, initiate even changes in the area that do not alter existing law if they will have a far-reaching and long-term effect on the position in the area, beyond the period when the holding of the area as a military area comes to an end for one reason or another, unless they are for the good of the local residents.[44]

Applying this test, Justice Kahan held that the change which the military commander wished to introduce was so far-reaching as to require special justification. He explained:

> When the area came under the control of the commander of the area, electricity was supplied by the petitioner, who is a local company. The result of using the option [to end the concession] will be that supply and distribution of electricity will be entirely in the hands of bodies outside the area, and given the importance of electricity in maintaining regular life of the public, this change has implications that go beyond the economic and technical aspects of the matter.[45]

As can be seen, while Justice Kahan retained the test according to which the determinative factor is the good of the local residents, in applying the test his approach was radically different from the one adopted in the *Electricity Co. (No. 1)* case. The good of the local residents is not to be gauged solely in terms of economic development and social welfare, but must also recognize political interests of the local population. That population could be worse off receiving a steady supply of electricity from an Israeli company than it would be receiving an inferior supply from a local company. Furthermore, the specific nature of the military government as a temporary institution has significant implications for its governmental powers. Such a government must generally refrain from changes that have far-reaching and long-term effects.

The full import of Justice Kahan's judgment in the *Electricity Co. (No.2)* case is apparent when one compares the approaches to the orders issued by the military commander and the Israeli minister of energy. Under Israeli domestic law East Jerusalem is subject to Israeli law rather than a regime of belligerent occupation, so the minister of energy was not subject to the restrictions placed on the powers of the military commander. The minister's status was not temporary. Furthermore, it was perfectly legitimate for him to use his power to further the political interests of the State of Israel, as defined by the executive branch of government. Justice Kahan therefore held that, in contrast to the order issued by the military commander on the West Bank, the order issued by the minister of energy was valid.[46]

The *Electricity Co.* cases represent two models of judicial decision-making in which the authorities claim that measures adopted to serve political interests of Israel further the welfare of the local population. Both models accept the majority view in the *Christian Society* case that the legitimacy of measures taken by the military depends on whether they were adopted for the good of the local population. However, the model followed in the first case ignores the political motives behind the measures taken by the military and emphasizes the short-term material benefit to the local population. The model followed in the second case displays a degree of skepticism toward the argument that steps with obvious political motives are adopted for the good of the local population. It regards the transience of the military regime as a serious constraint on that regime's governmental powers. Furthermore, and possibly most significantly, this model does not restrict the notion of the welfare of the local population to issues of material benefit. The wider political interests of the population protected by the notion of transience are regarded as a constraining factor on use of governmental powers.

Rhetoric and Decision-Making

One of the most comprehensive discussions of article 43 is to be found in Justice Barak's judgment in the *Ja'amait Ascan* case. The case involved a plan to build a major network of four-lane highways linking towns in the West Bank and Greater Jerusalem. The petitioners argued (1) that an occupying power may not build long-term projects in occupied territory and (2) that the highway system was being built to serve Israel's political interests, rather than to benefit local residents. In replying to the latter argument the authorities cited the enormous growth in the number of vehicles in the area since 1967, as well as the inadequacy of the existing network of roads to cope with the increased volume of traffic. They conceded that the highways would benefit the residents of Israel and would facilitate travel between Israel and the West Bank, but pointed out that a large number of West Bank residents travel to work in Israel. The authorities denied that there could be anything wrong in planning and building a project in cooperation with Israel, as long as the aim of the project, from the military government's point of view, is to further the interests of the area.

Before analyzing the facts of the case, Justice Barak summarized the principles that define the powers of a military government in occupied territory.

1. Under the Hague Regulations all decisions of the occupying power must be guided by one or both of two considerations: securing the legitimate security interests of the occupant in the occupied territory and ensuring the welfare of the local population. "The military commander may not consider the national, economic or social interests of his own country, unless they have implications for his security interest or the interests of the local population."[47]

2. Two factors determine the parameters of a military government's powers in occupied territory: (a) "the duty to act as a proper government that looks after the local population in all fields of life" and

    (b) the limitations imposed on a government of a temporary nature that does not exercise sovereignty, but rules under the laws of war.

3. Although the Hague Regulations were drawn up at a time when laissez-faire notions of government prevailed, when applying article 43 today, the relevant notions of public order and civil life are those prevalent in a "modern and civilized state at the end of the twentieth century."[48]

4. In applying article 43, it is essential to distinguish between short-term and long-term occupations. Even though the Hague Regulations were drawn up with short-term occupations in mind, article 43 can be applied to long-term occupations by taking account of the passage of time and of changing conditions in establishing the requirements of public order and civil life.

5. In a long-term occupation the military government's duty to ensure public order and civil life may require long-term investments that will effect changes that will remain after the occupation ends. Such investments are lawful provided they are carried out for the good of the local population and do not bring about material change in the basic institutions of the occupied territory.

In applying these principles in the specific case, Justice Barak held that the ultimate question was whether the planning had indeed been done only for the good of Israel, or whether the good of the local population had been a guiding factor. He "saw no reason to reject the respondents' stand" on this question.[49] The planning considerations were presented to the Court and it had no basis for doubting their authenticity. The petitioners had not refuted the evidence presented by the respondents. Justice Barak concluded that "from examining the material presented to us we see a picture of professional planning, which takes into account the conditions and needs of the area and not only the conditions and needs of Israel."[50]

Application of the "benevolent occupation" approach in this case reveals its inherent difficulties. In the first place, as Justice Barak himself mentions, a military government is not elected by the people and does not represent them. How then is it qualified to make highly controversial decisions regarding the "benefit of the local population"? Justice Barak noted that the solution to transportation problems adopted in the highway network approved by the planning council was not the only possible solution. He held, however, that because it was a reasonable solution, there was no basis for judicial intervention in the decision of the planning council.[51] How appropriate is the model of reasonableness, adopted from English and Israeli administrative law, when dealing with decisions made by bodies not politically accountable to the public for whose good they are ostensibly acting? Limiting the scope of judicial review over administrative action to questions of reasonableness rests on the theory that the government, of which administrative bodies are a part, is responsible to parliament for its actions and that, if its policies are misguided, the correct remedy is political rather than judicial. What place does this have in a regime in which the government is not politically responsible to the people it governs?

According to the Jordanian planning law in force when Israel occupied the West Bank in 1967, an institutionalized mechanism exists for public input in the planning process. In addition to the Supreme Planning Council, the law provides for district planning bodies. The military government disbanded the district bodies (in which local inhabitants play a central role in the planning process) and placed their powers in the hands of the Supreme Planning Council (which is composed solely of officials appointed by the military government).[52] One needs a certain amount of naivete to believe that this council is concerned exclusively with the good of the West Bank residents, rather than the political objectives of the Government of Israel.

The notion of "public benefit" is intimately connected to political objectives and interests. The model applied by Justice Barak is reminiscent of a colonial model of governors who know what is best for the natives. Development is assumed beneficial and large highways must be for the public good, as must improved connections between the Occupied Territories and Israel itself. There is, however, nothing inherently good about development the adverse consequences of which may override benefits. It is quite true that people may opt for development despite its adverse consequences, but should a temporary regime make this irrevocable decision?[53] Moreover, is improving connections between the West Bank and Israel necessarily for the good of the West Bank residents, on the not unreasonable assumption that many of these residents would prefer to break those connections?

Justice Barak's analysis raises another problem. Despite the Court's stated conviction that the planning was for the good of the local population, there is no lack of evidence to show that it was carried out as part of a general plan for the West Bank that was based on the planners' perception of Israeli interests. Even if it is indeed true that the planners were also concerned to meet the needs of the West Bank population, what was the *dominant* consideration? According to Justice Landau's analysis in the *Elon Moreh* case,[54] if the political interests of Israel were dominant, the decision should have been invalidated even if the planners thought that the plan would also serve the needs of the West Bank population.

The principles defined by Justice Barak establish a theoretical framework for gauging the parameters of a belligerent occupant's powers. They fail, however, to address the inherent difficulties involved in balancing the conflicting demands on any occupying army, whose primary concern is obviously to protect the security of its own forces and the military interests of its own country, rather than to cater to the needs of the local population. More important, they fail to address the difficulties of applying the benevolent approach in the political context of the West Bank and Gaza. Until the peace process gained momentum after the Labor Party returned to power in 1992, the political establishment in Israel refused to recognize that those territories were subject to a regime of belligerent occupation. Government policy was to adopt measures whose very object was to ensure that Israeli control over the Territories would not be temporary and that the dividing line between the Territories and Israel itself would be obliterated.[55]

The notion of transience as a constraint on the powers of the military in occupied territory, one of Justice Barak's principles in the *Ja'amait Ascan* decision, was applied by the Court in the *Elon Moreh* decision (discussed in the next chapter), and in the *Electricity Co. (No. 2)* case (previously discussed). In general, however, it has not served to limit the actions of the military. The dominant trend in the Court's decisions has been to rely on the benevolence of the military authorities.

The most glaring example of this trend is to be found in Justice Shamgar's monumental judgment in the *VAT* case. This case arose out of two military orders, promulgated on the West Bank and in Gaza, imposing value-added-tax (VAT) on most goods and services, as well as detailed bookkeeping procedures necessitated by the tax.[56] The tax was imposed simultaneously with introduction of the tax in Israel. For the first few years, bookkeeping procedures connected with the tax were not rigorously enforced in the Occupied Territories, but when the authorities began to enforce these procedures merchants from the West Bank and Gaza petitioned the Supreme Court. They argued: (1) that a belligerent occupant does not have the power to impose new taxes in occupied territory and (2) that the legislation introducing the new tax was inconsistent with article 43 of the Hague Regulations, as the tax had been imposed for the good of the Israeli economy rather than for the benefit of the residents of the Occupied Territories.

The major part of Justice Shamgar's opinion addresses the first argument.[57] Justice Shamgar surveyed different views on this question and reached the conclusion that there is no hard and fast rule of customary international law against imposition of new taxes in an area subject to a regime of belligerent occupation. This does not mean, however, that an occupying army may freely impose new taxes. The question must be examined according to the principles set down in article 43 of the Hague Regulations regarding changes in local law. In other words, the question is whether the new taxes were imposed in order to ensure "public order and civil life."[58]

In addressing the second argument Justice Shamgar reached the conclusion that the law introducing VAT was justified both in order to fulfill a military need and to ensure the welfare of the population. If the tax had not been imposed in the Occupied Territories after it was imposed in Israel, the free flow of goods, services, and labor that had been maintained between the Occupied Territories and Israel since 1967 would have had to be stopped, a step that would have had dire economic repercussions in the Territories. It was for the good of the local population that measures were taken to prevent such a situation; the military government had a direct interest in preventing an economic collapse that would make its task of maintaining public order much more difficult.[59]

Despite the logic behind the Court's reasoning, it is difficult to escape the irony of the "benevolent occupant" approach, as applied by the Court in the VAT case. The notion of "no taxation without representation" having been rejected by the Court, it proceeded to accept uncritically the authorities' argument that they had the good of the local population at heart when they imposed VAT, a tax not necessarily suited to the West Bank and Gaza economies.[60] As in the highway case, it takes a certain degree of credulity to believe that the dominant motive behind the imposition of VAT was the benefit of the local population rather than protection of Israeli economic interests. But even if one accepts this premise, the case exemplifies the bear's hug that Professor Dinstein warned against in his note on the *Christian Society* case.

PART II

CHAPTER FIVE

CIVILIAN SETTLEMENTS AND DEVELOPMENT PROJECTS

Establishment of Israeli civilian settlements in the Occupied Territories dramatically exposed the dissonance between government policies and the formal legal framework of belligerent occupation. According to the international law of belligerent occupation, the political status quo of occupied territories must be maintained so that their ultimate fate can be determined by political negotiation. In contrast, the political aim of settlements is to create facts that will predetermine the outcome of any negotiations by making Israeli withdrawal from the settled parts of the Territories politically unfeasible.[1] Furthermore, the existence in the Territories of a large number of settlers, who enjoy the full democratic rights of Israeli citizens and for whose benefit scarce land and water resources have been harnessed, has made the regime there much closer to a colonial regime than one of belligerent occupation.

POLITICAL BACKGROUND

Settlement in the Occupied Territories began soon after the end of the 1967 War.[2] In the initial period, during which the Labor Party was in power, government policy roughly followed the Alon Plan that sought to distinguish between areas heavily populated by Palestinians, which would eventually be returned to Jordan, and strategic nonpopulated areas, which would remain under Israeli control. The plan envisaged a line of strategic settlements along the Jordan valley and further settlements in the areas surrounding Jerusalem. After the 1973 Yom Kippur War, the Labor government came under pressure from the newly formed Gush Emunim settlers' movement to allow settlement in other areas of the West Bank. Some elements in the Labor Party supported the aspirations of this movement and a few settlements were allowed outside the original boundaries of the Alon Plan. When the Labor Party was defeated in the 1977 elections, there were twenty-four settlements on the West Bank (excluding Greater Jerusalem), with a total population of 5,000.

The Likud Government that came to power in 1977 was ideologically and politically committed to allowing and promoting Jewish settlement in all parts of the historic Land of Israel. Arguments for such settlements were not dressed in the strategic/security terms used by the Labor Party, but in religious/nationalistic terms. Settlement planning was directed by the Rural Settlement Division of the World Zionist Organization (WZO), headed by a member of the Herut Party, Matityahu Drobles. The first settlement plan, drawn up by the WZO and submitted in 1978, envisaged establishment of a chain of settlement "blocs" along the densely populated highlands of the West Bank. This plan stated quite clearly that the objectives of the settlements were to "reduce to the minimum the possibility for the development of another Arab state in these regions"[3] and to make it difficult for the local Palestinian population "to form a territorial continuity and political unity when it is fragmented by Jewish settlements."[4]

The Drobles plan was updated in 1980 and 1983. The amended plans called for establishment of Jewish settlements around and between Palestinian towns. In 1991 Housing Minister Ariel Sharon announced the "Seven Stars Plan," which called for establishment of new towns on the Green Line that separates the West Bank and Israel, with the declared intention of its consequent eradication.

The Israeli public was always divided on the prudence of establishing settlements in the Occupied Territories. Israelis who believed that resolution of the conflict with the Palestinians would necessarily involve withdrawal from all or most of the West Bank and Gaza argued that establishment of settlements would impede an eventual political agreement. Other arguments were that the settlements provoked resentment among Palestinians who felt their property and security threatened, that establishment of settlements encouraged nationalistic and chauvinistic tendencies among sections of the Israeli public, that the inevitable distinction between privileged Israeli citizens and Palestinians subject to occupation produced a system of apartheid, that the existence of settlements created a further source of friction between Israelis and Palestinians, and that investment of resources in the settlements diverted funds required for pressing needs in Israeli society.

On the other hand, large sections of the Jewish public in Israel supported the policy. Many did so on religious or nationalistic grounds.[5] Others subscribed to the view that the presence of Israeli settlements would enhance security or that the settlements would strengthen Israel's bargaining power in future negotiations.[6] As time passed and the government encouraged settlement of Israelis in the Occupied Territory by offering highly subsidized housing, many Israelis who settled there became supporters of the policy out of economic self-interest.

LEGALITY OF SETTLEMENTS

Arguments against the legality of Israeli settlements in the Occupied Territories may be divided into three categories:

1. *General Prohibition.* Article 49 of Geneva Convention IV prohibits transfer of part of the occupying power's civilian population into the occupied territory. While it may be argued that this prohibition does not apply to the purchase of land in the occupied territory by residents of the occupying country and establishment of residence there on land purchased or rented, the widely accepted view is that it does apply to establishment, or even promotion, of civilian settlements by the government itself.[7] Furthermore, under principles of customary international law an occupying power may only employ measures and promote projects in occupied territory if they serve one or both of two purposes: military needs or benefit of the local population.[8] Establishing civilian settlements in occupied territory in order to further the economic or political interests of the occupying power is incompatible with these principles.[9]

2. *Use of Private Land.* International law outlaws *confiscation* of private property by the occupying army,[10] but recognizes the power of the army to *requisition* land for the needs of the occupying army.[11] Expropriation of private land for establishment of settlements is clearly illegal. Use of requisitioned land may be challenged on a number of grounds. First, a civilian settlement is not a "need of the occupying army" for which requisition is permitted. Second, because the salient feature of requisition (as opposed to confiscation or expropriation) is its temporary nature, requisitioned land may not be used for a permanent settlement.

3. *Use of Public Land.* Under article 55 of the Hague Regulations, the occupying power must administer public property as a usufructuary. Establishment of a settlement, which changes the nature of the land use, is inconsistent with the notion of usufruct.

Given the political controversy over the settlements, the Supreme Court was reluctant to deal with the issue. It was especially reluctant to address general arguments that challenged the government's entire settlement policy (as opposed to more restricted arguments that could affect the legality of a particular settlement, but not of the whole policy).

The argument based on article 49 of Geneva Convention IV is a general argument of principle; its acceptance could have provoked a major confrontation with the government. It is unlikely that the government (especially one made up of parties with a strong ideological commitment to the Greater Land of Israel) would have abandoned its political program and ideology on the settlement issue in response to a decision of the Supreme Court. One can only guess what the reaction would have been to a judgment declaring all government-sponsored settlements in the Occupied Territories illegal; it might well have been legislation overruling the precedent or restricting the Court's jurisdiction in petitions relating to the Occupied Territories.[12]

It will be recalled that the Court offered two rationales for its refusal to address the legality of settlements under article 49 of Geneva Convention IV.[13] First, because article 49 does not reflect customary law it may not be relied on before the domestic courts of Israel. Second, given their political sensitivity *general* arguments relating to legality of settlements are not justiciable.

The Court itself has ruled that the Hague Regulations reflect customary international law that will be enforced by Israel's domestic courts. Thus, the first of these rationales does not apply to arguments resting on the Hague Regulations that relate to general limitations on the powers of an occupying power, requisition of private land, or use of public land. The Court addressed the issue of requisitioning private land for establishment of settlements in a number of cases. Its judgment in one of these cases forced the government to abandon use of private land for settlements. However, the Court made every effort to avoid ruling on the use of public land for settlements and on the general limitations on an occupying power. In doing so it resorted to two judicial doctrines. When a private individual attempted to challenge the use being made of land that had been declared public land, the Court denied his *standing* to raise this question.[14] When an attempt was made to confront the entire settlement policy of the government on the basis of the argument, inter alia, that establishing permanent settlements is prohibited under the Hague Regulations, the Court held that the matter was nonjusticiable.[15]

Although the Court was not prepared to tackle the settlement *policy*, it rejected the claim that every petition relating to settlements should be regarded as nonjusticiable; the political nature of settlements could not empower the authorities to take an individual's land without the right to challenge the action in court.[16] Thus, the main cases dealing directly with the settlement issue are cases of land requisition.

LAND REQUISITION

Rafiah Approach Case[17]

This case related to Northern Sinai, at the time in Israeli hands but subsequently handed over to Egypt under the terms of the peace treaty with Israel. The principles that guided the Court in this case were adopted in later cases dealing with requisition of land on the West Bank and in Gaza.

The *Rafiah Approach* case related to eviction of Bedouin who lived in the Rafiah Approach area, an area on the Egyptian side of the international border with Mandatory Palestine separating the Gaza Strip from the rest of Sinai.[18] The eviction followed a rise in attacks on civilians, both Israeli and Palestinian, mining of roads, and sabotage of buildings and installations. The military authorities claimed that it was necessary to create a buffer zone between Sinai and Gaza so as to make it more difficult for armed infiltrators to carry out attacks in Gaza or Israel or to send weapons or explosives. The military commander issued an order closing the area, although the Bedouin were still allowed to enter the area to cultivate their crops during the day. Compensation was offered for buildings and orchards that had to be evacuated.

Eviction of the Bedouin from their lands provoked a reaction on the Israeli left, especially among members of *Mapam* kibbutzim in the area, who were supposedly the immediate "beneficiaries" of the security zone created by the eviction. In a petition to the Supreme Court submitted on behalf of nine Bedouin sheikhs by a lawyer associated with the *Mapam* party, the central argument was that the military could have used other means to solve the security problems and that the real reasons behind the eviction were not security considerations but "political or settlement [considerations] that the respondents prefer not to provide."[19] The military authorities conceded that two *Nachal* outposts had been established in the area from which the Bedouin had been evicted, but insisted that the sole grounds for the eviction had been security considerations.[20] They detailed the measures that had been taken to turn the area into a buffer zone.

As this was one of the first cases in which the Court was asked to rule on the validity of a military order in the Occupied Territories (the order declaring the area closed), a number of questions arose (which have been discussed in other parts of this study).[21] The question that interests us at present is only the "taking" question and its relationship to settlement.

The security arguments for the government action were presented in an affidavit of General Israel Tal, a highly respected army general. For their part, the petitioners could provide no real evidence that the dominant considerations had not been the security considerations described in the affidavit. Although the settlement issue lay in the background, the authorities provided the Court with an excuse to avoid dealing with it. In his affidavit General Tal stated that there were three ways of protecting a buffer zone: (1) closing the area, preventing permanent presence of local residents, and erecting various obstacles such as fences; (2) establishing Jewish settlements and Jewish presence; and (3) a combination of these actions. Justice Landau declared that as "for the moment, at least" only the first of these measures had been adopted, he would "concentrate on examining the matter in this light, and will not deal with the question of settlement for security purposes outside the state's area of jurisdiction—a question that has its own legal aspects and was not discussed in the arguments before us."[22]

Having ruled that the military authorities have the formal power to close areas for security reasons, the question, in Justice Landau's view, related to the scope of judicial review in security matters. He held that "the scope of intervention of the court in the actions of military authorities that relate to security matters must necessarily be very narrow."[23] As he was persuaded that the military had acted in good faith for security reasons in closing the area and taking possession (as opposed to title) of the land, there was no room for the Court's intervention.

Like his colleague, Justice Witkon also regarded the issue as being the scope of judicial review over acts of the military. His view was that such review is limited to two questions: (1) whether the formal authority exists to perform the challenged act, and (2) whether the security argument was the genuine factor behind the military's decision. In examining the second question Justice Witkon stated:

> The petitioners argued before us that their eviction from their places of residence was not a security necessity and that the security considerations were no more than an excuse to enable the land to be prepared for Jewish settlement. The respondents argued that there was definitely a security necessity to evict the petitioners and the members of the Bedouin tribes from their places of residence, and that the presence and settlement of Jewish settlers in the evacuated areas serves the security needs of the district. There is no doubt that the respondents had the power to evict the petitioners, as long as they were acting for security considerations. It is clear that the fact that the same lands, in whole or in part, are designated for Jewish settlement does not negate the security nature of the whole action. The security considerations submitted that were reviewed in the judgment of my honorable friend, were not

refuted nor revealed to be fictional or camouflage for other considerations, when it was learnt from General Tal himself that the area (or part thereof) is designated for *settlement of Jews, which in itself, in this case, is a security measure* (emphasis added).[24]

The Court's attitude to the security question in this case is highly questionable.[25] According to the general jurisprudence of the Court, security considerations alone should not be accepted as justification for a given act. The harm to the rights of the individual must be properly balanced against the security need. Furthermore, under the proportionality test, even when security measures are justified, the least invasive measures should be adopted. As discussed in the chapters on security, the Court's refusal to examine the balance between security and other considerations and to apply the proportionality test characterizes its decisions in cases relating to the Occupied Territories.[26]

For the purposes of the present discussion, two aspects of the *Rafiah Approach* decision deserve emphasis. First, the Court was prepared to divorce the settlement intentions of the government from the decision relating to the eviction of Bedouin from their land. According to this approach, if the military can convince the Court that they acted for sincere security reasons (generally not a difficult task), the Court will not look beyond those reasons to examine how the decision relating to land fits into the government's general political scheme on settlement. Second, Justice Witkon, at least, was prepared to accept that Jewish settlement itself might be regarded as a legitimate security measure in certain circumstances. This became a major issue in the *Beth El* case.[27]

Beth El Case

The *Beth El* case[28] must be considered in its immediate political context. After the 1977 elections, a new government led by Menahem Begin replaced the government led by the Labor Party, which had been the dominant party in all Israeli governments since independence. One of Mr. Begin's first acts after the elections that brought him to power was to visit a controversial settlement that had been established by the *Gush Emunim* settlement movement against the better judgment of the outgoing Labor Prime Minister, and to declare that there would be many more such settlements.[29] However, by the end of 1978 and beginning of 1979, when the *Beth El* case was argued and decided, the political scene in the Middle East had changed radically. Egyptian President Anwar Sadat had visited Israel at the end of 1977, the Camp David Accords had been signed in September 1978, and intensive negotiations had followed on the terms of the final peace agreement between Israel and Egypt. In the Camp David Accords, Prime Minister Begin had agreed that Israeli settlements in Sinai would be disbanded and that Israeli settlers would be withdrawn from Sinai.[30] The final treaty, whose terms were based on the Camp David Accords, included a commitment by Israel to withdraw its civilians from Sinai.

The *Beth El* case dealt with the petitions of Palestinian landowners whose land had been requisitioned "for military needs" by order of the military commander and on which the civilian settlements of Beth El and Bekaot had subsequently been established. The government's reply to the petition was presented in an affidavit by a senior general who declared that under the government's security strategy civilian settlements were part of the regional defense plan. He also stressed the strategic importance of the locations of both settlements. Beth El controls both major highways and infrastructure. Given these strategic advantages, the army intended to construct fortifications in the settlement. Bekaot lies in a strategic position in the Jordan valley, blocking the main route for infiltration from Jordan and the Jordan valley to the rest of the West Bank and Israel itself.

Justice Witkon, who wrote the main opinion of the Court, realized that he could not ignore the political context in which the case was being decided. He therefore prefaced his opinion with the following comment:

> Affidavits and documents that prove the settlement activities on their land were presented on behalf of the petitioners. Affidavits by General Orly, Coordinator of the Activities in the Territories in the Ministry of Defense and by the Chief of Operations in the general staff, were presented on behalf of the respondents, and these affidavits, together with the statements of the State Attorney, constitute for us an authoritative expression of the government's position. These and nothing else. All of us know, of course, of the recent political developments in our region, of the peace negotiations, of the aspirations and hopes on the one hand and the anxieties and objections on the other, but it must be understood that a judicial institution does not deal with matters that still lie in the future. These we leave to the politicians. We are dealing with the rights of the present litigants according to the situation prevailing between Israel and the Arab countries. This situation is one of belligerency, and the status of the respondents in relation to the occupied territory is one of an occupying power.[31]

The petitioners conceded the power of the IDF to requisition land for military needs, but pressed for a distinction between the needs of the occupying army and the general security interests of the occupying power. Relying on article 52 of the Hague Regulations they claimed that only needs of the army of occupation justify requisition of private property.[32] The Court refused to adopt this distinction. It held that in light of the state of belligerency, the occupying power has the responsibility not only to ensure order in the occupied territory, but also to deal with dangers presented from the occupied territory to the territory of the occupying power itself. There could therefore be no real distinction between the narrow military needs of the occupying army and the wider security needs of the state.

In the *Rafiah Approach* case Justice Witkon had already expressed the opinion that a civilian settlement could fulfill a security need. In the *Beth El* case the Court adopted his opinion.[33] Relying on the evidence provided by the military, both on the security functions of settlements and the strategic importance of the Beth El and Bekaot sites, the Court held that these settlements fulfilled a security function.[34]

It seems to me that in its response to the petitioners' arguments the Court confused a number of issues. Because the main function of any army is defense of its own country, the Court was on firm ground in holding that the "needs of the army of occupation" should indeed include needs connected with defense of the occupying power's country. This does not mean, however, that all actions taken to further the security interests of the occupying power may be regarded as needs of the army of occupation. As the Court's view on the security function of civilian settlements reveals, adopting the broader view paves the way for actions that are incompatible with the occupying power's fundamental duty not to use the occupation as a means of acquiring territory by use of force.[35]

The petitioners argued that the use made of their land meant that it had in fact been confiscated rather than requisitioned. In response the authorities declared that the petitioners' *ownership* of their land had not been affected and that they were entitled to payment for its use. The Court accepted this highly formalistic distinction between requisition and confiscation. In support Justice Witkon cited von Glahn, who states that "a temporary use of land and buildings for various purposes appears permissible under a plea of military necessity."[36]

The big question then became whether establishing a civilian settlement could be regarded as temporary use of the land. Justice Landau conceded that this was a serious question, but accepted the statement made by government counsel that

> the civilian settlement will be able to exist in that place only as long as the IDF holds the land on the strength of a requisition order. This possession itself may one day come to an end, as a result of international negotiations which could end in a new arrangement that will gain force under international law and will determine the fate of this settlement, like all the other settlements that exist in the Occupied Territories.[37]

At the present time, when Israeli settlements on the West Bank and in Gaza have created a major constraint in the peace process between Israel and the Palestinians, the judges' views on the temporary nature of settlements may seem preposterous. As previously explained, however, the judges' approach should be seen in light of the immediate political context of the Court's decision. The judgment in the *Beth El* case was handed down on 15 March 1979. By that time the terms of the final treaty between Israel and Egypt that was to be signed on March 26 were public knowledge and the subject of heated political controversy. The main controversy centered on the stipulation that settlements established by Israel in Sinai would be disbanded. Some of these settlements, especially Yamit and Ophira, which had been established as "permanent settlements," had turned out not to be so permanent after all. The notion that the permanence of settlements is a relative concept that depends on political circumstances was therefore well founded in the political reality of the time. Nonetheless, the formalistic approach, which rests on the distinction between requisition and expropriation, was abandoned later in the *Elon Moreh* case.

Mattityahu Case

The *Mattityahu case*[38] reached the Court shortly after the *Beth El* decision was handed down. In March 1979, building began of a new settlement on land that had been requisitioned in 1977 in the vicinity of the village Na'alin. This settlement, Mattityahu, was planned as one of three settlements in the hills east of the Ben Gurion International Airport (the other two were on the Israeli side of the green line). Villagers from Na'alin, who claimed to have rights in the requisitioned land, petitioned the Court. In light of the *Beth El* decision their counsel did not attack the legality of settlements in occupied territory under international law. Instead he concentrated on the argument that security considerations were not the real reason for building the settlement. In order to prove this point, counsel submitted an affidavit in which General (Reserves) Mati Peled attempted to refute the security arguments for the settlement set out in an affidavit submitted to the Court by the general in charge of coordinating IDF activities in the Occupied Territories.[39]

In a brief decision dismissing the petition, Justice Landau stated that in the case of disagreement on professional-military questions, the Court would assume the sincerity of the considerations presented on behalf of the authorities responsible for security in Israel and the Territories. Extremely persuasive evidence would be needed to refute this assumption. Justice Landau analyzed General Peled's arguments against the settlement's security function and stated that he found them unconvincing.[40]

Justice Landau also dismissed the argument that the requisition order was invalid since the decision to make the order had been made by the Cabinet Committee on Security rather than by the military authorities. There was nothing wrong with the military carrying out policy set by the government, provided that their professional judgment did not dictate otherwise. He added, however, that the final decision on settlement had to be the government's, because political factors were involved too.[41] Thus, the government could conceivably recognize the military importance of a proposed settlement, yet decide that the settlement would not be established for political reasons. In the *Elon Moreh* case decided two months later, Justice Landau clarified that political considerations could play a negative role in stopping a settlement justified on security grounds; they could not be the dominant factor in deciding that a settlement should be established.

Elon Moreh Case

The petition in the *Elon Moreh* case[42] was submitted shortly after the peace treaty between Israel and Egypt was signed. Despite the similarity to the *Beth El* case, the same bench of five judges who had decided that case reached a different conclusion. It is therefore important to look at the facts of the *Elon Moreh* quite closely.

In January 1979, at the height of the controversy in Israel over the terms of the Camp David agreement and the fears of the Jewish settlers' movements that Jewish settlement in all the Occupied Territories was doomed, members of the militant settlers' movement, *Gush Emunim*, set up an unauthorized settlement in the area of Nablus, demanding that they be allowed to settle in the area. The government was highly sensitive to the charge that it was reneging on its political and ideological commitment to Jewish settlement in all of the land of Israel. At the same time it was eager to show that it, and not the settlers' movement, was setting policy. Government representatives managed to persuade the settlers to leave after promising that a settlement would be established in the area. The Cabinet Committee on Settlement subsequently examined potential sites for the settlement in the Nablus area and opted for a site on private land. The chief-of-staff then gave his approval for requisition of the land for military purposes and the Cabinet Committee on Security formally approved this decision. In an appeal to the full Cabinet submitted by the deputy prime minister, himself a former chief-of-staff, the Committee's decision was upheld by a majority vote. Significantly, however, both the minister of defense and the foreign minister, who had formerly served both as chief-of-staff and as minister of defense, joined the deputy prime minister in opposing the decision. Immediately after

the Cabinet decision was taken, an order was signed by the IDF commander on the West Bank requisitioning about 700 dunams of land "for
the needs of the army." Two days later Israeli civilians, with IDF backing, began preparing the requisitioned land for the new settlement of
Elon Moreh.

The government's decision met with serious public opposition.
Work on the site was delayed when demonstrators from the *Peace Now*
movement entered the site and prevented work. Later a large demon-
stration of Palestinians, led by the mayor of Nablus, was dispersed by
the IDF.

Owners of part of the requisitioned land petitioned the Supreme
Court, which granted both an order *nisi* and a temporary injunction to
stop work on the settlement. Because the petition was directed against
the Government of Israel and the minister of defense, the natural candidate to give the required affidavit presenting the government's position was the minister of defense. However the minister, General Ezer
Weizman, who had opposed establishing the settlement, told the prime
minister that he could declare that an army base was required in the
area for military purposes but could not give an affidavit supporting the
settlement on security grounds. The chief-of-staff therefore gave the
required affidavit.

The obvious starting point for the Court's analysis was its decision
in the *Beth El* case. In laying the groundwork for a different outcome,
Justice Landau stressed that the *Beth El* precedent did not imply that all
settlements in the Occupied Territories could be justified on grounds of
military need. The need had to be examined in every case.

The chief-of-staff, who serves as the government's main advisor on
military matters, claimed that the settlement would fulfill an important
function in regional defense. While the Court accepted that this was
indeed his sincere and honest opinion, it refused to follow the *Beth El*
precedent. The factual record revealed that under pressure from the
militant *Gush Emunim* settlers' movement the government, rather than
the military authorities, had initiated establishment of the settlement.
Even if the military subsequently concurred and supported the decision
for military reasons, the dominant consideration had been political.
This meant that the requisition order was invalid for two reasons:
under Israeli administrative law political grounds are an improper purpose for a decision by the military; under the rules of customary international law, land in occupied territory may only be requisitioned for
military needs.

In rejecting the view that the settlement was required for military
needs the Court was once again faced with a question that related to a
central tenet in the political philosophy of the government of the day.

Justice Landau stated that the Cabinet Committee and the majority of the Cabinet, who supported the decision, "were decisively influenced by grounds of Zionist outlook on the settlement of the whole of the Land of Israel."[43] Counsel for the government stated that the prime minister had asked him to inform the Court that he supported the right of the Jewish people to settle in Judea and Samaria. After quoting the prime minister's statement, Justice Landau stated:

> The view on the right of the people of Israel, which is reflected in these words, is well based in Zionist philosophy. However, the question which still remains before this court in this petition is if this view justifies taking the property of an individual in an area subject to a regime of military government, and . . . the answer to this question depends on the interpretation of article 52 of the Hague Regulations. I am of the opinion that the "military needs" mentioned in that article cannot, under any reasonable interpretation, include the national security needs in the broad sense, that I have just mentioned.[44]

In the *Beth El* case the Court extended the term "military needs" beyond the needs of the occupying army to include general security interests of the occupying power. In the *Elon Moreh* case the Court confined these security interests to those based on a rational, military/strategic analysis of the dangers the state faces, and the measures needed to counter them, rather than on ideological goals or outlook. In the political context of Israel, in which security considerations, *stricto sensu*, and ideological positions are often confused, this was a significant statement.

Justice Landau explained why the decision to establish Elon Moreh could not be justified as a military need. First, from the answers provided by the chief-of-staff to questions posed by the petitioners, it was clear that the army had neither initiated nor planned a settlement in the area of Elon Moreh. The *military* planning and strategy that had been proved in the *Beth El* case was lacking.[45] Second, in its decision to establish the settlement the Cabinet stated that in determining the site the views of the *Gush Emunim* settlers would, as far as possible, be taken into account. Justice Landau saw this as clear evidence that it was the pressure of *Gush Emunim* that spurred the government to decide on establishing the settlement.[46] Even if military authorities later considered that the settlement would fulfill a security function, the political factor was dominant. This was sufficient to invalidate the decision.

Finally, Justice Landau referred to the argument rejected in the *Beth El* case, namely that establishing a permanent settlement is inconsistent with requisition of land that is, by its very nature, a temporary measure. In the *Beth El* case the settlers themselves were not party to the proceedings and had not expressed their view on the issue.[47] In the *Elon Moreh* case the *Gush Emunim* settlers were given leave to join the proceedings. Counsel for the government did not contest their assertion that the prime minister had assured them that their settlement was as permanent a Jewish settlement as Dagania and Netanya.[48] Justice Landau drew the conclusion that the decision to establish the settlement met:

> an insuperable legal obstacle, because no military government may create in its area facts for its military purposes that are intended from the very start to exist even after the termination of military rule in that area, when the fate of the territory after the termination of the military rule is unknown.[49]

In Justice Landau's view this in itself provided grounds for invalidating the decision.

On the question of permanence, it is difficult to find a real difference between the settlements in the *Beth El* and *Elon Moreh* cases. The intention of permanence was not peculiar to *Elon Moreh*. It lay behind the entire settlement policy, whose political object was to create facts that would determine the future borders of the country. The fact that these intentions had been frustrated when the opportunity for peace with Egypt arose, and that settlements which had been established in Sinai were disbanded in the context of that peace treaty, in no way reflects on the original *intention* behind those settlements. The *Beth El* decision was handed down just before the signing of the peace treaty with Egypt, while the *Elon Moreh* decision was handed down seven months after the treaty was signed. The passage of time may have made it easier for the Court to reach a decision that would have been problematic whilst negotiations were going on for the removal of 'permanent' settlements.

The facts in the *Elon Moreh* case were not unique. Nevertheless, the Court diverted from its usual path of non-intervention. A number of possible explanations may be offered for its willingness to do so. In the first place, the split in the Cabinet over the decision to set up the Elon Moreh settlement was telling. The minister of defense, foreign minister, and deputy prime minister (all of whom had impressive military backgrounds) had opposed the settlement. The judges may also have had a hunch that the majority in the Cabinet supported establishment of the settlement for reasons of domestic politics rather the conviction that the settlement would serve the country's best interests. In these circumstances the judges felt they were on strong ground in rejecting the security argument.[50] Furthermore, the Court's decision did not challenge the entire Cabinet. Some ministers may well have regarded it as a decision that saved the government from itself.

Second, the *Gush Emunim* settlers joined the action and placed the ideological, rather than the security, argument before the Court. As Justice Witkon stated, this made it difficult for the Court to endorse the security argument accepted in the *Beth El* and *Mattityahu* cases. Finally, a feeling that the authorities had tried to mislead them may have influenced the judges. In his original affidavit the chief-of-staff had conveyed the impression that he himself had initiated establishment of the settlement, and that his recommendation had been brought before the Cabinet in case there were political objections. Only after the chief-of-staff had been asked by the Court to answer a questionnaire and further information had been submitted by counsel for the authorities did it become clear that the decision-making process had been the other way round. The political echelons had initiated the settlement and only then had the military given their approval. This provided the Court with a formal basis for deciding that the dominant reason for requisitioning the land had been political, rather than military. But it seems to me that the fact that an attempt had been made to mislead the Court could well have had a significant influence on its willingness to dismiss the government's arguments.

Aftermath of Elon Moreh

The *Elon Moreh* decision caused a major upheaval in the political arena.[51] There were even calls to ignore the decision or to legislate so as to undo its effects. Although the government was committed to continuing its settlement policy, these calls were ignored. After some hesitation, the order to dismantle the settlement was complied with by moving the settlers to a new site on a nearby hill.

In its decision the Court expressly refrained from ruling on the legality of settlements under international law. The only constraint placed on settlement related to requisition of private land for this purpose. While rejecting proposals for highly visible *Knesset* legislation, which would have attracted harsh domestic and international criticism, the government sought an alternative mechanism of pursuing its settlement policy. The mechanism adopted involved use of government or state land, rather than requisitioned private land.[52]

Following the *Elon Moreh* case, the authorities pursued an intensive policy aimed at defining and gaining control over state lands on which civilian settlements were subsequently built. As a result, the *Elon Moreh* case is the last decision dealing with requisition of private land for civilian settlements. Later decisions deal with the steps taken to declare land as state land and other aspects of the settlement policy, such as planning decisions, building of roads and expropriation of land for that purpose.

STATE LANDS

Legal Background

No comprehensive registration of land ownership existed for the West
Bank or Gaza in 1967.[53] Only one-third of the land had been registered.
Title in nonregistered land was proved either by title deeds (*koushan*) or
prescriptive use. Settlement of land rights in nonregistered land was suspended when the IDF entered the area.[54] The formal reason given was
the duty to protect the rights of absentees and of Jordanian citizens not
in the area.[55]

Soon after the occupation began, a military order was promulgated
dealing with state land.[56] Under this order the Custodian of Government
Property appointed by the military governor is empowered to take possession of government property and regulate its use.[57] Later a crucial section was added to the order stating that if the custodian certified property as government property, it would be so deemed unless proved
otherwise. In other words, once land is certified the onus is on those
who claim land rights to prove that the land is not state land. Claims are
heard by a special appeals committee, which deals with various decisions or actions of the military government.

During the 1970s a survey was completed of land registered in the
name of absentees or of the government and the Custodian of Government Property took possession of this land.[58] Following the *Elon Moreh*
decision the Cabinet decided that all uncultivated rural land would be
declared state land.[59] The onus would then be placed on individuals to
prove their rights in the land. This could be done only by producing a
koushan or by proving both possession and cultivation of the land for a
period of at least ten years.[60]

Thus began the policy of taking possession of large areas of land
declared state lands. Plia Albeck, the government attorney then in
charge of checking whether land could be regarded as state land, esti-
mated that approximately 40 percent of the land in the West Bank is
state land.[61]

The connection between widening the scope of state land and the
settlement policy of the Likud government was quite explicit. The Drobles plan of 1978, which formed the basis for the original settlement policy of the Likud government, declared: "State land and uncultivated
land must be seized immediately in order to settle the areas *between* the
concentrations of minority population and *around* them, with the object
of reducing to the minimum the possibility for the development of
another Arab state in these regions."[62]

Writing in 1985, Plia Albeck stated that approximately 90 percent
of the Israeli settlements in the Occupied Territories had been built on

state land. Although purporting to fulfill the occupying power's duty to preserve the right of the public in state land, such land was regarded as a resource to be used for settlement of nationals of the occupying power.

Court's Decisions

In *al-Naazer* v. *Commander of Judea and Samaria*[63] an attempt was made to challenge the state land system previously described. The petitioners argued that under Jordanian law regular courts decided land claims. In placing the jurisdiction over such claims in the hands of an appeals committee rather than the courts, the military governor had changed local law and thereby exceeded his authority under international law.

Justice Shamgar rejected this argument. He pointed out that under regulation 55 of the Hague Regulations the occupying power has a duty to safeguard the capital of public properties and administer them in accordance with the rules of usufruct. Local residents have no special rights in public property and the occupying power has a duty to protect such property against intrusion. Justice Shamgar cited experts in the field of international law who state that when doubt arises whether property is public or private, the presumption shall be that the property is public until ownership has been established.[64]

Justice Shamgar ruled that the substantive law regarding property ownership had not been changed and that land rights would be determined according to the prevailing law in 1967. Because military authorities are not subject to the jurisdiction of the local courts (which have general jurisdiction over land disputes), the appeals committee was authorized to deal with such disputes, thus giving local residents a remedy if they objected to certification of land as state land. Every appeals committee is composed of three members, at least one of whom must be a lawyer, and the order constituting the appeals committee states that in fulfilling their duties they are subject only to the authority of the law. In conclusion, Justice Shamgar stated, the military order authorizing the appeals committee to hear appeals against the declaration of land as government land gave local residents rights that they would not have had had the authorities relied exclusively on article 43 of the Hague Regulations.

The decision in the *Ayreib* case reveals part of the workings of the state land system. The petitioner claimed to have rights in land that had been certified as state land in Beit Icsa, a village near Jerusalem. A new Jewish settlement, Hadasha, was planned for this land.

The petitioner submitted his claim to the appeals committee, which recognized his rights over twenty-four of the seventy dunams in which he claimed title. The committee held that the rest of the land had been bought and registered by Jews in 1921 and that under Jordanian law it had passed to the Jordanian Custodian of Enemy Property after 1948. As such it was to be regarded as government land. On part of this land stood the petitioner's house that, the committee held, had been built without a building permit. The petitioner did not contest the committee's finding that his *koushan* (title deed) only related to part of the land, but argued that he had acquired rights over the rest of the land through possession.

The Turkish land law, which had been in force throughout the territory of the British Mandate, was still in force on the West Bank in 1967. It also remained in force in Israel itself until 1970. This law stipulates that title in *miri* land may be acquired by possession and cultivation over a period of ten years.[65] The Supreme Court rejected the argument that the practice in Jordan had been to ignore the requirement of cultivation and recognize title on the basis of possession alone. Relying on precedents from Mandatory times and Israeli courts prior to 1970, according to which cultivation is a necessary requirement, it held that as neither legislation nor precedent had been produced to show that this was not the situation in Jordan, the appeals committee had correctly applied the law.

The petitioner also argued that use of the land to build a new Jewish settlement was incompatible with the duty of an occupying power to administer public property as a usufructuary. However, the Court held that the petitioner lacked the standing or right to question the use of public land. It also stated that deciding whether the restrictions laid out in article 55 of the Hague Regulations should apply to land held by the Custodian of Enemy Property was not necessary in the instant case, nor was it pertinent to decide the fate of the land after the end of the occupation.[66] Finally the Court added:

> There is no place for complaining that the custodian [of government property] exercised his authority for an improper purpose. The conclusion that is reached from all the data before us is exactly the opposite. It was within the powers and duties of the custodian to put his hands on property in which the petitioner tried to unlawfully gain possession. As became apparent, the petitioner wished to extend his control over tens of dunams of land, which he never bought nor cultivated; and as this was land which was owned by others and which should have been protected originally by the Jordanian Custodian of Enemy Property, the custodian was entitled to exercise his authority, in order that the property be brought under the control and supervision of the person responsible.[67]

The impression gained from these two decisions, and especially from the dictum quoted from the second decision, is that the objective of the authorities in certifying state land, and taking control over it, was to protect the property so as to ensure that trespassers would not gain control over it. In a situation of belligerent occupation, public property should indeed be protected until the occupation ends and the public can once again decide on its use. It requires a fair degree of naivete to believe, however, that the sole, or even dominant, purpose of the authorities, including the Custodian of Enemy Property, was to protect public land for the benefit of the local public or the absentee sovereign. The dominant purpose was to find land that could be used for settlements and other projects that served Israeli political interests. This was the improper purpose to which the petitioner pointed.

The most glaring feature of these decisions is their total detachment from the context of the government's land-use policy on the West Bank. The Court presents the system of certifying state land as a form of benign action by military authorities eager to fulfill their obligations under international law. In reality, however, the picture is entirely different. Public lands are not regarded as land reserves that are first and foremost available for use of the local population; they are regarded as land reserves that serve Israeli interests (as perceived by those in power). Land reserves in the Occupied Territories are in effect administered by officials of the Israel Lands Administration set up under Israeli law to administer "government land" in Israel itself. These reserves are used for civilian settlements that are anathema to the local population and, to the extent that the government establishes them in order to encourage Israelis to settle there, are widely regarded as a violation of international law. Furthermore, Justice Shamgar cites article 55 of the Hague Regulations, which states that the occupying power must administer public property in accordance with the rules of usufruct. This means that the occupying power is entitled to enjoy the fruits of the land, but must not change its capital nature. Establishment of a permanent Israeli settlement would appear to be inconsistent with the rules of usufruct. Nevertheless, in the one case in which this argument was raised, Justice Shamgar refused to deal with it, questioning the standing of a private individual to challenge the use of public land. Later, when the same argument was raised in a petition submitted by the *Peace Now* movement, Justice Shamgar rejected the petition on the grounds that it was too general and therefore nonjusticiable.[68]

There is a clear disparity between the *Elon Moreh* and public land decisions. In the *Elon Moreh* case the Court held that the actual intention of the authorities was the determinative factor in examining the legality of their acts. If the intention in certifying land as public land is not to protect it under article 55 but to use it in contravention of that article, should this not be ground for questioning certification? Article

55 is cited to legitimize this system of gaining control over state lands; it is ignored when the argument is made that the very same article limits the use that may be made of such lands.

HIGHWAY PLANNING AND CONSTRUCTION

Background

Planning and building of roads and highways in the Occupied Territories are intimately connected with settlement policy. Until the mid-1970s, when settlement policy roughly followed the Alon Plan, north–south highways were built.[69] During the mid-1970s, when chances of a political settlement on the West Bank seemed remote, east–west highways were planned, as well as a northern highway from the coast through part of the West Bank to Jerusalem. After the Likud came to power, emphasis was placed on the building of highways that would integrate the West Bank and Israel. Once again planners were quite explicit about the connection between the highways and settlement policy. Thus, in a plan for highways prepared by the World Zionist Organization (WZO), it was stated:

> There would seem to be no need to say too much about the importance of an adequate net of highways in Samaria and Judea. . . . Although the matter is clear, the net of highways today (fifteen years after the Six-Day War) does not reflect the special character of the area as a central part of the country, nor help to exploit the enormous settlement potential of the area. Furthermore, it does not increase awareness of the area nor reduce the reluctance towards it of the majority of the Jewish population.[70]

The connection between the settlements and the highway plan was not only in their political objectives. The highways were planned to allow access roads to be built to Jewish settlements, thereby increasing the accessibility of these settlements from the main urban centers in Israel.

Court's Decisions

The *Tabeeb* case[71] dealt with expropriation of land for a highway. The expropriation was carried out under the Jordanian law regarding acquisition of land for public purposes that remained in force in 1967. Landowners whose land had been affected were entitled to compensation. The petitioners argued that the land, a small part of which belonged to them, had been expropriated in order to build a road that would provide access to a new Jewish settlement to be established in the area. The respondents admitted that the new road would provide access to the new settlement, but claimed that the road was part of a network of roads and highways planned for the West Bank in order to improve the flow of traffic by circumventing towns and other populated areas. The road would also improve transport to and from Arab villages in the area.

Although Justice Landau, who had been on the bench in the *Rafiah Approach*, *Beth El*, and *Elon Moreh* cases, was on the bench in the *Tabeeb* case, Justice Shilo, an acting Supreme Court judge, wrote the judgment. His view was that, under the *Beth El* and *Elon Moreh* precedents, the question was what the dominant consideration had been in expropriation of the land. After mentioning the planning considerations behind the highway scheme, he stated: "One must assume that the security and military authorities who undertook the task of planning and implementing this network of highways, the cost of which reaches huge sums, did not do so only in order to ease civilian transport and ecology, and that the main consideration from their point of view was military."[72]

Justice Shilo proceeded to describe the military advantages of the improved highway system both in the event of war and in case of attacks on army and civilian traffic by local residents. He mentioned prolonged and extensive planning carried out by the government corporation, *Tahal*, which had examined five alternative schemes in each of which cost factors and integration with the existing network were examined. His conclusion was:

> that the military and security considerations were dominant in choosing the present course, and there is therefore no problem with it from the point of view of international law. The consideration that benefit would also accrue to the future settlement *Tzavta* was minor and secondary.[73]

From the decision itself it is difficult to work out just how Justice Shilo reached this conclusion, as it is not clear whether the authorities had argued that military considerations had indeed been the dominant factor in planning the road network. This question was to trouble Justice Barak in the second round of the *Ja'amait Ascan*[74] case discussed below. Justice Barak examined the file and found that in the *Tabeeb* case, the head of infrastructure planning in the Ministry of Defense's unit for national security had given evidence that in planning the highways the military need was incorporated with the needs of the local population. However, Justice Shilo did not rely on this evidence. Instead he stated that "one must assume" that the military authorities would not have gone to all the trouble and expense of planning the highways if there was no military interest in them.[75] This is a most peculiar statement, for the military government is an arm of the Government of Israel, and as such it executes government policy in the Territories.[76] In the *Elon*

Moreh case, Justice Witkon ruled quite explicitly that the onus is on the military authorities to *prove* that taking of private property is required for military needs. In the *Tabeeb* case Justice Shilo mentioned that a civilian company did the planning, but this did not seem significant to him. Given the evidence submitted on behalf of the respondents, it may well have been reasonable for the Court to hold that there was indeed a military interest in the scheme. Yet Justice Shilo failed to explain his conclusion that this interest was the *dominant* consideration in the planning process.

Among the plans drawn up for the West Bank was a highway network that would connect places in Israel with West Bank towns and would facilitate traffic between areas north and south of Jerusalem. Part of this plan included an interchange between two highways. One highway joins Ben-Shemen (on the Tel Aviv–Jerusalem highway) with Atarot in north Jerusalem. Part of this highway is in Israel and part in the West Bank. The second highway joins Ramallah, Jerusalem, and Bethlehem. Most of this highway is in the West Bank, although a small part passes through Israel. The interchange planned in the Atarot area was to have three levels: one to connect the Ben-Shemen–Atarot highway with the Jerusalem–Bethlehem highway; a second to allow the Ben-Shemen–Atarot highway to continue on to Ma'ale Adumim (a huge urban settlement built on the West Bank near Jerusalem, on the road to Jericho), and a third to connect the service roads to the Jerusalem–Bethlehem highway.

In two cases challenging the legality of the Atarot interchange (and consequently that of the entire highway network), the petitioner was a cooperative whose objective was to construct a housing estate for teachers in the Ramallah district. To carry out this scheme it purchased land near Atarot, the industrial area of greater Jerusalem on the Jerusalem–Ramallah road. As the cooperative realized that there was not much chance of obtaining planning approval for a residential suburb in the area, it did not initially apply for permission for the whole project. Instead, members of the cooperative applied separately for permits to build houses in the area. Only after the individual applications were approved and construction was started on three houses did the planning authorities realize that the applications were part of a wider housing scheme. The matter was brought before the Supreme Planning Council, which decided to revoke the building licenses. The cooperative subsequently submitted a detailed plan for the entire project, which was rejected. The main reasons given were the proximity of the project to the industrial area of Atarot, and that the land was needed for the interchange already in advanced stages of planning. Under the plan, part of the land in the area was to be expropriated and building restrictions were to be placed on other land in the area.

The cooperative attacked the decisions to revoke the building licenses and reject the detailed plan.[77] The Court held that the licenses were invalid under local planning laws because the statutory requirement that licenses conform to a detailed plan and parcellation scheme had not been met. The Supreme Planning Council was therefore authorized to revoke the licenses even in those cases in which building had begun.

The Court also rejected the claim that approval had been denied to the detailed plan for political reasons. It held that all the considerations taken into account by the planning authorities were relevant planning considerations. The Court took the view that the petitioners were to blame for the situation, which they had brought upon themselves by concealing their real intentions. It added, however, that the planning authorities were also at fault, as they should have checked whether the individual license applications were consistent with the existing plan. Although it refused to express an opinion whether the petitioners who had started building should be entitled to compensation, it stated "that it only would be fair and just if the respondents would now help the petitioners to find alternative land on which they could plan and build their suburb."[78] So ended round one of the litigation.

The highway plan had not yet received planning approval when the cooperative's detailed plan was rejected. While the first round of litigation was still in progress, the planning procedure went ahead. The Supreme Planning Council heard the cooperative's objections to the plan after judgment had been given in the first round of the litigation. When its objections were rejected and the plan was approved, the cooperative submitted a second petition to the Supreme Court in which it attacked both the decision to approve the plan and the expropriation of part of its land that was included in the plan.[79]

The petitioners' case rested on two main arguments. First, that because the highway network had been planned in the interests of Israel and not in the interests of the residents of the West Bank, it was an unlawful use of power by a belligerent occupant. Second, that a belligerent occupant, whose rule is by its very nature temporary, may not plan and construct projects that have long-term effects. In reply the authorities argued that the highway system was being built for the benefit of West Bank residents. They pointed to the enormous growth in the number of vehicles in the area since 1967, and the inadequacy of the existing network of roads to cope with the increased volume of traffic. The authorities admitted that the highways would benefit the residents of Israel and would facilitate travel between Israel and the West Bank. They pointed out, however, that a large number of West Bank residents travel to work in Israel. They argued that the position that existed at the beginning of the occupation could not be frozen, and that it was the duty of the military government to further the interests of the local population in all walks of life, including transportation.

Justice Barak divided his decision into a number of sections. First, he set out the normative basis for examining the acts of the military government. Having categorically declared that the applicable legal standards are the rules of belligerent occupation as developed in customary international law, he stated that the military government must be guided in its decision by one of two considerations: military need or benefit of the local population. In the planning context this means that planning may not be carried out only to serve the interests of the occupying power. If the planning of the highway network and interchange were done only for the good of Israel, the military government had exceeded its power. The real question was, however, whether the planning had indeed been done only for the good of Israel, or whether the good of the local population had been a guiding factor.

Analyzing the factual issue of the motivations behind the planning, Justice Barak held there was no basis for doubting the authenticity of the planning considerations presented by the authorities. The petitioners had presented no evidence to refute that presented by the respondents.[80]

As we have seen, in the *Tabeeb* case the Court decided that expropriation of private land for the building of a highway was legitimate because the new highway fulfilled a military need. Justice Barak wondered if there had not been military considerations in favor of the highway system in the case before him. However, he noted that while in the *Tabeeb* case the authorities had submitted evidence that military need had been a factor, in the case before him they had rested their entire argument on the interests of the local population. Justice Barak expressed surprise that military need had not been cited again as a consideration behind the planning and wondered how a line of argument adopted in one case was not mentioned in another. This did not, however, lead him to doubt the sincerity of the considerations presented to the Court. Instead, his conclusion was that he would assume that the military factor had not been a planning consideration.

As previously stated, this decision seems inconsistent with the *Elon Moreh* approach. Despite the Court's declaration that it was convinced the planning was for the good of the local population, it would seem that the plan was part of a general plan for the West Bank that was based first and foremost on the planners' perception of Israeli interests.[81] Even if the planners were also concerned to meet the needs of the West Bank population, the Court should have identified the *dominant* consideration. According to Justice Landau's reasoning in the *Elon Moreh* case, if the dominant consideration were the political interests of Israel, the decision should have been invalidated even if the planners thought that the plan would serve the needs of the West Bank population as well.

CONCLUSIONS

There is clearly a glaring disparity between the political objectives of government settlement and developments policies in the Occupied Territories and the Court's legal reasoning. Alongside the broad political explanations for this disparity, one must also consider the particular nature of judicial decision-making. Courts are called upon to deal with a specific dispute and not with general government policy. Within the framework of a concrete dispute, they must base their decisions on the facts and arguments presented by the parties. Unless the interested party succeeds in proving the specific connection between the political context and the decision taken by the authorities in his or her case, it is all too easy for courts to ignore that context. One of the reasons for the petitioners' success in the *Elon Moreh* case was that they managed to prove the political dimensions of the *specific* decision to establish a settlement on their land. In other cases, the petitioners based their arguments on general government policies, without proving the close connection between those policies and the exigencies of the concrete case. This made it easier for the Court to ignore the wider political context and base its decisions on narrow arguments of security or public benefit presented by the authorities.

The Court has never ruled on the general arguments relating to the legality of establishing civilian settlements in the Occupied Territories. It has left open the question whether establishing these settlements is compatible with article 49 of Geneva Convention IV, or with the powers of an occupying force under rules of customary international law. Hence the Court's jurisprudence on settlements and related issues rests on a dubious assumption of legality.

With the notable exception of the *Elon Moreh* case, the Court refused to interfere in decisions connected with land-use and settlement decisions. I have already argued that the facts in the *Elon Moreh* case were not really unique. The path taken in that case could have been followed in other cases. The Court could have relied on the dominant motive in order to block use of public land for settlements and prohibit expropriation of private land for highways; it could also have relied on the insuperable obstacle mentioned by Justice Landau in the *Elon Moreh* case, that a belligerent occupant may not "create in its area facts for its military purposes that are intended from the very start to exist even after the termination of military rule in that area."[82] It did neither. *Elon Moreh* remains the exception that proves the rule: the Court provided legitimization for government actions that are highly questionable, not only on political grounds, but on legal grounds as well.

CHAPTER SIX

RESIDENCY AND FAMILY UNIFICATION

In previous chapters I reviewed the Court's attitude to the legal status of the Occupied Territories. I shall now review the status of the Palestinian residents of the Territories. This question has arisen in two major contexts: residency status and family unification.

RESIDENCY

The Palestinian residents of the Occupied Territories are not Israeli citizens. On the West Bank, many residents acquired Jordanian citizenship after the West Bank's 1950 annexation by Jordan. Residents of Gaza did not generally acquire Egyptian citizenship before 1967 and until establishment of the Palestinian Authority pursuant to the Oslo Accords they had no recognized citizenship.

The status of residency does not protect persons against deportation under regulation 112 of the Defence Regulations.[1] However, only persons who endanger the security of the area may be deported under these regulations. No power exists to deport a resident unless the security test of the regulations is met. Thus, so long as a resident remains in the Territories his or her right of residency is retained. However, what about a resident who leaves the Territories? Does that person have a right to return and reside there?

The approach taken by the authorities, and accepted by the Court, has been that so long as a person retains resident status, he or she may enter the Territories and reside there. Once this status is lost, a person has no right to reside in the Territories and is totally dependent on the discretion of the military authorities. The question of loss of residency is, therefore, of crucial importance.

The pattern for dealing with loss of residency was set in *La'afi* v. *Minister of Interior*.[2] This case concerned people who claimed residency in areas surrounding Jerusalem (in which Israeli law was applied in June 1967). However, the principles laid down by the Court were followed in subsequent cases dealing with residents of the West Bank and Gaza.

The petitioners in the *La'afi* case were husband and wife. After their marriage in 1960 they lived in part of the village of Beit Tzefafa that was occupied by Jordan until 1967.[3] Before the marriage the husband had begun to work in Kuwait, returning every year for a month or two. In 1962 the wife spent some time in Kuwait with her husband, but subsequently returned to Beit Tzefafa. She was included in the census carried out immediately following the Six-Day War but soon thereafter she and her three children joined her husband in Kuwait. The family remained in Kuwait for four years, after which the wife's mother applied for a permit that would allow them to return and remain in Beit Tzefafa. The application was turned down. The family was later given permission to visit the area, and while there they renewed their application for permanent residents' status. When this application was rejected, they petitioned the Court.

The Court held that the petitioners had set up home in another country for a period of four years, and even if they had done so for economic reasons, once they took up residency in another country they lost their residency status in the land in which they had been born and in which all their family lived. As the Court put it, "the simple fact is that they preferred to raise their children in Kuwait rather than rebuilding their house in Israel."[4]

Having lost their residency status, the petitioners were dependent on the minister of interior's discretion. This discretion is virtually absolute. The Court will only interfere if there is proof that corruption or bad faith was involved. In this case the authorities explained that they were following a general policy not to grant applications such as that of the petitioners unless family unification was involved.[5] The Court refused to interfere in this policy.

One argument did give the Court some difficulty. The petitioners pointed to two similar cases of people from their village who had received permanent residence status. One of these had been the daughter of the mukhtar. They argued that this meant that the decision not to grant them residency status was tainted with discrimination, hence justifying judicial intervention in an administrative decision. However, the Court took the line that: "The argument of discrimination does not hold in matters such as these, as they are not cases of maintaining equality between fellow citizens, but the authorities of the state are acting towards those on the outside and the state itself, as it were, is facing those who wish to settle in it permanently."[6]

The result was that even though the Court was amazed that the authorities had admitted that favoritism (in Israeli parlance "*protekzia*") had been behind the granting of permanent residency to one of the individuals named by the petitioners, this was insufficient ground to grant such status to the petitioners as well. The Court summarized its attitude as follows:

> In spite of our negative reaction in the matter of the mukhtar's daughter, I do not think that this diversion justifies another diversion in the petitioners' matter, for such a decision by us would totally destroy the dams that the Ministry of Interior sought to construct with its policy. The decision in the petitioners' matter is difficult, but vital interests of the state prevent their return after they built their house in another country.[7]

The Court failed to explain what these "vital interests of the state" were. In a later case dealing with the related question of family unification, the Court referred to "political circumstances" that lay behind the decision not to allow residents of surrounding countries to reside permanently in Gaza.[8] Once again the Court failed to be more explicit about the nature of those political circumstances. In the absence of an explanation, it seems fair to assume that the "vital interests of the state" and the "political circumstances" are related to a restrictive immigration policy for Palestinians, part of the attempt to maintain a "demographic balance" between Jews and Arabs in the territories under Israeli control.

As previously stated, the decision in the *La'afi* case rested on Israeli law, since Beit Tzefafa had become part of greater Jerusalem in which Israeli law had been applied in June 1967. In the *Al-Teen* case[9] a similar question arose in relation to the West Bank. The petitioner had been brought up in Beit Jala. She was registered in the 1967 census but in 1968, when she was only sixteen years old, her parents took her to Amman. There she married and subsequently accompanied her husband to Kuwait. Four years later she returned to the West Bank for a visit and asked the military authorities for permission to stay in the area with her husband and children. When her application was rejected she petitioned the Court.

The Court held that the petitioner had left the area of her own free will (or at least the free will of her parents/guardians) and had established a new domicile in Kuwait. When she came back to visit her parents and expressed her desire to remain, she was no longer "a returning resident, but a tourist who wishes to settle in occupied territory."[10] The area had been declared a closed area and the petitioner had no right to remain in the area unless the military commander gave his permission.

The petitioner argued that according to article 9 of the Jordanian Constitution every Jordanian citizen has the right to choose his or her place of residence in the country and that, as this article was in force on the West Bank in 1967, it still applied. Thus, any citizen who had been a resident of the West Bank was entitled to live there. The Court rejected the argument. It held that under the rules of international law, laws promulgated by the military commander to promote the security of his forces have precedence over the local constitution and laws. The order closing the West Bank and making entrance conditional on a permit from the military authorities serves the security interests of the military and it is therefore to be preferred to any contrary rule in the local constitution or laws.[11]

The pattern set in the *La'afi* and *Al-Teen* cases was followed consistently. Residents of the Territories who take up residence in another country automatically lose their residency status in the Occupied Territories. Because the Territories have been declared a closed area, such "former residents" must receive permission to visit their families in the area and require a permanent resident's permit to live there. The legal basis for the military order closing the area lies in the powers of the military commander under international law to promulgate orders needed to protect the security of his forces. However, the grounds for an individual decision refusing a permit to enter or live in the area need not be security grounds. The military authorities may set policy on the granting of permits and the Court will not interfere in the authorities' discretion.[12]

The test for losing residency status is whether the person can be seen to have taken up residence in another country. The test is objective and depends first and foremost on the period of time spent in the other country. In some cases this period of time has been ten years or more,[13] but, as we have seen, spending four years abroad with one's nuclear family may be regarded as sufficient evidence of residency there.[14] The Court sometimes refers to another place having become the "center of one's life."[15] In judging whether this criterion has been met the Court takes into account factors such as raising a family or acquiring citizenship, but the major factor remains the length of time spent in the other country.

FAMILY UNIFICATION

Family unification is sometimes tied to the residency issue. This is the case when the person who wishes to unite with his or her family in the Occupied Territories is a former resident who wishes to reestablish residency there. In many other cases, there is no connection with the residency question. The person wishing to live in the area was not previously a resident of the Occupied Territories, but bases his or her request to live in the area on a family connection, usually marriage, with a resident.

The Court's approach to the family unification question was articulated in the *Al-Teen* case reviewed above and has been followed consistently, with a single exception. The Territories are occupied territories that were declared closed areas under military orders promulgated when the IDF took control. In such areas, the military commander has discretion to decide whether outsiders will be allowed to enter the area and under what conditions. The Court will not interfere in policy set down by the military commanders. Because the outsiders who wish to enter the area have no right to enter and the decision is purely discretional, the Court will not interfere on the strength of an argument of discrimination between different applicants. It will only interfere if there is evidence of arbitrariness, lack of good faith, or extreme unreasonableness.

The Court explained the way it perceived the legal situation in the *Taiah* case:

> Entrance to the area of Judea and Samaria depends on receiving a special permit, both because of the special status of the area as occupied territory as well as the military legislation that turned the whole area into a closed area (Order Regarding Closed Areas (Area of Judea and Samaria) (No.34), 1967). When territory that was in the hands of one country passed through war to the control of the army of another country and that army establishes a military government in the said territory, that military government is entitled to prohibit or limit the entrance of people into the territory held by it, as the interests and needs over which it has responsibility require. As far as the area of Judea and Samaria is concerned, this authority is expressly stated and regulated in Order 34 that was mentioned above.
>
> The said authority relating to regulation of entering and leaving the area includes the power to regulate both movement whose purpose is temporary sojourn, as well as movement regarding changing one's place of residence.[16]

The military authorities have the power to ban entrance of all non-residents to the area. They may, according to their discretion, allow the entrance of some, and may set policy defining the criteria of entrance. Such policy may restrict entrance permits "only to cases which are exceptional from the humanitarian point of view and to cases in which the authorities themselves have a security, political or social interest in a given application."[17]

Until the early 1980s the authorities declared that their policy allowed for granting residence status to minor children and spouses of local residents.[18] Later this policy was changed and marriage or child–parent relationship were no longer regarded as sufficient basis for granting an application. The Court accepted the legitimacy of the policy according to which marriage of a resident to a nonresident was not a good enough reason for allowing the nonresident to live permanently in the area.[19]

The Court was not always happy with the attitude of the authorities, but made it clear that it does not sit as an appeals committee against their policies or individual decisions. It perceives its duty as judging whether the authorities were acting within their powers, and not whether the policy is to be commended. In *Allah* v. *Minister of Defense*[20] the petitioner was a woman who had been brought up in a West Bank village but had married and settled with her husband in Kuwait in 1960. After her husband's death in 1973, she received permission to visit her family in the area. She visited on a number of occasions together with her minor children and applied for permanent residency status. When her application was turned down, she petitioned the Court. By the time the case was heard the petitioner had left the area, but the Court nevertheless asked to hear the response of the authorities "mainly concerning the humanitarian side of the affair." After hearing the response, the Court dismissed the petition, holding that the authorities were not legally bound to grant a resident's permit to the petitioner, who had lost her residency status. Nevertheless, it saw fit to remark that the petitioner's desire, after her husband's death, to return to the area in which her family lived was not unreasonable and stated "that the respondents would do well to consider her matter and to review it with the sympathetic approach which it deserves."

In one case, the *Samara* case,[21] the Court was prepared to go even further. The petitioner was born in a West Bank village, but left in 1962 to work in Germany. He returned periodically to visit his family and on one of the visits met a resident of the area to whom he was married in 1968. The wife continued to reside in her village and the husband would visit her there. An attempt to settle in Germany failed and the wife returned home. Over time, the couple had four children. The petitioner's first application for permission to reside permanently in the area was accepted, but the petitioner was ill in Germany at the time and could not take advantage of the permission granted. All subsequent applications were rejected. The last application was rejected "for security reasons," but when the petitioner challenged the decision in court the authorities admitted that there were no specific security reasons for denying the petitioner permanent residency status. The petitioner's application had been rejected because he did not meet prescribed criteria, which the authorities were not prepared to divulge to the petitioner.

The Court once again accepted that the military commander has the full authority to close, and to regulate entrance to and exit from, the area. Relying on the *Al-Teen* case the Court held that no right to family unification in the area existed. However, all applicants have the right that "the refusal to grant them a permit . . . be based on proper considerations."[22] Rejecting the argument that the military commander's considerations were nonjusticiable, the Court held that the commander's decisions are subject to the same scope of review as the decisions of the minister of interior regarding entrance to Israel itself.

The Court accepted that determining the criteria for family unification and their implementation in practice was "a sensitive matter that is connected to state security and foreign relations." It was therefore only natural that the Court would not replace the commander's discretion with its own. However, "when the commander had acted illegally, it is proper for us to intervene."[23]

Had the commander acted illegally? Counsel for the authorities stated that had the petitioner's case been an isolated one, the military commander would have granted his application. However, the commander feared that if he approved the petitioner's application, he would have to approve many similar applications. The Court decided that the commander's fear was unjustified and that "his decision rejecting the application is therefore faulty and should be revoked."[24] It explained that there were a number of factors that, in isolation, could easily exist in other cases, but when taken together they made the petitioner's case unique. First, the petitioner was the spouse of a resident, as opposed to a more distant relative; second, the couple could not build their home in Germany, which was not an Arab country and in which the customs and culture were strange to them; third, the original reason provided for rejecting the application, that there were some specific security problems relating to the petitioner, was not well based, and there was no security reason for denying permanent residency to the petitioner; finally, the petitioner's original application had been approved and it was only because of an illness that he was unable to take advantage of it. The Court's conclusion was that "this combination of circumstances shows that the respondent's decision to refuse a permit in this case, in which the humanitarian nature is blatant, and the characteristics of which are highly unusual, is unquestionably flawed and is therefore tainted with administrative arbitrariness."[25]

In important respects the *Samara* case represents an entirely different approach to that adopted in all the other family unification cases.[26] The Court was not prepared to accept that mere implementation of a policy on immigration to the area is sufficient grounds for rejecting an individual application. It also recognized that an applicant has the right that a refusal to allow him or her permanent residence be based on proper considerations. The Court itself must examine whether this right was respected, and is therefore forced to examine whether the considerations of the authorities were proper. Had the Court followed this approach in the earlier *Taiah*[27] case, it could easily have ruled against the authorities by deciding that insufficient weight had been given to the humanitarian factor (rather than merely recommending that the authorities reconsider the application in a sympathetic manner). On the other hand, the Court itself pointed out that it was only the combination of factors that made the *Samara* case unique. Furthermore, it was not prepared to question an immigration policy that denied family unification, but merely to hold that the reasons given by the authorities for departing from their own policy were unfounded. It is far from clear what the position would have been had the commander decided that no applications whatsoever would be approved.

In later cases the Court seemingly followed the *Samara* approach of examining each individual case on its merits. However, in all cases the result reached was to uphold the authorities' decision. In *Khalil* v. *IDF Commander of Judea and Samaria* the Court referred to the *Samara* case, but stressed the material difference between that case and the petitions before it. Thus, it pointed out that the petitioner in the *Samara* case had received permission to reside in the area and had not been able to take advantage of it because of his illness. It also pointed out that since the *Samara* case "a few years have passed and the policy of the authorities in the Occupied Territories has changed in the meantime."[28] In *Awwad* v. *Head of Civil Administration*,[29] the Court stressed that it was not

> sitting as an appeal instance against the committee, which deals with family unification, and we do not replace the committee's or area commander's discretion with our own. The intervention of the High Court of Justice is justified, only if in examining the guide-lines, the process or the decision itself, a flaw is found that meets the criteria that we have established for ourselves for the purpose of reviewing the acts of a statutory authority.[30]

The most comprehensive attempt to persuade the Court that a local resident has the legal right to have his or her nonresident spouse residing permanently in the area was made in the case of *Shahin* v. *IDF Commander in Judea and Samaria*.[31] The petitioners, residents of the West Bank and Gaza, requested permanent residency status for their wives, who were residents of Jordan and Egypt. They attached opinions by two foreign professors of international law, who took the view that international law protects the integrity of family life and that the right to have a nonresident spouse live with one may be regarded as a corollary of this right. The Court's judgment, written by the president of the Court, Justice Shamgar, is devoted to an analysis of these opinions.

The main thrust of Justice Shamgar's judgment is based on two points. First, that international law does *not* impose a legal obligation on a country to allow entry of noncitizens, even if they are married to residents or citizens of the country. Demands for family unification have always concentrated on the duty of countries to allow citizens and others to *leave* their borders so as to unite with their families elsewhere.[32] Second, even if such a right were recognized in normal conditions, it would not apply in cases of belligerent occupation, especially if the non-residents were residents of countries in a state of war with the occupying country.[33] Neither the Hague Regulations nor Geneva Convention IV contain provisions regarding the obligation to admit nonresidents to occupied territory. The Court stated:

> The accepted practice in the past and in the present shows that when a state of war exists, strict restrictions are usually placed on freedom of movement, that are far greater than those in practice in Judea and Samaria and Gaza, into which many have been allowed to enter as tourists or within the framework of family unification.[34]

In the *Shahin* case the authorities admitted that the policy on family unification had been changed in the mid-1980s. Whereas previous policy toward wives and children of local residents had been liberal, current policy was that all such requests would be rejected unless there were exceptional humanitarian considerations or the military government had an interest of its own in approving the request. The change was in response to the assessment that family unification had become a method of fairly large-scale immigration into the area.

The Court accepted the power of the military government to change its policy. It rejected the argument that the military authorities had to provide individual objections in each specific case and held that they could adopt a general policy based on the common features of the phenomenon, although they retained the duty to examine whether there were exceptional circumstances in every individual case.[35]

The Court placed its decision within the context of belligerent occupation and the ongoing conflict between Israel and the Arab countries. In concluding his judgment, Justice Shamgar remarked:

> The question before us, in effect, was not whether to give effect to marriage, but whether the authorities have a duty to permit wide-scale movement, that encompasses thousands of people, from one side of the cease-fire lines to the other, and whether the policy, which the respondent . . . set for himself, according to which he would grant a permit

only in special and exceptional cases and not in the many cases in which a man from Judea and Samaria or from Gaza wishes to effect a change in the permanent residence of a woman from the neighboring countries, whom he married when she visited as a tourist in the occupied territory or when he left for a visit in one of the neighboring countries. . . .

We all hope that peace will also solve these problems, but their immediate solution at the time of war, by allowing movement of many—and not just a few individuals—*into* the area occupied by the IDF, cannot be the cause for intervention by this court.[36]

In summary, the Court accepted the power of the authorities to close the Occupied Territories. In practice, the authorities have allowed movement to and from the Territories, both of residents and nonresidents. This practice does not affect the power of the authorities. By permitting something that they are not legally obliged to permit, the authorities have not relinquished the power to regard the area as closed. They have the discretion to decide who shall be allowed to enter the area and who shall be allowed to take up permanent residence there. Permission granted to a nonresident to reside in the Territories is an act of grace and not a right. It is therefore not a sound argument that the authorities discriminated against an individual by allowing others in like circumstances permission to stay in the area. Once it is clear that an application was turned down according to the guidelines of existing policy, the Court will not examine whether the individual circumstances justify deviation from that policy.

The Court was on fairly firm legal ground in rejecting the notion that a country has a general obligation under international law to grant permanent residence to noncitizens or nonresidents, or to allow family unification within its borders.[37] It would also seem that an occupying state may indeed declare occupied territory a closed area to which entrance is prohibited, although use of this power should be determined by the two objectives that must guide an occupying state in all matters: security and benefit of the local population. Obviously, the occupying power may deny an individual access to occupied territory if it has sound military or security reasons for doing so. It may also restrict entry if allowing it would be harmful to the interests of the local population (e.g., straining existing employment opportunities). Yet may the occupying power restrict immigration for reasons connected with the political dimensions of the dispute between it and other countries? In cases of family unification, the Court has never demanded what it has demanded in other contexts, namely that the decisions of the military government be motivated either by military or security considerations, or by the good of the local population.

Furthermore, even if the occupying power does retain wide discretion to set immigration policy for the occupied territory, what restraints apply to this discretion once the occupying power does in fact allow entrance into the area? The principle of nondiscrimination must guide any occupying power; there is no good reason why this principle should not apply to issues of residence and family unification.

Professor Dinstein has argued that the approach of the Court should be exactly the opposite of the approach adopted in the *Shahin* case. Instead of a presumption that the husband, wife, or minor children will *not* be allowed permanent residency status unless they can show that their case is exceptional, the presumption should be that residents are entitled to have their spouse and minor children living with them unless there is a specific reason (such as security or economic factors) to deny permission.[38]

A highly significant factor about the family unification cases is the way in which the Court relied on the fact that the regime on the West Bank and in Gaza is one of belligerent occupation. This was viewed as a major factor explaining the legal basis for the policy adopted by the authorities. This was not accompanied by the type of caveat that at one time accompanied all decisions resting on the law of belligerent occupation. Perhaps the reason was that this is one area in which the law of belligerent occupation was relied on by the authorities to justify their policies, rather than by petitioners interested in challenging acts or policies of the authorities.

PART III

CHAPTER SEVEN

SECURITY POWERS

BASIC ISSUES

Arguments of security or military necessity underlie many of the issues discussed in the preceding chapters. Until the argument was rejected in the *Elon Moreh* case,[1] the authorities successfully argued that requisition of private land for establishment of civilian settlements could be justified on security grounds. The Court also held that security considerations justified expropriation of land for constructing highways. In the *VAT* case,[2] the Court went even further and held that imposition of *VAT* in the Occupied Territories, following its introduction in Israel, could be explained on the basis of security demands.

We must now consider specific security measures used by the authorities. Two features characterize these measures: (1) their declared purpose is to contain a security risk and (2) they involve severe restrictions on the rights or liberties of the individual. Some of the measures (such as house demolitions) are declaredly punitive; others (such as administrative detention or curfews) are declaredly preventive, although their effect is obviously punitive. A significant proportion of the petitions submitted to the Supreme Court by residents of the Territories relate to such security measures.

In this chapter I address a number of issues connected to the use of security powers. I begin by discussing the reality of the security concerns that faced the authorities, the dynamics of security arguments in a highly loaded political situation, and the general approach of the Supreme Court in reviewing security questions. I then proceed to review the

Court's attitude on two questions that touch on general arguments relating to the legality of security measures: (1) whether the Defence (Emergency) Regulations, 1945, on the basis of which many of the security measures (such as deportations and house demolitions) are carried out were still in force in the West Bank and Gaza when the IDF entered those areas in 1967, and (2) whether the provisions in the local law in the Territories are subject to the principles of international law that place constraints on a belligerent occupant. In the chapters that follow I discuss the Court's decisions relating to curfews, administrative detention, interrogation practices, house demolitions, and deportations.

REALITY OF SECURITY CONCERNS

Whatever one's view of the prolonged occupation or of the policies followed by various governments both in the specific context of the Occupied Territories and in its general conflict-management strategy, so long as no political decision is made to withdraw from all the Territories the military authorities are confronted with the realities of the situation there. These have always included a host of security concerns. Some, such as the security of Israeli settlements and settlers, were the direct result of government policies and actions. Others were a function of the very nature of the IDF's presence as an occupying force in the Territories, which is anathema to the local population. These were paramount in the initial stage of the occupation during which there was some armed resistance. They were also dominant after the *Intifada* started in December 1987 and the IDF met with wide-scale violent demonstrations, throwing stones and Molotov cocktails at vehicles and other targets, tire-burning on major highways, and other forms of low-scale violence to which no army of occupation could remain indifferent.[3]

Another major concern relates to actions of terrorist groups against civilian targets in the Occupied Territories and in Israel itself. The border between the Occupied Territories (especially the West Bank) and Israel cannot be sealed, and it is not difficult for a resident of the West Bank who decides to carry out a terrorist attack against a civilian target in one of Israel's towns or cities to reach his or her destination. Terrorist attacks against targets in Israel have at times imposed an enormous burden on the security authorities whose mission is to protect the security of the Israeli public.

The military authorities cannot be oblivious to security threats and are forced to adopt measures to contain them. In a society that prides itself on adherence to the rule of law and fundamental human rights standards, any such measures should conform to accepted legal principles and rules of international humanitarian law. The object of this study is not to examine whether it would have been possible to maintain a long-term occupation without resort to repressive measures of one sort or another, whether the security strategies adopted by the military were effective, or whether alternative strategies could have been adopted, but how the Court reacted to arguments that these standards, principles, and rules were not being respected.

DYNAMICS OF SECURITY ARGUMENTS

Maintaining a clear distinction between legitimate security concerns and political considerations is never easy. It is especially difficult in a conflict situation, like the Israeli–Palestinian one. Even after the State of Israel was established, this conflict retained its character as a struggle between two ethnic/national communities that both claim rights in the same land.[4] In such a context, each side may regard actions taken to further its strategic aims in the struggle as actions connected to its collective security. A good example is the security argument that was raised to justify establishment of Jewish settlements in the Occupied Territories.

The connection between political strategies and perceptions of security is not confined to the inherent difficulties in distinguishing between the two. Actions that are overtly political may provoke a reaction that leads the authorities to adopt measures that they subsequently attempt to justify on security grounds. In some cases the Court has been a party to this process.

A case in point is the *Beit Hadassah* case.[5] Beit Hadassah is a building in the center of Hebron that belonged to Jews before 1948. After 1948 the property was taken over by the Jordanian Custodian of Enemy Property, who leased it to an organization that sublet part of it to shopkeepers. After the Likud came to power in 1977, tremendous pressure was placed on the government to allow Jews to settle in Hebron itself, especially in Beit Hadassah. A group of Jewish women settlers eventually took over the upper floor in the building and refused to leave. The government yielded to pressure and decided to establish a *yeshiva* (religious academy) in the building. It was warned by a senior legal advisor that care should be taken that settling the upper floor of the building with Jewish residents would not create a nuisance for storekeepers on the ground floor. In 1981 a number of Hebron residents, including one of the storekeepers in Beit Hadassah, petitioned the Supreme Court to order eviction of the Jewish settlers who, they claimed, were not only trespassers, but had been harassing the storekeepers.[6] The Court was perturbed by the complaints of harassment and stressed that they had to be properly investigated, but it ruled that the petitioners had no property rights in the building and could therefore not challenge the settlers' right to be there.

A few years later, storekeepers in the building petitioned the Court. By this time another floor had been added to the building in order to allow more Jewish settlers to live there. The complaint related to a fence that had been constructed around the building that restricted access, including to the ground-floor stores. All persons wishing to gain access to the shops had to undergo a special security check, a factor that obviously had a deleterious effect on the petitioners' businesses. The petitioners claimed that the real intention behind the fence was to pressure them into selling their businesses.

The argument of the military authorities was that

> considering the large number of people, who would in the future live in Beit Hadassah, and the importance of the house as a symbol of the renewed Jewish community in Hebron, and to the history of bloodshed, that accompanied this process, the [authorities] reached the conclusion that it is essential to take steps that will ensure that no attempt will be made to use violence against the tenants of Beit Hadassah.

They claimed that the fence and security checks were an essential security requirement. In accepting this argument the Court stated that the military authorities had the power to take all measures necessary to protect the settlers in Beit Hadassah, and as the danger toward these settlers was severe, the measures were justified.[7]

This case illustrates the logic of the Court's analysis when faced with the results of political measures whose legality is questionable. The legality of the government decision to settle Israeli citizens in the Occupied Territories is not examined; their presence there later becomes a fact justifying security measures that impinge upon the local population. As in the *VAT* case examined in chapter 4, the law is dragged behind the measures of *de facto* annexation.

SCOPE OF REVIEW IN SECURITY MATTERS

Courts all over are reluctant to interfere in executive discretion in security matters, especially in times of national crisis, in which a society sees itself threatened by external or internal enemies.[8] The U.S. Supreme Court, often regarded as the prime example of an activist court, has in times of national crisis consistently bowed to executive discretion and refused to interfere in decisions that have afterwards been recognized as serious violations of fundamental human rights.[9]

It is not difficult to find reasons for the reticence of courts in security matters. First, the attitude that at times of crisis the "general interest" should be preferred to the rights of individuals is not limited to the executive branch of government. On the contrary, it is likely to be widely shared. There is little reason to expect that the attitudes of judges on this issue will be radically different from those of Cabinet ministers, or of the public at large.[10] Second, when a court interferes with an executive decision it must be prepared to bear the responsibility for the outcome. Courts sometimes give explicit expression to their refusal to accept such responsibility. More often they do not mention this factor, but it is no doubt a conscious or subconscious element in their decision-making process. Third, research on decision-making in face of uncertainty reveals a bias in favor of omissions (i.e., failure to act) rather than commissions (i.e., performance of a positive act).[11] Non-intervention of a court (an omission) rather than intervention (a commission) would seem to be perfectly consistent with this general bias.

As a general rule of thumb one can surmise that the bigger the chance of a link existing, or being perceived to exist, between a specific court decision and the materialization of a concrete security risk cited as the grounds for the executive action, the less likely that the court will be prepared to interfere in that action. The greater the danger that a court could be charged with hindering security, or with responsibility for actual "security problems," even when there is no way that a direct link could be established between its decisions and those problems, the more reluctant a court will be to interfere with executive decisions. There are, however, clear exceptions to this rule of thumb. One example is the Israel Supreme Court decision outlawing all use of force in interrogation of terrorist suspects,[12] notwithstanding the security services' persistent argument that such a restriction would hinder efforts to combat terrorism.

There are a number of ways a court can deal with its natural reluctance to interfere in security matters. One is to limit the scope of its review so that it does not have to look into the substantive decision of the executive. This approach was adopted in the early jurisprudence of the Supreme Court of Israel,[13] but was later abandoned. The older generation of judges gradually became wary lest the wide security powers enjoyed by the executive be used for improper purposes. They were therefore prepared to examine whether security considerations were indeed the real reasons for exercising security powers. On the other hand, once they considered that the executive perceived the issue to be one of security, they did not consider it within their province to review the decision on its merits. The following statement of Justice Landau in the *Beth-El* case is typical of the attitude adopted by these judges:

> the spheres of intervention of this court in the military considerations of the military government are very narrow, and the judge as an individual

will certainly refrain from placing his views on political and security matters in place of the military considerations of those who are entrusted with defense of the state and with maintaining public order in the occupied territory.[14]

In the 1980s the Court extended its scope of review even further. There were probably a number of reasons for this development. First, the trauma of the Yom Kippur War, in which the myth that the Israel Defense Forces are infallible was tragically shattered, may well have encouraged the Court that blind faith in the decisions of the security establishment could no longer be maintained in any sphere.[15] Second, broadening the scope of review in security matters fitted into a general trend of the Court to extend the net of judicial review.[16] Finally, the judges largely responsible for the change were the new generation of judges who adopted a highly activist approach to judicial review in general.

The rhetoric of the Court in recent years suggests that there is no difference between the scope of judicial review in security matters and in other matters.[17] Justice Barak presented the prevailing view when he said:

> In the past the security character of administrative discretion discouraged judicial review. Judges are not security staff, and they should not interfere in security considerations. Over the years it has become clear that when it comes to judicial review there is nothing special about security considerations. . . . Just as judges are qualified and bound to examine the reasonableness of professional discretion in every sphere, they are qualified and bound to examine the reasonableness of discretion relating to security. The approach is therefore reached that there are no special limitations on the scope of judicial review over administrative discretion relating to matters of security.[18]

The change in rhetoric did not necessarily reflect a greater willingness actually to intervene in decisions made on security grounds.[19] Nevertheless, it had important implications. Foremost among these was the potential inhibitive impact on decision-making within the executive. The type of case in which the Court has serious doubts whether security considerations were the genuine grounds for the decision became far rarer. The fact that the authorities have to present the Court not only with the formal legal basis for the security measure, but with the grounds for using the measure in the specific case, must have some effect on the decisions themselves. Nevertheless, the potential discrepancy between rhetoric and action cannot be ignored.

VALIDITY OF DEFENCE REGULATIONS

In 1945 the British Mandatory authorities promulgated the Defence (Emergency) Regulations, 1945. Based on the Palestine (Defence) Order-in-Council, 1937, the immediate aim of these regulations, which applied to the whole of Mandatory Palestine, was to provide the authorities with wide-ranging powers needed, in their view, to crush the uprising of the Jewish underground movements.[20] Among the measures included in the regulations are administrative detention (regulation 111), deportations (regulation 112), and forfeiture and demolition of houses (regulation 119). Although their promulgation by the British had met with a spate of criticism from leaders of the Jewish community in Palestine and especially from members of the Jewish Lawyers Association,[21] the military authorities in the Occupied Territories resorted to many of the measures provided for in the Defence Regulations.

Various arguments have been directed against the use of the Defence Regulations by the military authorities. Some arguments have been directed against the validity of the regulations on the West Bank and Gaza when the IDF entered those areas in 1967. Others have been directed against the validity of specific provisions, particularly regulation 112, which deals with the power to deport on security grounds.

Revocation of the Defence Regulations

Three days before termination of the British Mandate over Palestine, an Order-in-Council was signed in London and tabled in the UK parliament. The Palestine (Revocations) Order-in-Council, 1948, declared that the Palestine (Defence) Order-in-Council, 1937, was repealed as from 14 May 1948 (the last day of the British Mandate).[22] As the Defence Regulations were promulgated under the power given to the High Commissioner in the Order-in-Council of 1937, revocation of the Order–in–Council meant that the Defence Regulations were also revoked.

The Palestine (Revocations) Order-in-Council, 1948, was published in the Government Gazette in London but not in the official Palestine Gazette. In the *Na'azal* case[23] the Supreme Court held that failure to publish the order in the Palestine Gazette meant that the order was a "hidden law" that had no validity. The Court relied on Military Order No. 160, enacted in 1967, and on general legal principles. Military Order No. 160 declares that a "hidden law" has never had any validity.[24] The Court held that this principle would have applied even if Military Order No. 160 had not been promulgated.

This reply of the Court evades the main question, which is whether according to the laws in force in the area *before* 1967, the Palestine

(Revocations) Order-in-Council, 1948, was regarded as valid, even though it had not been published in the official gazette.[25] If the answer were negative, the question would become whether the military commander could revive legislation that was not valid when the occupation began.

Furthermore, the Court's approach would seem to pervert the purpose of the principle against hidden laws. This principle rests on the notion that individuals should not be punished for failing to conform to norms unless they could have known in advance what the norms were and what the punishment would be in case of deviance. Should this same principle apply to a case in which the authorities *divest themselves* of far-reaching powers to impose restrictions on the liberties of the individual? What principle, besides requirements of form, demands that a law directed toward the authorities alone, which in no way restricts the freedoms or rights of individuals, must be published outside the halls of government? One can well imagine a court interested in protecting the rights of the individual adopting an approach in favour of the validity of any law that restricts or abrogates the Defence Regulations.

Jordanian Constitution

In the *Awwad* case [26] an attempt was made to challenge the validity of regulation 112 of the Defence Regulations, which empowers the military authorities to deport a person on security grounds. The petitioner argued that regulation 112 had by implication been repealed by the Jordanian Constitution of 1952.

The Court ruled that the chain of validity of the Defence Regulations on the West Bank had remained unbroken from the time they were promulgated by the British until they were employed by the IDF after 1967.[27] It then proceeded to examine the argument that deportations are inconsistent with the prohibition against exile from the realm of a Jordanian citizen in article 9 of the Jordanian Constitution. Justice Sussman pointed to article 128 of the Constitution that declares that all laws existing at the time the Constitution was enacted would remain in force. He held that, according to accepted rules of interpretation, regulation 112 of the Defence Regulations was therefore not affected by the Constitution.[28]

In the *Kawasme II* case Justice Sussman's view was questioned by Justice Landau, who thought that article 128 of the Jordanian Constitution could be read with an implied proviso, whereby it does not abrogate unqualified civil rights such as the right guaranteed by article 9.[29] The conclusion should ostensibly have been that regulation 112 was no longer valid when the IDF entered the West Bank in 1967 and could therefore not be relied on by the military commander. Justice

Landau avoided this conclusion by relying on Military Order No. 224 (the Interpretation Order), promulgated by the IDF military commander in 1968.[30]

The Interpretation Order states that "in order to remove any doubt" emergency legislation is not impliedly repealed by later non-emergency legislation; it may only be repealed by express provision. Furthermore, the order declares that emergency legislation in force in the area on 14 May 1948 remained in force unless expressly repealed. Justice Landau rejected the petitioners' argument that regulation 112 had no validity, because it

> ignores section 3 of the [Interpretation] Order which stipulates that the point in time for the continued force of emergency legislation is not the time when the Order was published, in February, 1968, but 14.5.48. On that day . . . regulation 112 was by all accounts in force in the whole of Eretz-Yisrael, and it was never expressly abrogated . . . afterwards. . . .

> The conclusion is that from the point of view of domestic law, that was applied in Judea and Samaria, regulation 112 remains in force to this day.[31]

The problem with this view was mentioned by Justice Haim Cohn, who dissented from Justice Landau's opinion.[32] Justice Cohn agreed with Justice Landau that regulation 112 was impliedly repealed by article 9 of the Jordanian constitution and that only the Interpretation Ordinance could have saved it. Unlike Justice Landau, however, he thought that the source of validity of regulation 112 had important legal implications: the Interpretation Order, as part of the military legislation, is subject to judicial review and if it is inconsistent with customary international law, it may be regarded as invalid.[33]

According to customary international law, the law in force in occupied territory must be respected by the occupying power.[34] The relevant cut-off point for determining whether any given law was in force must obviously be the period immediately preceding the beginning of the occupation. If regulation 112 was repealed in 1952, the real question had to be whether a military commander in occupied territory possesses the power to promulgate legislation that institutes deportations. In a system in which legislative power is unbridled, the legislator may enact an interpretation law that retroactively declares laws to have been in force even if they had in fact been repealed in the past. However, as the Supreme Court itself has conceded on more than one occasion, the legislative power of a military commander in occupied territory is not unbridled. Under the guise of an interpretation order passed "to remove doubts," the military commander may not resurrect a measure that he lacks the power to institute by passing an express law.[35]

The majority judges in the *Kawasme II* court took a very narrow view of the relevant legal framework, limiting themselves to the *internal* rules of the domestic legal system (that include military orders). The Court followed this approach yet again in the *Na'azal* case. Taking its cue from the majority view in the *Kawasme II* case, the Court refrained from dealing directly with the argument that under the Hague Regulations the legislative power of the military commander of an occupied area is limited and may not be used to introduce the measure of deportations.

The decisions on the continued validity of article 112 of the Defence Regulations in the *Awwad* and *Kawasme II* cases relate to the West Bank. In the *Maslam case*,[36] a similar argument was raised concerning the validity of regulation 112 in Gaza. The petitioners argued that the power to deport had been impliedly repealed by the Egyptian military government in Gaza when it enacted the Basic Law for the Gaza Strip, 1955, and the Constitution of Gaza, 1962. Both the Basic Law and the Constitution guaranteed freedom to choose one's place of residence and freedom of movement "within the framework of the law." The Basic Law left all Mandatory laws in force "provided they are not inconsistent with this basic law." The petitioners' argument was that as the power to deport is inconsistent with the freedom to choose one's place of abode and with freedom of movement, it must be seen as having been abolished by the Basic Law.[37]

The Supreme Court rejected this argument. It held that because both the Basic Law and the Constitution protected freedom of abode and of movement "within the framework of the law, it is obvious that if there is a statute that curbs freedom of abode or freedom of movement, it will prevail, and such a provision is to be found in regulation 112 of the Defence Regulations, that are valid in Gaza according to the provisions both of the Egyptian regime and the Israeli regime relating to the continuity of the law."[38]

Once again it seems that the Court's reasoning is questionable. The provision that all persons enjoy freedom of movement and freedom to choose their place of abode "within the framework of the law" obviously means that in exercising these freedoms persons may not perform illegal acts, such as trespass. It hardly means that the authorities retain all former powers to restrict these freedoms.

The main characteristic of the Court's approach in all decisions on the validity of the Defence Regulations has been narrow formalism. The Court has not perceived itself as a judicial body that should play an expansive role in trying to protect basic rights against violation by government, but as a body that must support the foundation of military legislation in the Occupied Territories.

PRIMACY OF LOCAL LAW

One of the arguments raised by the authorities to counter challenges to the legality of security measures under international law was that the restrictions imposed on an occupying power under the laws of belligerent occupation only restrict that power's *legislative* capacity, but not its power to implement laws that were in force when the occupation started. Taken one step further, this argument holds that as the belligerent occupant must respect existing law, it may even be obliged to implement the measures provided for under the local legal system.

In the *Sakhwill* case,[39] the first reported decision dealing with sealing or demolishing a house, the petitioners argued that sealing the room in a house that belonged to a person convicted of harboring a terrorist was contrary to Geneva Convention IV. The Court refused to enter into the question of whether the convention was binding because there was "no contradiction between the provisions of that convention . . . and use made by the respondent of authority given to him according to a statutory provision that was in force when the area of Judea and Samaria was controlled by the state of Jordan and which to this day remains in force in the area of Judea and Samaria."[40]

The notion that the substantive provisions of Geneva Convention IV do not restrict a belligerent occupant in employing local legislation that was valid when the occupation began was later fully articulated in the *Jabar* case.[41] In this case it was argued was that punitive house demolitions are contrary both to the Hague Regulations and Geneva Convention IV. In support of this argument, counsel submitted an opinion of the ICRC regarding interpretation of article 53 of the Geneva Convention.[42] The Court held that article 53 was irrelevant since house demolitions are carried out under a provision of local law that remained valid under article 43 of the Hague Regulations (discussed in chapter 4) and article 64 of Geneva Convention IV (which states that the penal law of the occupied territory shall remain in force).[43]

The reasoning of the Court rests on dubious grounds. First, the accepted view is that restrictions placed on a belligerent occupant apply notwithstanding empowering provisions in the local law.[44] The provisions of the two conventions cited by the Court are obviously meant to *protect* the local population; citing those provisions to justify use of measures aimed against that population is an abuse of their meaning and intention.[45] Article 64 of the Geneva Convention, cited by the Court, states that the penal laws of the occupied territory shall remain in force "with the exception that they may be repealed or suspended by the Occupying Power in cases where they constitute a threat to its security or *an obstacle to the application of the present Convention*" (emphasis added). This hardly supports the notion that local law frees the Occupying Power from its duty to respect the provisions of the Convention. Finally, article 68 of the Convention allows the occupying power to impose the death penalty for certain offences "provided that such offences were punishable by death under the law of the occupied territory in force before the occupation began." The inclusion of this proviso is clear evidence that the assumption of the Convention is that, unless otherwise stated, the provisions of the Convention have precedence over the law in force at the time of occupation.

Although I have separated discussion of the Court's stand on the continued applicability of the Defence Regulations as part of the local law on the West Bank from its view that limitations placed on the occupying power under international law do not affect its power to employ local law, there is an obvious connection between the two issues. Given the Court's view that only military legislation is subject to scrutiny under the standards of international law, it becomes essential to decide whether the formal source of a given measure (such as deportations or demolitions) is local law or military legislation. The theory adopted by the majority of the court in the *Kawasme II* case was that the basis for the validity of regulation 112 of the Defence Regulations is the Interpretation Order. Thus the "law in force argument" could not be a legitimate argument for rebutting the claim that deportations are outlawed under the international law of belligerent occupation. It may be for this reason that the Court raised this argument in house demolition but not in deportation cases.

CHAPTER EIGHT

LIBERTY AND SECURITY OF THE PERSON

LIMITATIONS ON FREEDOM OF MOVEMENT

Restrictions on freedom of movement of residents in the Occupied Territories may be imposed in a number of ways. The most drastic restriction takes the form of a curfew that restricts the right of all people in a given area to leave their homes during stipulated times.

In all cases in which attempts have been made to challenge such restrictions, the military authorities have replied by explaining their grounds for fearing serious breaches of public order unless the restrictions are maintained. They invariably present the Court with evidence (part of it classified) on which their assessment is based.

The pattern of the Supreme Court's decisions on restrictions of movement is clear. It expresses concern with the implications of the restrictions, and often urges the authorities to reconsider whether the restrictions are still necessary, but it has consistently refrained from interfering in these restrictions.

In the case of *Shawe* v. *IDF Commander in Gaza*,[1] the petitioners challenged a night curfew that had been imposed in the whole Gaza area soon after the *Intifada* started.[2] They argued that the curfew was too broad to be regarded as a legitimate preventive measure and that it served, in fact, as a punitive sanction. The Court accepted that a curfew must not be used as a punitive measure. However, it stated that the commander had sworn that the curfew was required to ensure security and maintain public order. The Court held that it had no adequate grounds for intervening in the commander's considerations, nor for fixing the areas in which the curfew could be lifted or relaxed. It therefore dismissed the petition, although it declared that the respondent should examine the need for the curfew periodically, "taking into account the difficulty caused to the population."[3]

An attempt by the Court to pressure the authorities to consider relaxation of curfews, without taking responsibility for interfering in their operational decisions, stands out in the *Panous* case.[4] The military commander had issued orders imposing a general curfew on a number of towns for the period of one month. He claimed that the curfew was needed to allow the military authorities to carry out a specific operation.[5] While the Court accepted that there were legitimate grounds for the curfew, it held that it should have been limited to two weeks, after which time the need for the curfew would be reconsidered.[6] It therefore issued a decision limiting the curfew order to the two-week period, after which it would elapse "unless a new order based on substantial grounds that justify it was issued, or the circumstances justify shortening the period."[7] Although the Court was not prepared to take the responsibility for ending the curfew, it made it more difficult for the military authorities to renew it. A similar approach was adopted in the *Insh el-Usra Society* case.[8]

Severe restrictions on movement were also the focus of the *Barcat* case.[9] In this case the petitioners' son had died while in police custody. The authorities released the body to the parents, but the military commander issued an order that the funeral be held at night and attendance restricted to the deceased's family. The family petitioned the Court to allow them to hold the funeral during daytime in the presence of all the local residents.

The military commander presented the Court with evidence that in previous funerals of persons who had died at the hands of the security forces, there had been serious disturbances despite assurances given beforehand by local leaders. Furthermore, the security services provided evidence that nationalistic elements were actually planning a large event that would include breaches of the peace.

The Court conceded that the issue of the burial concerned both respect for the deceased and the dignity of his family. The military commander could not use his powers to restrict the circumstances of the funeral unless there were strong grounds for doing so. In this case, the Court held that it had been proven that there was a high probability that if the funeral were to take place during the day there would be serious disturbances. It held that in these circumstance the commander's decisions was reasonable and there were no grounds for the Court to interfere.[10]

The Court's approach in these cases typifies its approach in cases in which it is asked to interfere in the discretion of the military commander. Once the Court has established that the commander has the power (under local law or military orders) to take a specific decision, it invariably refuses to intervene in that decision.[11] The one apparent exception is the case in which severe restrictions are placed in advance on freedom of movement or other liberties. In such cases the Court may be prepared to restrict the period during which the *original* closure order remains in force. However, it expressly declares that the military commander may issue another order if it is needed under the conditions prevailing when the first order expires. Thus, the Court is not a full party to the commander's decision, but it does not assume responsibility for preventing the commander from taking measures that he claims to be necessary.

ADMINISTRATIVE DETENTION

Extent of Use

Administrative detention has been one of the measures used on a large scale by the military authorities in the Occupied Territories. In the spring of 1970, 1,261 Palestinians were being held in administrative detention, 220 of whom had been detained for over a year.[12] By 1971 the number of detainees had dropped to 445.[13] During the 1970s approximately forty Palestinians were held as administrative detainees every year. During the years 1982–1985, use of administrative detention was suspended; use of the measure began again in 1985. After the *Intifada* began in December 1987, the measure was used on a massive scale. From December 1990 to October 1991, 1,590 Palestinians were held under administrative detention.[14] After the Oslo Accords extensive use was also made of the measure. In September 1997 there were 509 Palestinians in administrative detention. As a result of pressure, this number was radically reduced and by September, 2000 only five Palestinians were being held as administrative detainees.[15]

Legal Basis: Local Law

According to article 111 of the Defence Regulations, the military commander has the power to place a person under detention if he is of the opinion that detention is needed to protect the defense of the land or public security. The detainee has the right to challenge the detention before an advisory board (which recommends to the military commander whether to maintain the detention order or to revoke it). The advisory board must also review the detention every six months, even if the detainee does not appeal. In substance, these provisions were also included in a military order promulgated by the military commander after 1967.[16]

The Defence Regulations, which, according to the Court's jurisprudence, are valid in the Occupied Territories, are also still valid in Israel itself. However, in the matter that concerns us here, important changes have been made in the Israeli system. Under a statute enacted in Israel in 1979, article 111 of the Regulations was abrogated and replaced by a system of preventive detention that is subject to strict judicial review.[17] Following the amendment in Israeli law, the law in the Occupied Territories was modified too. In 1980 the Orders Concerning Security Provisions in Gaza and the West Bank were amended to incorporate features of the Israeli system.[18] Under the revised Order 378, if the military commander has reasonable grounds for believing that security of the area or public security demand that a specific person be held in detention, he may order that person's detention for a period not exceeding six months, which may be extended. The detainee must be brought before a military judge within ninety-six hours of his arrest; the judge may uphold the detention order, revoke it, or shorten the period of detention. If the order is upheld, it must be reviewed within three months. The judge's decision is subject to appeal before the president of the military court.

After the *Intifada* started, the authorities responded by placing hundreds, and later thousands, of Palestinians in detention. Because they could not bring all these detainees before a judge within ninety-six hours, Order 378 was again amended.[19] The main change was to eliminate review by a military judge and replace it with the right of appeal against the detention before an advisory board. This system was revised after a short while to provide for a right of appeal before a military judge.[20]

The law on administrative detention expressly states that the reviewing judge is allowed to examine privileged evidence.[21] Before doing so the judge must decide whether there is justification for maintaining the privilege. If that decision is negative, the evidence is revealed to the detainee and his or her counsel. On the other hand, if the judge decides that the privilege is justified, the judge may take the evidence into account when reviewing the detention order itself. This means that a person may be interned without being informed of the reasons for the internment.

Legal Basis: International Law

International law does not rule out administrative detention in a situation of belligerent occupation. On the contrary, article 78 of Geneva Convention IV expressly states that "if the occupying power considers it necessary, for imperative reasons of security, to take safety measures concerning protected persons, it may, at the most, subject them to assigned residence or to internment." However, under article 6 of the

Convention, this article and the other articles dealing with internment cease to apply one year after the general close of military operations.[22] It has been argued that when these articles no longer apply administrative detention can only be justified if it would be permitted in a state of emergency under international human rights law.[23]

Even if one ignores the one-year limitation in Geneva Convention IV, or takes the view that after one year administrative detention may be allowed if it would be permissible in a state of emergency in non-occupied territory, it is clear that use of administrative detention is subject to stringent conditions. Firstly, such detention may be used only when considered necessary "for imperative reasons of security."[24] Furthermore, because this is the most extreme security measure allowed by Geneva Convention IV, under the principle of proportionality it may not be used when less severe measures are available to contain the security risk. There must be an effective system of review so that the detention of every detainee will be reviewed every six months.[25] Finally, the conditions of detention must meet the standards laid down in great detail in section IV of Geneva Convention IV.

Court's Decisions

In its capacity as a High Court of Justice the Israeli Supreme Court is an instance of last resort; it will not entertain a petition unless the petitioner has exhausted all other remedies. The Court has adhered to this principle in its approach to administrative detention. Because the law regulating administrative detention provides for a review mechanism, the Court will not hear a petition challenging administrative detention until this review mechanism has been exhausted.[26] The Court has refused to allow circumvention of this principle by petitioners who have attempted to challenge the alleged *intention* of a military commander to issue an administrative detention order.[27] The Court has also stressed that it is not a court of appeal against the decisions of the military judge who reviews the detention order: it will only interfere if there is a serious flaw in the proceedings or on the record.[28]

The Court has never entertained arguments against the legality under international law of the system of administrative detention maintained in the Occupied Territories. In the *Ketziot* case it conceded the inherent difficulties of administrative detention, but merely mentioned that such detention is permitted under Geneva Convention IV. The president of the Court, Justice Shamgar, described the system of administrative detention as follows:

> An administrative detainee has not been convicted of an offence and is
> therefore not serving a sentence. He is imprisoned on the basis of a

decision by a military-administrative authority as an exceptional emergency measure, on imperative security grounds. . . . The detention is
aimed at preventing and frustrating a security danger that derives from
the acts the detainee is likely to commit, when there is no reasonable
possibility of preventing these acts by regular legal steps (criminal proceedings) or by an administrative measure whose consequences are not
as severe.[29]

While stressing that detention can be justified only on imperative
security grounds when there is no less severe preventative measure available, the Court has seldom been prepared to examine whether these
stringent conditions have been met. The reason given is that there is a
review mechanism to examine these questions and it is not the function
of the Court to serve as an appeal instance against the reviewing military judges. Thus, the general approach of the Court has been to stress
procedural aspects of the review process but to refrain from intervening
on the merits. The Court's original position was that it would not as a
matter of course review the privileged evidence examined by the military
judge. It would do so only if it could not learn from the military judge's
decision itself on what grounds the detention was upheld,[30] or if the petitioner raised a concrete argument that justified looking at all the evidence.[31] However, the Court later modified its practice and was prepared
on occasion to examine the privileged evidence in order to see whether
the decision of the military judge was well founded.[32]

The Court has been reluctant to set clear substantive standards for
reviewing administrative detention. It has ruled that administrative
detention must not be used when the detainee could be placed on criminal trial,[33] or when less drastic means would effectively contain the danger to security.[34] It has also emphasized that a person may not be detained
for his views.[35] The general test is whether there is evidence of "activities
that lead or are likely to lead to violence and danger to security."[36]

In the *Katamash* case the petitioner had been charged before a military court with hostile activities. After a pre-trial detention of nine
months, the military judge released him on bail. An appeal was lodged
against this decision. At the same time the military commander issued
an order placing the petitioner in administrative detention. The petitioner argued that the administrative detention was a way of circumventing the decision to release him on bail. The Supreme Court held
that the administrative detention could not be justified if the only evidence before the military commander who issued the detention order
was the evidence before the judge who had released the petitioner on
bail. On the other hand, the detention would be legal if the military
commander had based his decision on additional evidence which
revealed that the petitioner would endanger public security if he were

free. On the strength of the military judge's decision and the affidavit of the military commander, the Court held that the latter's decision was not based on the same evidence as that of the military judge. It therefore upheld the administrative detention.

A similar approach was taken by the Court when dealing with renewal of a detention order, after the period of the original order had been shortened by a military judge. The Court held that the military commander may not renew such an order unless the military judge specifically shortened the period in order to give the commander a chance to reconsider the need for the detention toward the end of the shortened period, or if there is new evidence or a change in circumstances that substantially increase the risk in releasing the detainee.[37]

As in the other security cases, the Court has rarely intervened in the discretion of the military commander to issue an administrative detention order or that of the military judge to uphold such an order. However, there have been exceptions. In *Zaid* v. *IDF Commander in Judea and Samaria*[38] the Court examined the privileged evidence and ordered the immediate release of the petitioner. No explanation was given either for the decision to examine the privileged evidence or for the decision to order release of the detainee.

The Court's main concern has been for the procedural aspects of administrative detention. In the *Ketziot* case the Court dealt with petitions from administrative detainees who were held in a special camp set up in Israel for the large number of detainees held during the *Intifada*. The majority on the Court rejected the argument that under international law administrative detainees had to be imprisoned in the occupied territory and not in the territory of the occupying power.[39] On the other hand, the Court dealt at length with the petitioners' argument that there was a long delay before appeals were heard. Although the Court found that there had not been undue delay in the specific cases of the petitioners, it laid down ground rules for appeals. The Court stated that even though the law that required bringing the detainee before a judge within ninety-six hours had been replaced by a system of appeals, it was of the essence that the appeals should be heard promptly. Counsel for the authorities had informed the Court that 28 percent of the appeals were partially or wholly successful.[40] In the Court's view this proved that administrative detention without effective judicial review could lead to mistakes in fact or law that resulted in persons being kept in detention without material basis. The Court held that appeals should be heard within two to three weeks and that if the existing judges could not cope with this demand, more judges should be appointed to hear appeals.[41]

The Court also gave detailed guidelines to the military judges as to procedure in reviewing detention orders. As in almost all cases most of the evidence is privileged and cannot be revealed to the detainee or his or her counsel, it is incumbent on the reviewing judge to examine the evidence with great care. The judge should consider whether part of this evidence could be revealed to the detainee and counsel without endangering security interests. The judge should first hear the open evidence presented by the authorities and the response of the detainee and counsel. The judge should then examine the privileged evidence and give the detainee and counsel an opportunity to make submissions or clarify points the judge may wish to raise in the light of the privileged evidence. Immediately thereafter the judge should deliver a decision or announce the date on which it will be delivered.[42]

The guidelines set by the Court are not regarded as binding. Shortly after it laid down the guidelines, the Court ruled that it would not interfere in the decision of a military judge who had deviated from the guidelines unless the deviation caused substantial injustice.[43]

In the *Ketziot* case the petitioners also complained of the harsh conditions in the detention center. In order to examine these complaints, the Court visited Ketziot and the judges met with detainees and heard their complaints in person. The Court stressed that because the detainees were not convicted prisoners, they were entitled to better conditions than ordinary prisoners, referring to the ICRC Commentary on Geneva Convention IV and its view that the conditions of internees should be similar to those of prisoners of war.[44]

The Court discussed the conditions of detention in great detail. It criticized the overcrowding and demanded that it be ameliorated. It also held that some of the disciplinary measures imposed by guards were unacceptable. Furthermore, it instructed the authorities to consult qualified Muslim religious authorities as to the arrangements for prayer and gave directives regarding the availability of newspapers and delivery of letters. Finally, the Court stated that a court was not the appropriate body to monitor prison conditions. It recommended that the authorities establish an advisory board that could monitor conditions in Ketziot on a permanent basis and make recommendations to the authorities on changes that should be implemented.[45]

In concluding this discussion of administrative detention, it should be noted that this is the one security measure that has not only been used against Palestinians. Administrative detention orders have occasionally been issued against Israeli settlers in the Occupied Territories. Attempts by these detainees to have their detention orders overturned by the Supreme Court have been no more successful than attempts by Palestinians. Thus, in both the *Federman* and *Citrin* cases, the Court held that less drastic restriction would not have effectively met the security danger posed by the detainees' activities. The administrative detention orders were upheld.

Summary

The Court's decisions in the administrative detention cases reveal a pattern that runs through its decisions on other security measures. The Court has not given detailed and careful consideration to the arguments that the system of administrative detention in the Occupied Territories is inconsistent with international law. On the contrary, international law has been used to legitimize the measure. No mention has been made of the restrictions placed on its use, nor was an attempt made to examine whether these restrictions are respected in practice. The Court has been very reluctant to examine whether detention is justified in specific cases and has generally left this question to be decided in the internal review procedure before a military judge. However, by opening its doors to review of individual decisions, looking at the evidence, and even interfering in the rare case, the Court has sought to constrain use of administrative detention while leaving the final responsibility for the decision on release of a detainee in the hands of the authorities.

The Court has strengthened the standing of the military judges' decisions. It has also set guidelines for the reviewing military judge, but has not been prepared to regard the failure of a reviewing judge to follow these guidelines as a flaw that vitiates the decision. The Court has also been prepared to go to some lengths to examine allegations regarding the conditions of detention and make recommendations for improvements. It has not, however, demanded that conformity with international standards is a condition of detention.

INTERROGATION PRACTICES

The interrogation practices of Israel's security service have been a major concern of domestic and international human rights groups and of the international community. Although the controversial interrogation methods have been used mainly, although not solely, against Palestinian residents of the Occupied Territories, no argument was ever raised that they could be justified in terms of Israel's role as an occupying power. Interrogations most often take place in Israel itself and the attempts to provide legal justification for the interrogation practices were based on norms of the Israeli domestic legal system, rather than on the laws in the Occupied Territories or the international law of belligerent occupation. From a strictly legal perspective, the Supreme Court's decisions on this issue are therefore not really within the scope of this study, which concerns the Court's jurisprudence relating to the Occupied Territories. Yet the interrogation methods have a clear *political* connection to the Occupied Territories, since the acts of violence they were designed to contain are wholly or partly a function of the control by Israel of a hostile population in occupied territory. I shall therefore include a brief discussion of the issue here.[46]

During the first twenty years of the occupation, serious allegations were made concerning use of force in interrogation of Palestinians suspected of hostile activities. The authorities consistently denied these allegations, both in court and in reply to press and NGO reports. In 1987 it was revealed that an Israeli army officer who belonged to the small Circassian community had been convicted of security offences on the basis of a confession extracted through force by interrogators of the General Security Service (GSS). In response the government set up a judicial commission of inquiry to examine the methods of interrogation of the GSS and to recommend methods and guidelines for interrogations, "taking into consideration the special needs of the struggle against hostile terrorist activities."

The Commission of Inquiry, chaired by the former president of the Supreme Court, Justice Moshe Landau, found that since the early 1970s the GSS had used force in interrogations and had systematically lied when challenged in court. The Commission strongly condemned the behavior of the GSS. Nevertheless, the GSS managed to convince the Commission that limiting methods of interrogation to accepted police practice would mean that "effective interrogation would be inconceivable"; interrogators would be unable to obtain the information needed to frustrate planned terrorist acts.

In setting principles and guidelines for future interrogations the Commission considered three possible approaches: (1) rejecting use of force in all cases, however crucial it was to obtain information relating to planned terrorist attacks; (2) maintaining the position that the law prohibits all use of force while accepting that law enforcement authorities would turn a blind eye when the interrogators acted outside the law; and (3) establishing guidelines for use of special interrogation methods where essential in order to extract information that would lead to frustration of planned acts of terror.

The Commission was convinced that, in light of Israel's security situation, the price to be paid for adopting the first approach would be too high. It rejected the second approach as hypocritical. It therefore opted for the third approach, according to which, when other forms of pressure were not efficacious in obtaining crucial information from suspected terrorists, special interrogation methods could be used, including nonviolent psychological pressure and even a moderate degree of physical pressure.

The Commission attempted to base legal justification for use of moderate physical pressure in interrogations on the defense of necessity in criminal law. The argument was that if an interrogator used moderate physical pressure against a suspect to prevent the greater harm likely to be caused to innocent persons by a terrorist act, the interrogator would not be criminally liable.

The Commission divided its report into two parts. In the first part, which was published, it laid out the general issue and its principled recommendations.[47] In the second part, which has never been published, it laid out guidelines and constraints for the GSS regarding interrogation methods. It recommended that these guidelines be reviewed periodically by a ministerial committee. The Commission apparently assumed that if the use of force were strictly regulated it could be contained and "excesses" would be prevented.

While the government decided to adopt the Commission's recommendations, they were severely criticized in many quarters. It was argued that even though the Commission had expressly stated that methods amounting to torture were never to be allowed, it had in fact licensed torture, which is absolutely prohibited under international law. Lawyers also argued not only that the defense of necessity does not apply to interrogations, but that a defense against criminal liability, which by its very nature must be examined *ex post factum* within the individual circumstances of a specific case, does not provide a basis for governmental power to violate individual rights and freedoms.[48]

Fate would have it that the *Intifada* began a short time after publication of the Landau Report. A comprehensive study published by a leading Israeli human rights organization three years later showed that the use of methods that could fairly be described as torture had become widespread in interrogation of Palestinian detainees.[49]

Several attempts were made to challenge both the legality of various interrogation methods used by the security services and the Landau Commission's legal theory on the basic of which the authorities sought to justify these methods. In the first major attempt, a petition was submitted to the Supreme Court in 1991 on behalf of a human-rights NGO and a Palestinian who had been interrogated by the authorities. The petitioners asked the Court to forbid use of nonviolent psychological pressure and moderate physical pressure permitted by the Landau Report, to forbid interrogators from using methods of pressure permitted in the secret part of the Commission report, and to order publication of this secret part of the report.[50]

The Court held that questions regarding the legality of interrogation measures could only be examined within the context of a concrete case. Such a case could arise if the validity of a confession extracted by use of the "special" interrogation methods were challenged in court, or if a member of the security services were charged with acting illegally. The

Court therefore refused to rule on the questions of principle raised by the petitioners. It also refused to order publication of the secret part of the Landau Report.[51]

This decision of the Court was highly problematic. The Landau Commission itself explained that use of pressure was not meant to obtain confessions for criminal proceedings, but to extract information needed to frustrate terrorist activities. The authorities were unlikely to charge a person if the evidence against him or her consisted of a confession extracted by use of force. Furthermore, because the authorities held that interrogations using the methods permitted by the Landau Commission were legal, an interrogator using those methods would not be prosecuted. Thus, the chances of examining the legality of the methods permitted by the Landau Commission in the type of cases mentioned by the Court were negligible.

Alongside the "general" petition already mentioned, a large number of petitions were submitted to the Court on behalf of individuals arrested in circumstances in which it was considered likely that "special" methods of interrogation would be employed. In these cases counsel applied not only for rulings on the legality of the interrogation methods allegedly being used against their clients, but for interim injunctions against use of these methods until the case had been decided. In most of these cases the authorities claimed that they had no intention of using the methods or that the interrogation had ended. The Court therefore stated that there was no need to issue an interim injunction.[52] In a few cases the authorities conceded that they were using special methods, but, claiming that such methods were essential in the fight against terrorism, they asked the Court not to grant the interim injunction or even to revoke an injunction that had already been granted.

In the *Balebisi* case,[53] the authorities applied to the Court for revocation of an interim injunction to prevent use of physical force in interrogation of the petitioner two weeks after it had been granted. They submitted an affidavit that the petitioner had confessed to having planned the attack at a junction near an army base in which two suicide bombers and twenty-one Israeli citizens had been killed. The petitioner had provided information on another bomb that had been hidden and the authorities claimed there was a high probability that the petitioner had further information about planned terrorist activities. They argued that it was essential that they be allowed to proceed with the interrogation without being bound by the terms of the interim injunction.

Counsel for the petitioner did not contest the information provided by the authorities, but argued that even if the information were correct the injunction should remain in force, especially in regard to use of shaking.[54] The Court held that since the petitioner's counsel had not contested that there was a high probability that the petitioner possessed information regarding planned terrorist attacks, it had to assume that by obtaining this information the authorities could save lives. It therefore decided that there was no longer any justification for the injunction. The Court took care to stress, however, that revocation of the injunction did not imply that the authorities could use interrogation measures that were illegal. It even pointed to the restrictions applying to the necessity defense under the Criminal Code.

In *Khamdan v. General Security Service*[55] the authorities once again applied for revocation of an interim injunction against use of force in an interrogation. They claimed that the petitioner had information regarding imminent terrorist attacks and that it was essential that they be allowed to use methods of interrogation that, they claimed, did not amount to torture and were covered by the necessity defense. After examining the classified evidence, the Court stated it was satisfied that the authorities had information on which they could base a well-founded suspicion that the petitioner could provide them with most essential information that could avoid a serious tragedy, save human lives, and prevent egregious terror attacks. Following the *Balebisi* precedent, the Court revoked the interim injunction, stressing that this did not imply that the authorities could use illegal methods of interrogation. It also stressed that it had no information on the methods of interrogation and would express no opinion about them. Furthermore, revocation of the interim injunction did not imply that the Court was taking a position on the issues of principle regarding the defense of necessity and its scope.

In the *Mubarak* case[56] the petitioner argued that four methods of interrogation were being used against him, each of which amounted to torture: tying his hands behind his back in a painful position; hooding; playing loud music, and sleep deprivation. In reply to his application for an interim injunction the authorities tried a different tack to the one taken in the previous cases: they argued that the measures were not meant to pressure the interrogatee but were required by the interrogation. The first three measures were to prevent him from attacking his interrogators and establishing contact with other interrogatees; the petitioner was deprived of sleep because of the long period of time he had to wait before being interrogated. They also assured the Court that all efforts were being made not to cause any unnecessary discomfort to the petitioner. In a decision that stretches credulity to its outer limits, the Court accepted this reply and refused to issue a temporary injunction (subject to the remark that handcuffing the petitioner in a painful position is unlawful).

The decisions in all these cases were interlocutory. The Court left open the question of the legality of the measures used, and in the first two cases it specifically stated that the authorities must act within the confines of the law. Nevertheless, the decisions are important in assessing the Court's initial position on the use of force in interrogations.[57] Revocation of the interim injunctions in the *Khamdan* and *Balebisi* cases necessarily implied that use of force in interrogations could be legal. The Court's caveat that the authorities must act within the law was meaningless when the very question was whether the approach and guidelines of the Landau Commission on which the authorities relied were compatible with domestic and international legal norms.

The explanation for the Court's timidity in these cases obviously lies in the unenviable situation in which it was placed. During 1996, when the three decisions were handed down, there was a series of suicide bombings in which a large number of civilians were killed and many more were injured. In each of the cases the Court heard evidence by senior members of the General Security Service who were adamant that they could not obtain the information necessary to frustrate further attacks unless they were permitted to use the interrogation methods allowed by the Landau Commission.[58] The covert message was clear: if it tied the hands of the investigating authorities, *the Court* would be held responsible for any future terrorist attacks.

After the interim injunctions were refused or revoked, the petitions in these cases were left pending. A significant number of additional petitions by interrogatees were submitted. These were joined by petitions submitted by human-rights NGOs that tried once again to challenge the legal theory on which the Landau Commission based its justification of "special" methods of interrogation, including use of moderate physical force.

Some of the petitions were submitted in 1994, 1995, and 1996. The Court held a number of hearings on these petitions, but dragged its feet and refrained from finalizing the hearings and delivering judgment. In the intermediate period, both the State of Israel and the Supreme Court itself were subject to severe criticism by domestic and international NGOs and by international forums for the methods used in interrogation.[59] Eventually, in September 1999, an expanded bench of nine justices, headed by the Court's president, Justice Aharon Barak, delivered its opinion, which must be regarded as one of the most courageous ever delivered by the Court.[60]

In its decision the Court mentions the difficult situation the State of Israel faces in having to contain terror, and the authorities' claim that information extracted from some of the individual interrogatees had led to frustration of terrorist attacks. However, it accepted the legal arguments against use of force and other methods of pressure in interrogations. The Court held that while necessity could possibly serve as a defense in a specific criminal case, it does not arm the investigating authorities with the power needed to use "special" methods of interrogation. Because there was no other legal basis for such power, neither the government nor the GSS had the authority to "lay down guidelines, rules or permits for use of physical means in the course of investigating those suspected of hostile terrorist activity."

The Court added that its decision was based on the law at the time judgment was delivered. Were the law to be amended, the position could be different, although every amendment would have to meet the demands of the Basic Law: Human Dignity and Liberty.

The main impression one gets from reading the Court's decision is that the authorities did not have an arguable legal case. The Court presents the answers to the legal issues, including the Landau Report's necessity defense theory, as if they were almost self-evident. The question that arises is therefore twofold. First, if it was so clear that the authorities lacked the power to use physical force and other methods of pressure in interrogations, why did it take the Court so long to hand down a decision? Second, why did it revoke the interim injunctions in the *Khamed* and *Balibisi* cases and refuse to grant such an injunction in the *Mubarak* case?

It is not difficult to find an answer to these questions. In fact, the answer was provided by the Court itself. At the end of judgment, having ruled that the methods of interrogation that the General Security Service claimed essential in its struggle against terrorism are illegal, the Court stated:

> Deciding these applications weighed heavy on this Court. True, from the legal perspective, the road before us is smooth. We are, however, part of Israeli society. Its problems are known to us and we live its history. We are not isolated in an ivory tower. We live the life of this country. We are aware of the harsh reality of terrorism in which we are, at times, immersed. The apprehension that our decision will hamper the ability to properly deal with terrorists and terrorism, disturbs us. We are, however, judges. We demand that others act according to the law. This is equally the standard that we set for ourselves.

This says it all: the legal position is clear, but the Court identified with the dilemma facing the security authorities. While it could not deliver a judgment legitimizing the methods of interrogation, as long as it could tolerably do so it simply preferred not to deliver judgment at all.[61] What forced the Court to deliver its decision when it did is not clear. Reduction in the number of terrorist attacks, together with international condemnation of the State of Israel and the Court itself, probably helped. It is also possible that the realization that the "special"

methods of interrogation had become almost standard practice in interrogation of Palestinians, and were certainly not limited to the classic
"ticking-bomb" situation generally cited in discussions of the necessity
defense, encouraged the Court to "do the right thing."[62]

The Court's decision in the GSS interrogation methods case would
seem to signal a departure from the pattern described in other parts of
this study. In contrast to that pattern, the Court here took a clear and
unequivocal position on a substantive question of principle. The decision was not restricted to the particular circumstances of a concrete case,
but related to measures employed by the authorities as a matter of policy. I do not wish to detract from the importance of this decision, nor
from the courage manifested in handing down such a decision despite
persistent claims by the highest echelons in the security establishment
that the methods employed were essential tools in the struggle against
militant and highly motivated ideological terrorists. Nevertheless, a
number of points should be noted.

First, when asked to intervene in *real time* on the basis of the same
arguments that it eventually accepted, the Court desisted. In the case in
which it eventually handed down a ruling, the Court was not required
to interfere in an ongoing interrogation. The reluctance of courts to
interfere in real time in major security decisions, even in face of com-
pelling arguments contesting their legality, would seem to be an inherent
feature of judicial decision-making.[63] The classic example is probably the
1944 *Korematsu* case,[64] in which the U.S. Supreme Court refused to
interfere in a military order that excluded all persons of Japanese ances-
try from a designated area in California. As will be seen in the discussion of house demolitions in chapter 9, this pattern has been followed
by Israel's Supreme Court on other occasions.

Although the Court certainly did rule that specified interrogation practices of the General Security Service were illegal, it based its decision on formal grounds of the domestic legal system, namely that the interrogators
had not been given statutory authority to depart from the usual rules of fair
interrogation. The Court did indeed mention standards of international
law, according to which all forms of torture and cruel, inhuman, and
degrading treatment or punishment are prohibited without exception, but
it refrained from stating whether all, or any, of the methods used by the
authorities were covered by this prohibition. It specifically left open the
possibility that the law would be changed by the *Knesset,* which could
decide that the special security difficulties of the State justify legislation
empowering use of physical force in interrogations, provided such legislation meets the demands of the Basic Law: Human Dignity and Liberty.[65]

I began this discussion by explaining that the issue of interrogations
does not really belong in a discussion of the jurisprudence on the Occu-

pied Territories. The path the Court opened for parliamentary change of
the law illustrates this point. Legislative power in the Occupied Territories is in the hands of the military commanders, not the *Knesset*. In exercising this power the military commanders are subject to the international law of belligerent occupation. Had the Court ruled that security
measures employed in the Occupied Territories (such as deportations
and house demolitions) are prohibited under international law, the military commanders would have lacked the power to change the law. The
ultimate responsibility for lack of such measures would thus have been
the Court's. In the case of interrogations, dealt with under the domestic
legal system of Israel, the Court sought to dilute its responsibility for the
situation created by its legal ruling by stating that the ultimate decision
on permissible interrogation methods is in the hands of the legislative
authority, which represents the people.

CHAPTER NINE

HOUSE DEMOLITIONS

House demolitions and deportations are the most extreme security measures used against individuals by the military authorities. The frequency with which the authorities have employed house demolitions has varied over the years. According to official sources, 1,265 houses were demolished in the first fourteen years of the occupation.[1] Use of the measure diminished in the late 1970s and early 1980s;[2] after the start of the *Intifada*, its use increased. According to an NGO report, from the beginning of the *Intifada* until the end of November 1991, the number of houses demolished was 443 and the number of houses fully sealed was 277.[3]

Sealing and demolition of houses have generated a large volume of petitions to the High Court of Justice. Although some of these petitions were submitted during the mid-1970s, the first judgment of the Court was not delivered until the middle of 1979.[4] Petitions submitted prior to this case were settled before the decision stage, generally when the authorities declared that they had no intention of demolishing the petitioner's house.[5]

LEGAL BASIS

The formal legal authorization for house demolition or sealing is to be found in regulation 119 of the Defense Regulations, 1945. This regulation states:

> A military commander may, by order, direct the forfeiture to the government . . . of any house, structure or land from which he has reason

145

to suspect that any firearm has been illegally discharged, or any bomb, grenade or explosive or incendiary article illegally thrown, or any house, structure or land situated in any area, town, village, quarter or street the inhabitants or some of the inhabitants of which he is satisfied have committed, or attempted to commit, or abetted the commission of, or been accessories after the fact to the commission of, any offense against these regulations involving violence or intimidation or any military court offense; and when any house, structure or land is forfeited as aforesaid, the military commander may destroy the house or the structure or anything in or on the house, the structure or the land. Where any house . . . has been forfeited . . . the military commander may at any time by order remit the forfeiture.

The sanction provided for in this regulation is composed of two elements: forfeiture of the house, structure, or land and demolishing or otherwise dealing with the forfeited property. The regulation itself mentions only the most extreme measure—demolition—but after ordering forfeiture the military commander may decide on a less extreme step, such as sealing all or part of the house. This sanction may be imposed if the property itself was used as the base for shooting firearms or throwing grenades, explosives or firebombs. However, it may also be imposed because inhabitants of the town, area, village, quarter or street in which the house is situated were implicated in violent offenses. In practice, the military authorities have not imposed the sanction unless the person involved in the violence was an inhabitant of the house that was to be forfeited and sealed or demolished.[6]

In the early years of the occupation, the authorities claimed that house demolitions were only used when the inhabitants of the house were connected to the offense committed by a member of the family.[7] I have no way of checking whether this policy was indeed followed at that time. What is clear, however, is that since 1979 (when the Court delivered its first decision relating to house demolitions), no connection has been required between the occupants of the house and the *offense* (as opposed to the offender). The Court itself has explicitly ruled that the measure may be employed even when the other members of the household were not aware of the acts of the perpetrator.[8]

NATURE OF SANCTION

As a starting point for a discussion of house demolitions, it is essential to distinguish between demolition of a house as an operational or preventive measure and its demolition as a punitive reaction to commission of an act. In the latter case the authorities do not claim that the house itself interferes with military operations or that the site is needed for military purposes. Regulation 119 appears in the Part 12 of the Defense Regulations that deals with "Miscellaneous Penal Provisions." Demolition of a house under this regulation is therefore clearly a punitive sanction imposed in response to an act committed by one of the inhabitants of the house.

As a punitive measure, house demolitions violate a number of fundamental legal principles. In the first place, despite its severe punitive nature, the sanction is imposed by administrative decree rather than by a court. In some cases the sanction is imposed after a person has been convicted in court, but in many cases it is imposed before conviction, so that neither the guilt of the individual suspected of committing the offense nor the appropriateness of the punishment is determined by a court of law. The measure does not replace ordinary criminal sanctions such as imprisonment; it may be imposed as an additional sanction.[9] Second, the main victims of the punishment are seldom the perpetrators of the acts of violence; rather, the victims are members of their families. In virtually all cases, the perpetrator of the act has been detained and faces a long prison sentence, possibly even life; has managed to avoid apprehension by fleeing the country;[10] or is dead, in some cases having intentionally killed himself when setting off the bomb that provided the basis for applying regulation 119.[11] The perpetrator is not necessarily the owner of the house sealed or demolished, but is most often a son of the owner or tenant.

In addition to the clear disparity between the sanction provided for in regulation 119 and accepted principles of penal law, there are weighty arguments that the sanction violates both international human rights law and international humanitarian law.[12] Purposeful destruction of a family home may constitute violation of the right to respect for privacy, family, and home, and may also constitute cruel and inhuman treatment or punishment.[13] Article 46 of the Hague Regulations forbids confiscation of private property,[14] while article 23 prohibits destroying or seizing enemy property, unless such destruction or seizure is imperatively demanded by the necessities of war.[15]

Article 53 of Geneva Convention prohibits destruction of real or personal property of the state or individuals "except where such destruction is rendered absolutely necessary by military operations." While he was attorney-general of the State of Israel, Meir Shamgar argued that demolition of houses fits the exception relating to military operations because it is a form of "effective military reaction" that is necessary as a deterrent.[16] This argument is not convincing. Article 53 refers to destruction rendered necessary by *military operations*. A distinction must be drawn between military operations and punitive action by the military aimed at maintaining *security*. Shamgar based his interpretation on the ICRC Commentary on Geneva Convention IV that refers to "imperative military requirements," but this must be read in the context of the Convention itself which makes a clear distinction between *military* operations, requirements, or considerations and requirements or considerations of *security*.[17] The ICRC has clarified that the term "military operations" must be restricted to "movements, maneuvers, and other action taken by the armed forces *with a view to fighting*" and does not extend to action taken as a punishment.[18] Furthermore, in order to fit the exception, the destruction must be rendered *absolutely necessary* by military operations. The military may be able to argue that house demolition is effective as a general deterrent (though many would doubt this), but it would be stretching credulity beyond reasonable limits to argue that such demolitions are rendered absolutely necessary.

Both the Hague Regulations and Geneva Convention IV prohibit collective punishment.[19] Article 50 of the Geneva Convention expressly prohibits imposition of punishments on a protected person for an offense he or she has not personally committed.

PROGRESSION OF COURT'S DECISIONS

Looking at the progression of the initial cases decided by the Supreme Court would seem to suggest that the authorities were well aware of the inherent deficiencies in the measure provided for in regulation 119. If the chronological order of the Court's reported decisions on use of this measure is any indication, the authorities adopted a step-by-step method, allowing a case to reach the decision stage only after less extreme use of the measure had already been upheld in a previous case.[20] In the *Sakhwill* case, the Court upheld *sealing* the *room* in a house that had been used by a person *convicted* of an offense.[21] The room that was to be sealed had been used to hide a wanted person and store explosives. The next decision, in the *Khamed* case, dealt with *sealing* the *rooms* of two persons who had not yet been convicted, but had confessed to serious acts of terrorism.[22] Once again, the premises had been connected to the offense: one of the accused had used his room to store grenades that he had later thrown at a bus; the other had hidden ammunition next to the house. This decision was followed by the *Khamamara* case in which the military commander had decided to *seal* the whole *house* of a family whose sixteen-year-old son had confessed to throwing hand grenades at soldiers.[23] This time there was no connection between the act and the house.

Soon after the *Khamamara* case was decided, the Court was asked to intervene in a decision to *demolish* the entire houses of two families whose sons had confessed to a brutal murder.[24] There was no connection between the houses and the murder, and the Court itself mentioned the irreversible nature of the measure. Nevertheless, it held that the severity of the acts committed "enabled the military commander, acting on the considerations of a reasonable military commander, to take the drastic measure of demolition."[25] Shortly after this decision, the Court once again upheld an order to *demolish* the houses of persons who had confessed to participation in terrorist acts that had caused the deaths of three people and injury to many more.[26] Since this case was decided, the Court has upheld demolition in numerous cases in which one member of a household has committed acts involving violence against soldiers, Israeli civilians, or Palestinians accused of collaborating with the Israeli authorities.

SUBSTANTIVE ARGUMENTS AGAINST HOUSE DEMOLITIONS

The Court's initial response to arguments that house demolitions are contrary to principles of international law was to deny that these principles apply to a measure based on local law.[27] In later cases, the Court made a rather feeble attempt to refute the claim that house demolitions are usually a form of collective punishment.[28] It based this attempt on two arguments: (1) that the sanction is not collective and (2) that it is not punitive.

The first attempt to refute the collective punishment argument was made in the *Dujlas* case.[29] The Court's answer to the argument was phrased as follows:

> There is no basis for the petitioners' complaint that demolishing the house involves an element of collective punishment. . . .
>
> The object of the regulation [119–D.K.] is "to achieve a deterrent effect," and this effect, by its very nature, must apply not only to the terrorist himself but also to those surrounding him, [and] certainly the members of his family who live with him. . . . He must know that his heinous acts will not only harm him, but that they are likely to bring great suffering to his family. From this point of view the above sanction of demolition is no different from the punishment of imprisonment which is imposed on the head of a family, a father to small children, who will remain without a supporter and breadwinner.[30]

Even though the Court has repeated it on a number of occasions,[31] the parallel between the suffering caused to a person's family by his imprisonment and the suffering caused by demolition of the family home is unconvincing.[32] A prisoner's family may suffer because of imprisonment but they do not suffer the same penalty as the prisoner himself. Furthermore, the *direct aim* of imprisonment is to deny freedom of movement to the perpetrator of an offense; suffering caused to others may be an inevitable consequence of the imprisonment, but it is not its aim. If the effect of the culprit's imprisonment on his family could be neutralized, the aim of the punishment would not be frustrated. On the other hand, when a person has already been apprehended and is no longer living in a house (and is in fact liable to life imprisonment), and especially when he has been killed, the *immediate aim* of demolishing the house is not to deny rights or freedoms of that person but to cause suffering to his family. This could conceivably be effective as a general deterrent (though, of course, it may also be counterproductive), but the objection to collective punishment is not that it is not an effective deterrent, but that it is cruel and inhuman.

The only voice on the Court that has been receptive to the collective punishment argument has been that of Justice Cheshin.[33] In several dissenting opinions, Justice Cheshin has taken the view that demolishing a house is illegitimate if the sanction offends the fundamental legal principle that no one may be punished for the crime of another. In his first two opinions on this issue, the conclusion drawn by Justice Cheshin was that the authorities could not demolish a house shared by a number of families, the son of only one of which had been involved in a terrorist act. The demolition (or sealing) could only be carried out on that part of the house in which the culprit had lived with his nuclear family.[34] While these opinions were a step in the right direction, they did not solve the problem of collective punishment, since they allowed demolition of the immediate family's residence without any proof that its members had been involved in the culprit's act. Justice Cheshin realized the disparity between his principled approach and its application in these decisions. He therefore eventually went further and took the view that the authorities could not demolish or seal the home of a suicide-bomber's immediate family.[35] In the *Ghanimat* case, Justice Cheshin explained his view in the following way:

> The first petitioner is the wife of the suicide-murderer and the mother of his four minor children. The wife and children live in the same apartment in which the suicide-murderer lived, but nobody claims that they were a party to the act which he planned to do—and did: the murder of innocent souls. Nobody even claims that they knew of his planned act. If we demolish the apartment of the terrorist we will destroy at the same time—and with the same strokes of the axe—the apartment of the wife and children. In doing so we will punish the wife and children even though they committed no crime. We should not act in such a manner.[36]

Justice Cheshin's voice has been alone in a judicial wilderness. Although the majority on the Court has declared that regulation 119 does not give the military commander the authority to use house demolitions as a form of collective punishment,[37] they have adopted a very narrow definition of the term. This became obvious in the *Sabeach* case[38] in which the authorities had decided to demolish the family home of a suicide bomber. One of the family's arguments was that the authorities should demolish or seal only the room in which the bomber had lived. The Court found such an argument unconvincing in suicide-bombing cases because "for a terrorist who is planning to blow himself up and commit suicide the fear that the army could afterwards only seal his private room, or even demolish it, would serve no deterrent function. In such a situation the respondent's [demolition] order would lose all meaning."[39]

Even if one adopts a narrow definition of the term collective punishment, according to which demolishing the family home of a young person who committed a serious act of violence is not included, there can be little doubt that such a demolition is a departure from the principle of individual responsibility. This, in itself, would seem to imply a significant departure from accepted principles of penal law. As previously stated, it is also incompatible with international law.[40]

In discussions of house demolitions in the early years of the occupation the claim was raised that the measure could, in certain circumstances, be regarded as a form of reprisal, outlawed under article 33 of Geneva Convention IV.[41] In rejecting this claim the authorities argued that the measure is a punitive measure.[42] Furthermore, the Court's initial reply to arguments against the validity of regulation 119 based on principles of international law was the "law in force argument," in support of which it cited article 64 of Geneva Convention IV according to which the *penal* laws of the occupied territory shall remain in force.[43] In the *Sakhwill* case the Court referred to the measures provided for in regulation 119 as "extraordinary *punitive* action,"[44] while in the *Khamamara* case the Court referred to regulation 119 as a "*punitive* provision."[45] Nevertheless, in a number of cases the Court has tried to justify judicial approval of a measure that would seem to include all the elements of collective punishment by denying that use of the measure is a form of punishment.

This approach, the first hint of which appears in the Abu *Alahn* decision,[46] was presented in the *Shukeri* case[47] in the following way:

> The authority given to a military commander under regulation 119 is not the authority for collective punishment. Exercising it is not designed to punish the family of the petitioner [the brother of a person convicted of a brutal murder and the attempted murder of a bus-load of people—D.K.]. The authority is administrative, and its exercise is designed to deter and thereby to maintain public order.[48]

The idea that describing the object of house demolitions as general deterrence implies that it is not a punitive measure was articulated more clearly in a number of later cases. Thus, for example, in the *Abu Kabita* case, the Court stated: "We were informed that the attacks on persons suspected of collaborating have recently become more severe, and the measure taken—*which is not a form of punishment but of prevention*—is important to prevent the spread of these phenomena."[49]

The notion that the object of house demolitions is not to punish the perpetrator, but to deter others, was stressed by the Court in cases in which the perpetrator was a suicide bomber who died when exploding the bomb in a bus or crowded street. In the first case dealing with the decision of a military commander to destroy the house of the suicide bomber's nuclear family, it was argued that in such circumstances the measure had to be seen as collective punishment. In reply the Court said:

> The object of using the powers granted to the military commander, according to regulation 119 (1) . . . is to deter potential terrorists from carrying out their murderous acts, as an essential measure for maintaining security. . . . Imposition of the said sanction does indeed have a severe punitive effect, which harms not only the terrorist, but also others, generally members of his family who live with him, but this is not its aim and this is not what it is intended to do.[50]

Despite the fact that the idea has been repeated in various forms in a number of decisions,[51] it is difficult to understand the sophistry involved in describing the object of demolitions as prevention rather than punishment.[52] One of the most widely accepted aims of punishment is general deterrence.[53] It should therefore be obvious that the objective of general deterrence does not mean that a measure causing pain, suffering, or deprivation of a right is not a form of punishment. The measure of house demolitions has all the elements of legal punishment: it is an evil deliberately inflicted for an offense against a legal rule by a human agency that is authorized by the legal order whose laws have been offended.[54] When imposed pursuant to regulation 119, it is not imposed to prevent use of the house itself for violent activities, which in certain circumstances may certainly be regarded as a preventive measure,[55] but to deter potential perpetrators from committing like offenses.[56]

In the *Shukeri* judgment[57] previously quoted, the Court explained that the power to decide on house demolitions is an administrative power.[58] Describing the power to impose the sanction in this way does not diminish its punitive character. The nature of a sanction is not determined by the type of state organ authorized to impose it. On the contrary, the type of organ authorized to impose a sanction should be determined by the nature of the sanction. The appropriate organ to decide that a punitive measure should be imposed is a judicial body. Indeed, one of the fundamental flaws of regulation 119 is that the power to impose the measures described therein is in the hands of a military commander rather than a judicial body.[59]

The only alternative to describing demolition of the house of a person who has committed an offense as a punitive measure is to characterize it as a form of reprisal, or "quasi-reprisal."[60] As already mentioned, the authorities strenuously objected to the claim that house demolitions are a form of reprisal. By denying the punitive nature of demolitions in order to escape the implications of collective or non-individual punishment, was the Court in fact unwittingly undermining the authorities' reply to the reprisal argument?

Other arguments that house demolitions are incompatible with international law received scant attention in the Court's initial decisions on use of this measure. Nevertheless, the Court constantly refers to these decisions as precedent for the view that the measure is compatible with international law.[61] The Court has never considered on their merits the substantive arguments against house demolitions that rest on the prohibitions on confiscation and destruction of property.

INTERPRETING REGULATION 119

In addition to its reluctance to accept arguments based on international law, the Court refused to adopt an interpretation of regulation 119 that would limit its scope of application. Regulation 119 states that the military commander may direct the forfeiture of a house situated in an area, town, village, or street, "the inhabitants or some of the inhabitants of which he is satisfied have committed . . . any offense against these regulations involving violence." In the *Khamri* case, the petitioner argued that one member of a household cannot be regarded as "some of the inhabitants" of the house. The argument was that the term "some of the inhabitants" implied that at least two of them had been involved in the act of violence.[62]

The term "some" may indeed mean more than one of the members in a group, and this argument presented one possible way of reading of the text. Had the Court been looking for a way to restrict the application of regulation 119, it could have accepted this meaning of the term. It did not do so. Instead it held that there is "neither a linguistic nor substantive basis for interpreting the term 'some of the inhabitants' as referring to persons residing in the house whose number must necessarily exceed one."[63]

The reference not only to the linguistic, but also to the *substantive* basis for interpreting regulation 119, shows that the Court is more concerned with the "governmental rationale" of the measure than with limiting the application of a measure that is wholly inconsistent with accepted legal values. This becomes even more apparent when one considers the Court's remark that accepting the petitioner's argument would mean that a house inhabited by two persons could not be demolished if only one of them was involved in violations of the Defence Regulations. Justice Barak stated that this conclusion was totally unfounded "both from the point of view of the wording of the regulation and from the point of view of the legislative policy that lies behind it."[64]

Consistent with its approach not to use interpretation as a device to restrict application of regulation 119, the Court adopted a liberal interpretation of the term "inhabitant" in cases in which students live away from home during the school year. In the *Khamri* case the Court held that the fact that two sons had lived away from their parents' home while they were at school did not prevent them from being inhabitants of their parents' home during vacation.[65] The Court added that it did not have to decide if the sons would be regarded as inhabitants of their parents' house while they were at school in another village. Nevertheless, the Court later understood the precedent as providing that "it is sufficient for there to be residence from time to time, that is to say during the school vacations, in order to establish the element of regulation 119 that enables exercising the power thereunder."[66]

Other attempts to persuade the Court to depart from a literal reading of regulation 119 also failed. The Court rejected the argument that the military must have evidence that the inhabitants of the house who were not directly involved in the acts of violence at least knew of those acts or participated in committing them, "as the existence of such knowledge or participation does not flow from the text of the regulation."[67] It held that there need not be a connection between the act committed and the house to be demolished or sealed because the text of regulation 119 distinguishes between the case in which the house was used for the offense and the case in which the perpetrator was merely an inhabitant.[68]

The Court refused to demand that the person who committed the act of violence be convicted in court before the sanction under regulation 119 may be applied.[69] Citing a precedent that deals with the evidential basis necessary under Israeli administrative law for an administrative body to exercise its powers in a way that affects the rights of an individual, the Court held that the question is whether a reasonable person would regard the evidence as sufficient.[70] It is true that regulation 119 empowers use of the sanction "if the military commander is satisfied" that the person has committed the offense. However, given the severity of the sanction and the irreversibility of demolitions, one possible way of reading the provision would be to say that the commander may only be satisfied that a person has committed an offense if that person has been convicted in court.[71]

The ruling of the Court that the sanctions provided for in regulation 119 may be imposed prior to conviction does not imply that the Court has been prepared to uphold use of those sanctions when there is any serious doubt whether the person alleged to have committed the act of violence actually did so.[72] The important point is, however, that once again the Court refused to adopt an interpretation of regulation 119 that would restrict the broad powers given to the military commander according to a literal reading of the regulation.

In recent cases, heard after enactment in Israel of the Basic Law: Human Dignity and Liberty, the Court has conceded that even if it may not invalidate regulation 119,[73] the regulation must be interpreted and applied according to the principles of the Basic Law. This means that measures offending protected rights must be used for a worthy purpose and must meet the proportionality test.[74] However, the Court has held that deterrence is a worthy purpose.[75] Use of the proportionality test will be considered below.

PROCEDURAL CONSTRAINTS

While the Court has refused to accept substantive arguments against the legality of house demolitions, it has placed procedural constraints on use of the measure. First, the Court issues a temporary injunction in every case in which use of the measure is challenged, pending review of the decision to employ the measure in the specific instance. The military authorities are then required to explain to the Court why they have decided on the measure. It is fair to assume that the mere existence of judicial review and the knowledge they will have to explain their actions in court have a restraining influence on the military authorities.

Until 1989 the chance of judicial review depended largely on the prior knowledge of the tenants that the house was to be demolished. In a number of cases family members of persons who had been arrested on serious charges petitioned the Court merely because they feared that the measure would be used without prior notice.[76] In *Zaid v. IDF Commander in Judea and Samaria*,[77] the authorities informed the Court that they were preparing directives to grant a hearing before exercising the powers in regulation 119 "except in severe and exceptional cases." The Court stated that it was not expressing an opinion on these directives, but thought that regulating the matter was important.

Following a 1988 case in which the authorities had demolished houses in the village of Beita without a prior hearing and had subsequently conceded that they would grant a hearing before demolishing any other houses in that village, the Association for Civil Rights in Israel (ACRI) submitted a general petition regarding hearings. ACRI argued that according to the principles of Israeli administrative law there is a duty to grant a hearing to the occupants of a house prior to demolition and to allow them reasonable time to petition the Court if their arguments against the demolition are rejected in the hearing. In 1989 the Court accepted this argument, rejecting the authorities' demand that they be allowed to deny a hearing in "severe and exceptional cases."[78] The Court accepted that in such cases the authorities could seal the house pending the hearing, as this was a reversible sanction.

The Court admitted only one exception to the hearing requirement in demolition cases: the case of "operational-military circumstances in which judicial review is incompatible with conditions of place and time or the nature of the circumstances."[79] The example given was the case in which a military unit is performing a military operation, in the course of which it must remove an obstacle, overcome resistance, or react immediately to an attack.

The narrow limits of this exception to the hearing requirement were later undermined in the *al-Boureij* case.[80] Following the brutal lynching of a soldier who had mistakenly driven into the al-Boureij refugee camp, the military commander decided to widen the main road, which required demolishing thirty premises. He did not claim that the inhabitants of these premises had been involved in the murder and declared that the measure was not a punitive one carried out under regulation 119, but a measure based on the power of a military occupant to requisition land for military needs.[81] The commander even conceded that compensation would have to be paid to the owners of the requisitioned property. Nevertheless, one of the main grounds for the ruling that a hearing must be granted prior to demolition is the irreversible nature of the measure. ACRI once again petitioned the Court, arguing that the authorities were duty-bound to follow the hearing procedure whatever the aim of the demolition. The Court accepted that the hearing requirement is not restricted to use of demolition as a punitive measure; it applies even when premises are to be demolished because of the hindrance they cause.[82] It nevertheless repealed a temporary injunction against the demolition being carried out prior to a hearing. The Court held that a hearing may be denied "when there are important and urgent basic interests of maintaining order and security and preventing danger to human life."[83]

This does not fit the "operational-military operations" exception. By recognizing the power of the authorities to deny a hearing on the basis of their assessment of urgency unconnected to operational constraints, the Court considerably limited the scope of the hearing requirement. One could even argue that in effect it accepted the argument that was rejected in the previous case, namely that a hearing need not be granted in "severe and exceptional cases" that in the commander's assessment demand "a swift deterrent response, within a short and reasonable time of the event."[84]

The decision of the Court to require a hearing before demolitions and to reject the "severe and exceptional cases" exception was handed down in response to a general petition that did not relate to any specific case. The way the Court circumscribed its own ruling is revealing. The issue here was a particular case in which the authorities, in the name of security, demanded freedom from procedural constraints. The military authorities presented legal values as fundamental as the right to a hearing as a hindrance to their efforts to protect security. The Court was capable of dismissing this argument when the matter was presented as a theoretical question, but it balked at enforcing the right to a hearing in specific circumstances. It was obviously not prepared to bear responsibility for a decision that the military would claim had hindered their efforts to maintain order. This reluctance to take responsibility for interfering in concrete decisions is characteristic of the Court's approach in reviewing specific cases. That approach must now be examined.

REVIEW OF INDIVIDUAL CASES

The hearing requirement, coupled with the Court's standard practice of staying every demolition pending judicial review, derives from the Court's willingness to examine the factual evidence in each and every petition relating to house demolitions and sealing. The executive-mindedness of the Court, apparent in handling of arguments against the legality of the measure itself, is also generally apparent in the Court's review of individual cases. The Court has decided over one hundred cases, but only in very few of these did it interfere in the decision to employ regulation 119. In one case the Court overruled a demolition order on jurisdictional grounds when it ruled that the culprit could not be regarded as an inhabitant of the house.[85] In another it remitted the case to the military commander for reconsideration, after finding that some of the facts on which he had based his decision were unsupported by evidence.[86] The only cases in which the Court interfered with a decision on the merits of the case by restricting the scope of the sanction under regulation 119 were the *Jabrin*,[87] *Hodli*,[88] and *Turkmahn*[89] cases (discussed later). The first two of these cases were limited in scope, but the *Turkmahn* decision signaled a change in direction, which had a discernible restraining influence on use of house demolitions by the military authorities.

In its initial decisions in petitions relating to sealing or demolishing a house, the Court adopted a strictly formalistic approach: regulation 119 was in force before 1967 and remained in force thereafter; the discretion to decide on use of the regulation is in the hands of the military commander; and if the formal conditions laid down in the regulation for use of that discretion pertain, the Court will not interfere.[90] This formalistic approach, which ignores the distinction between the existence of formal power and the way such power is used, does not characterize the *rhetoric* of all the decisions. The rhetoric stresses the examination of the military commander's decisions on their merits. But beyond rhetoric, for a long time the Court displayed great reluctance to interfere in the use made of regulation 119.

The Court frequently mentioned the duty of the commander to weigh conflicting considerations when deciding on use of his powers under regulation 119.[91] In a few cases it even enumerated the factors that he must consider, over and above the need for "law and order," including the personal involvement of members of the household in the act in response to which the sanction is to be employed.[92] However, evidence of involvement was not required as a necessary condition for use of the sanction and the Court accepted that it may be imposed even when there was no such involvement.[93] Severity of the acts themselves was regarded as sufficient grounds for imposition of the sanction, provided the culprit was an inhabitant of the house to be sealed or demolished.[94]

The horrific nature of many of the acts that led the military authorities to impose the sanctions provided for in regulation 119 may have helped the Court overcome any inhibitions it might have had in supporting these sanctions.[95] Suicide bombings claimed the lives of many innocent persons. The authorities, desperate to act in face of enormous social anxiety and insecurity, argued that sealing or demolition of the family home was the only measure that could deter potential suicide bombers. In these cases the Court always set out the background in great detail.[96]

The standard answer to the argument that the burden of the sanction is not borne by the perpetrator of the acts has been to stress the severity of the acts as a balancing consideration against the harm to others caused by the sanction.[97] This answer did not enable the Court entirely to sweep aside the sanction's problematic nature. It addressed this question in a number of ways. First, as previously seen, the Court tried to legitimize the sanction by drawing a parallel to other forms of punishment in which the family of an offender suffers.[98] Second, it emphasized that the powers provided for in regulation 119 were all given to the military commander solely "to enable him to fulfill his duty as the person responsible for public order and the security of the area, by deterring real and potential disturbers of public order."[99] After the *Intifada* started, the sanction was imposed in some cases in response to brutal murders or assault of local Palestinian residents suspected of collaborating with the military authorities. The Court stressed the military commander's duty to protect the local population.[100]

In a number cases, the Court attempted to lessen its responsibility for upholding imposition of the sanction by suggesting that the military commander reconsider his decision. In the *Khamamara* case[101] the Court dismissed a petition to enjoin a house-sealing order that left an entire family homeless and without a source of income (since the house had served as their place of business). The discomfort the Court obviously felt about this result did not lead it to interfere in the decision of the military commander. However, as the sanction imposed was not the most extreme measure of demolition, the Court saw fit to mention that forfeiture of the house was not final. The authorities could eventually repeal the forfeiture and allow the tenants to restore the house. The Court added that the petitioners could approach the commander to repeal the order and stated that it had been assured any such application would be considered on its merits.[102] In some cases, while refusing to interfere in the decision of the commander, the Court left a temporary injunction in force for a short period in order to allow time for reconsideration by the commander.[103]

The combination of formalism in interpreting the wording of regulation 119, understanding for the deterrent rationale behind it, and reluctance to interfere in the discretion of the commander to utilize his powers, manifests itself in the attitude taken by the Court to sealing of rented premises. In the *Al-Jamal case*,[104] the petitioner asked the Court to enjoin sealing a house that he had leased to a tenant. The order to seal the house had been issued because of the involvement of the tenant's son in throwing Molotov cocktails. The petitioner argued that the "remoteness of the connection between him and the person who had committed the security offenses negated the material justification for use of regulation 119."[105]

The Court held that the wording of the regulation allowed it to be used even if the person who committed the offense was a tenant. It refused to hold that application of the regulation in this situation was unreasonable, explaining that the deterrent effect that the commander wishes to achieve would be frustrated if a potential terrorist could avoid use of the sanction by living in rented premises. The Court found it easier to reach this decision, as the result—sealing the house—was reversible.

In a later case, the petitioner once again contested use of regulation 119 to seal rented premises because of acts of tenants or their families. The Court held that the family connection between the perpetrator of the offenses and the owner of the house was close enough to justify an order sealing the house. However, it referred to the situation of a rented house, stating that despite previous rulings of the Court that regulation 119 could be used against a rented house, it wished to leave the matter for further consideration. The Court added: "I tend to think that in the light of the very severe effect of imposing the sanction provided for in regulation 119 . . . it is proper for this court to establish a number of boundaries and also to interpret it narrowly, when it comes to the categories of people who are likely to be harmed by it."[106]

This was the first hint of an alternative approach according to which the Court would not only express platitudes about the duty of the military commander to weigh all relevant factors before deciding to use his powers under regulation 119, but would take upon itself to set boundaries to the discretion of the commander. The breakthrough in adoption of this approach came in the *Turkmahn* case.[107]

Muhamed Turkmahn had been convicted of shooting a couple, killing the husband and wounding the wife. He was sentenced to life imprisonment plus fifty years. The authorities decided to demolish the three-room house in which Turkmahn had lived with his mother and seven unmarried siblings. A married brother and his family shared the house. Justice Barak held that the commander's discretion was subject to the test of proportionality, according to which the severity of the act committed and the need for deterrence must be balanced against the suffering caused to those against whom the sanction is employed. In applying this test, Justice Barak adopted the distinction between the nuclear and extended family of the perpetrator drawn by Justice Cheshin in his initial decisions on the collective punishment issue. He held that demolishing the whole house would be a disproportionate measure, as it would affect not only the perpetrator's mother and unmarried siblings, but also the married brother and his immediate family. As it was not technically possible to demolish part of the house, the Court held that the authorities could only seal two of the rooms, leaving the third room intact for the married brother and his family.[108]

The approach of the Court in the *Turkmahn* case raises a number of questions. First, why is the suffering of the immediate nuclear family less worthy of consideration than that of the "separate" family of the married brother? The military commander had conceded that none of the family members were aware of Turkmahn's activities. Second, what distinguished this case from the dozens of others in which the Court had made no attempt to examine proportionality?[109] The Court provided no answer to these questions.

The *Turkmahn* approach did not eliminate the inherent difficulties of punitive house demolitions. It did, however, narrow application of the sanction. Following the Court's decision in this case the authorities limited the sanction to the home of the perpetrator's nuclear family. When this home was part of a larger building this usually meant that the home was sealed, rather than demolished.[110] In such cases the Court held that the sanction met the proportionality test.[111]

EFFECTIVENESS OF THE SANCTION

In a number of cases an attempt was made to attack the use of demolitions by questioning their effectiveness as a general deterrent.[112] The legal theory behind this argument is that use of a measure whose aim is to deter in circumstances in which it has no deterrent effect is an unreasonable use of governmental power. In one case the Court intimated that total ineffectiveness of the measure as a deterrent could indeed lead to the conclusion that use of the power was unreasonable.[113] However, the Court has never accepted the argument that the measure is ineffective as a deterrent.

In *Aga* v. *IDF Commander in Gaza,* the petitioners' counsel requested statistical information from the authorities relating to the number of attacks on collaborators and the number of houses that had been demolished following such attacks. She explained that she wished to show that house demolitions did not affect the number of attacks against collaborators and that use of the sanction as a reaction to such attacks was therefore unreasonable. The Court refused to adjourn the case or to order the authorities to supply the information requested. It held that the information would not help in ascertaining the effectiveness of the measures provided for in regulation 119 and explained:

> We are talking about a complex set of facts and factors that influence considerations of punishment and deterrence, and the statistical data requested will not clarify those matters. In particular, one cannot assess the effect of the above factors of punishment on the attacks on collaborators, without the possibility of examining the rate of attacks in a situation in which such punitive measures are not taken.[114]

The Court was correct in stating that it is extremely difficult methodologically to examine the effectiveness of the measure as a deterrent.[115] However, in these circumstances the question becomes one of burden of proof. Does the commander have to show the effectiveness of the measure, or does the person challenging the commander's decision have to prove its ineffectiveness? Had the Court taken a rights-minded approach, it would surely have held that to justify use of such an extreme measure, the commander must prove both its effectiveness as a deterrent and the lack of alternative effective measures.[116] Instead the

Court held that it would not interfere in the commander's assessment that the sanction is indeed effective.[117] In some cases it went even further by intimating that the commander's assessment was justified.[118]

The question of effectiveness became an important issue in the suicide-bombing cases, in which the Court ruled that demolition of the bomber's house is justified because of its deterrent value. Until the spate of suicide bombings in early 1996, it was the declared policy of the authorities that if a terrorist had been killed during a shoot-out, or in the attempt to apprehend him, they would not demolish his family's home.[119] They claimed that this policy had to be changed when it came to suicide bombings because the threat of death was no deterrent for potential suicide bombers. In response to the argument that even in such cases demolitions would not be an effective deterrent, the Court said:

> Even if we assume, that in suitable circumstances the Court may intervene in the military commander's assessment regarding the effectiveness of a measure, by preferring the opinion of an opposing expert, the circumstances in which the disagreement of opinion was brought before us do not create a basis for such intervention. Whatever the personal impression of the judge may be, based on his understanding and experience, he is in no position to hold positively that refraining from demolishing the houses of suicide bombers will not encourage potential candidates to overcome their final hesitations about taking part in such attacks. From my point of view, it is sufficient that we are dealing with an unknown variable, against which there stands the chance (even if it be a small chance) that using the measure may possibly save human lives, in order to prevent us from intervening in the assessment and decision of the respondent.[120]

CONCLUSIONS

Despite the sanction's harshness and its incompatibility with accepted principles of penal law and rules of humanitarian law, the Court displayed a marked reluctance to entertain arguments against the legality of punitive house demolitions. It refused to adopt a strict interpretation that would limit the scope of regulation 119 and consistently legitimized use of this regulation in the military authorities' attempts to control a hostile population.

By opening its doors to judicial review and placing procedural constraints on the authorities, the Court did indeed have a restraining influence on use of the sanction. However, having legitimized use of the sanction in dozens of cases, the Court was not prepared to reconsider its principled stand in later years. Instead it attempted to curb the sanction's impact on innocent people by employing the proportionality test.

Although this test does not eliminate the inherent objections to house demolitions, it widened the Court's restraining influence.

It would seem that the Court's decisions on house demolitions typify its jurisprudence on the Occupied Territories. The Court has not seen itself as a body that should question the legality under international law of policies or actions of the authorities, or should interpret the law in a rights-minded fashion. On the contrary it has accepted and legitimized policies and actions the legality of which is highly dubious and has interpreted the law in favor of the authorities. The Court's main role has been bolstering procedural requirements and interfering on the margins so as to prevent "excesses."

CHAPTER TEN

DEPORTATIONS

One of the most controversial security measures used by military commanders in the Occupied Territories has been deportation of residents on security grounds. The most extreme use of this measure was the deportation in late 1992 of 415 alleged activists of the *Hamas* and *Islamic Jihad* movements. This deportation, and the unsuccessful attempt to stop it by petitioning the Supreme Court, received worldwide attention.

As in the case of house demolitions, the period immediately following the 1967 War saw fairly widescale use of deportations. According to an official government statement, in the period between 1967 and 1977, 1,180 persons were deported from the Occupied Territories, sixty-eight of whom were residents deported on security grounds.[1] In later years the policy on deportations varied according to conditions in the Territories and the attitude of the incumbent minister of defense.[2] According to an NGO report, from the beginning of the *Intifada* until November 1991, sixty-six residents of the Territories were deported on security grounds.[3] There have been no deportations since the deportation of the 415 alleged *Hamas* and *Islamic Jihad* members in December 1992.[4]

The first attempt to challenge a deportation order by petitioning the Supreme Court was made by a Palestinian resident of East Jerusalem in early 1971.[5] Since then the Court has heard a fair number of petitions challenging this type of deportation. In many cases deportees refrained from seeking judicial review, either for political reasons or because of an assessment that their chances of succeeding were negligible. In some cases deportees withdrew their petitions before the decision stage. Sometimes this withdrawal was part of an out-of-court settlement, according to which the deportee would leave for a fixed period of time after which he or she would be allowed to return to the area. In a few cases deportees withdrew their petitions after the Court dismissed their applications to allow them access to privileged evidence.

LEGAL BASIS

Part X of the Defence (Emergency) Regulations, 1945 deals with "Restriction Orders, Police Supervision, Detention and Deportation." Regulation 108 provides that no order shall be made under that part of the regulations unless the competent authority is of the opinion that "it is necessary or expedient to make the order for securing the public safety, the defense of the land, the maintenance of public order or the suppression of mutiny, rebellion or riot."

The power to deport a resident is defined in regulation 112 (1), which states: "The government shall have power to make an Order, under its hand (hereinafter in these regulations referred to as a 'Deportation Order') for the deportation of any person from Palestine. A person in respect of whom a Deportation Order has been made shall remain out of Palestine as long as the Order remains in force."[6]

Regulation 112 (8) provides that any person against whom a deportation order is issued may appeal to an advisory committee that "shall consider and make recommendations to the government in respect of any such deportation order."

The pattern of the Court's decisions on the deportation question is similar to the pattern in house demolition cases. The Court dismissed all substantive arguments against the legality of deportations although, in contrast to the house demolition decisions, it discussed these arguments at some length. There were also two important dissenting opinions on substantive questions. The Court was somewhat more receptive to procedural arguments and made some attempt to bolster the procedural rights of deportees before the advisory committees. In assessing the legitimacy of specific decisions to deport, the Court's principled position moved from refusal to review those decisions on their merits to examination of the grounds for the decisions. However, this examination did not lead the Court to intervene in the decisions made by the military authorities. It upheld the deportation orders in all cases, although on one occasion it recommended that the political echelons reconsider the deportation decision.[7]

SUBSTANTIVE QUESTIONS

Substantive arguments against deportations rely on one or more of the following:

1. The validity of regulation 112 of the Defense Regulations on the West Bank or in Gaza in 1967.

2. The legality of deportations from occupied territories under international law.

3. Restrictions on the country of destination.

The argument under the first point and most of those under the second were discussed in the preceding chapters. In this chapter I shall confine the detailed discussion to those aspects that have not been discussed.

International law

The main legal argument against deportations from occupied territory rests on article 49 of Geneva Convention IV. As we saw in chapter 3, although the widely accepted view is that this article means what it says—namely that all deportations of protected persons from occupied territory are prohibited—the majority in the Supreme Court held that article 49 does not apply to deportation of individuals on security grounds. I shall not discuss the majority view again. Suffice it to say that the *Afu* decision,[8] in which the Court dealt at length with this question, is one of the most controversial of the Court's decisions on any substantive issue relating to the Occupied Territories. The majority's judgment in that case has neither enhanced the Court's prestige nor bolstered its image as a judicial decision-making body capable of interpreting international documents relating to the Occupied Territories in an objective fashion.

In chapter 3, it was pointed out that given its ruling that article 49 is part of conventional law that will not be enforced in Israel's domestic courts, the Court need never have expressed its opinion on the interpretation of article 49. This was indeed the approach of the majority in the *Kawasme II* decision, which preceded the *Afu* decision.

In the *Kawasme II* case all three judges on the bench accepted that if the prohibition against deportations in article 49 is not part of customary international law, it may not be enforced by a domestic court. However in a bold and imaginative dissenting opinion, Justice Cohn held that each provision of Geneva Convention IV must be examined to see whether it expresses a rule of customary law, conventional law, or possibly a mixture of the two. His analysis of article 49 led him to the conclusion that it contains a "nucleus of customary international law that has in fact been in practice for ages in all parts of the world."[9] This nucleus is the rule of customary international law that a state is duty-bound to allow entry to its own citizens; it may not, therefore, deport them. To the extent that article 49 prohibits deportation of foreigners, it expresses a rule of conventional law that may not be enforced before the domestic courts. On the other hand, as far as citizens of occupied territories go, the article adopts a principle of customary international law that has precedence over the legislation of the military commander and will be enforced by domestic courts.[10]

Justice Cohn stated that this principle of international law is generally discussed in texts dealing with times of peace, but that he had found no authority for holding that it is suspended during times of war or occupation.[11] Furthermore, Justice Cohn argued that residents of the Occupied Territories who are Jordanian citizens may not be deported to Jordan, even if that country agrees to accept them. Because the border between the Occupied Territories and Jordan may be crossed only with a permit of the authorities on both sides, residents of the Territories must be regarded as "quasi-citizens" of their permanent place of residence.[12] Justice Cohn's conclusion was that the deportation orders issued against the petitioners were incompatible with a principle of customary international law and should be regarded as null and void.[13]

The majority in the *Kawasme II* case did not contest Justice Cohn's proposition that customary international law prohibits deportation of a person from his or her country of citizenship. They held, however, that this rule only holds between states that have peaceful relations between them. It does not apply in a situation of war or of belligerent occupation.

Attempts in later cases to persuade the Court to adopt the dissenting view of Justice Cohn were unsuccessful. In dismissing such an attempt in the *Na'azal* case,[14] Justice Shamgar accepted the view expressed by Professor Dinstein in an article written in response to the Court's opinion in *Kawasme II* case.[15] In that article Dinstein argued that, contrary to the view accepted by all the judges in the *Kawasme II* case, even in peacetime the prohibition against deportations in customary international law is only against *arbitrary* expulsion or exclusion of a citizen from his or her country. While he sympathized with the attempt of Justice Haim Cohn to further human rights by arguing for a general prohibition against deportations in customary international law, Dinstein pointed out that even those human rights conventions that recognize a general right against expulsion allow suspension of that right during wars or other emergencies. He also took issue with Justice Cohn's view that Jordanian citizens may be regarded as "quasi-citizens" of the Occupied Territories.

In *Satiha* v. IDF *Commander in Gaza*,[16] the Court was forced to deal with an attempt by petitioner's counsel to distinguish between the legal situation in Gaza and on the West Bank (which had been discussed in the previous cases). The argument was that following the peace treaty between Israel and Egypt, Gaza was no longer subject to a regime of belligerent occupation and the position there should be determined according to customary international law that applies in times of peace. Because all the judges in the *Kawasme II* case had agreed that in times of peace a country may not deport its own citizens, permanent residents of Gaza could not be deported.

The Court rejected this argument. Like the Court in the *Na'azal* case, it referred to Dinstein's article "which proves that the general prohibition against deporting a citizen from his country was only accepted in regional treaties, but that various countries, including England, object to the existence of this custom."[17] The Court added that the prohibition that had evolved in customary law, even at times of peace, only relates to arbitrary deportation.[18]

Since the *Na'azal* and *Satiha* cases, the only substantive argument against deportations that the Court discussed at any length was that resting on article 49 of the Geneva Convention IV.[19] The Court refused to modify the stand, taken by the majority in the *Kawasme II* case, that the prohibition against deportations in article 49 is part of conventional law that may not be enforced by domestic courts.[20] The majority also held that even were it able to enforce the prohibition on deportations, article 49 would not prevent the type of deportations carried out from the Occupied Territories. As we saw in chapter 3, according to the Court's reading, article 49 only applies to deportations of the type carried out by the Nazis.

Limits on Country of Destination

In a number of cases the argument against deportation was based on the statelessness of the deportee, or on conditions in the country of destination. It is not always clear from the judgment itself whether the legal basis for the argument was international law or principles of Israeli administrative law relating to the reasonableness of governmental discretion in the individual case. Nevertheless, because the argument is a general argument of principle, it will be discussed here.

In *Marar v. Minister of Defense*, the petitioner argued that a deportation order could not be issued unless there were a country willing to receive the deportee. The Court's answer to this argument was purely formalistic. Regulation 112 recognizes the power to deport any person from Israel and states that once a deportation order has been given the deportee must remain outside the country as long as that order remains in force. Justice Cohn concluded that "it makes no difference whether there is another country in which he may remain. The authority is general and unrestricted, and we cannot restrict it through judicial interpretation."[21]

Justice Cohn was prepared to assume that the security authorities would carefully consider to which country a person would be deported and that "they will choose a state that is bound to accept the deportee under international law or its own laws, a state to which the deportee chooses to go or the state from which he arrived in Israel."[22]

The authorities claimed that the petitioner was a Jordanian citizen and that Jordan therefore had an obligation to accept him under international law.[23] The petitioner did not deny that he was a Jordanian citizen but argued that the manner in which deportees were deported to Jordan endangered their lives. His life would be in special danger because of the civil war in Jordan at the time. As a member of a Palestinian organization that was anathema to the Jordanian authorities, he would be placed in a dangerous situation; in these circumstances his deportation should be regarded as a form of extradition. Justice Cohn's reply was as follows: "We do not suspect the security authorities of being eager or even interested of extraditing to Jordan, or to any foreign country, a person who is liable to be persecuted or punished there for his political views, whatever they may be."[24]

Justice Cohn added that the Court had no reliable evidence on the manner in which deportations to Jordan were carried out. However the authorities were well aware that the deportation orders were not death sentences and they would do everything in their power to avoid endangering the deportees' lives.[25] Nevertheless, the "mere fact" that there was a civil war, or any other war, in a given state could not prevent the security authorities from deporting a person to that state. If the Court were to decide otherwise it would never be possible to deport a person to "one of the countries that constantly declare that they are waging war against Israel."[26]

The last statement gives some indication of the somewhat cavalier fashion in which the Court disposed of the petitioner's arguments. The petitioner's argument related to the civil war that was raging in Jordan at the time, and to the specific danger to him if he were to be deported to Jordan in this situation. He made no general argument that the "mere state of war" between two countries implied that one of those countries could not deport persons to the other. Yet the answer of Justice Cohn rests on the implication of accepting an argument that was never made.[27]

In *Shahahin v. Minister of Interior*[28] the deportee claimed that he was stateless and that the authorities had a duty to avoid endangering his life in carrying out the deportation. Although the deportation order against the petitioner was based on his status as an infiltrator rather than on regulation 112, the Court accepted that this made no difference when it came to the way the deportation would be carried out, and that the *Marar* precedent was therefore relevant. It proceeded to quote with approval from the opinions in that case.[29]

The Court also stated that it had required the authorities to relate to the possible risks to the deportee involved in his deportation. In reply the Court had been referred to a document issued by the head of the International Law Section in the military advocate-general's department, which adopted directives laid down by the government relating to the manner in which deportations would be carried out. Since the authorities declared that they would act according to these directives, the Court saw no reason to intervene.

The *Marar* precedent was relied on once again in the *Maslam* case,[30] in which the deportees were refugees from Gaza who claimed to be stateless. The authorities informed the Court that the destination would be determined according to the conditions at the time the deportation was carried out in an attempt to ensure the safety of the deportees. They added that if the deportees were to choose a country that would agree to accept them, they would be deported to that country. The deportees refused to accept this as an adequate reply. They argued that as stateless refugees they could not be deported, and that furthermore the military commander "was duty-bound to inform them to which country he intended deporting them, how he would ensure that that country agreed to accept them, and how he would ensure their physical and economic existence during the period of their exile."[31]

The Court referred once again to Justice Cohn's formalistic approach in the *Marar* case, which relies solely on the wording of regulation 112. It conceded that the fact that the deportees were stateless might affect implementation of the deportations since "if the petitioners do not choose to go to a specific state, which agrees to accept them, there is no state that is bound to accept them under international law or its own laws,"[32] and added that the military commander was aware of this situation. Nevertheless, this did not affect the way the Court perceived its own role. Following both the *Marar* and *Shahahin* precedents, it relied on the authorities to protect the safety of the deportees and saw no grounds for judicial intervention.

The approach of the Court on the country-of-destination question is indicative of two features of its jurisprudence: reluctance to use international law as a source of norms limiting the discretion of the authorities and reluctance to interfere in decisions on security-related issues. I shall return to these features in my concluding chapter.

PROCEDURAL QUESTIONS

Under regulation 112, a person served with a deportation order is entitled to have the order reviewed by a special advisory committee appointed by the military commander who makes the deportation order.[33] The procedural questions that have reached the Court relate to the duty of the authorities to allow a hearing by the advisory committee and to the nature of the proceedings before that committee.

Duty to Allow a Hearing

Until the *Hamas Deportation* case,[34] the most important case dealing with the right of a hearing before the advisory committee was the *Kawasme* case,[35] which reached the Court on two occasions.[36] The first round of the case related to the legal implications of a failure by the authorities to respect the procedural requirements of regulation 112. Given the importance of this case, it will be reviewed in some detail.

On the evening of 2 May 1980 six Jewish yeshiva students on their way home from prayers at the Grave of the Patriarchs were murdered in Hebron. The following day the military commander of the area issued deportation orders against the mayor of Hebron, Fayd Kawasme, the mayor of Khalkhul, Muhamed Milhelm, and the chief Shari judge in Hebron, Sheikh A-Tamami, who also served as a preacher in the main mosque of the city. The deportees were arrested by the military, but were not informed of the deportation order. They were taken to a helicopter and told that they were being brought to a meeting with the minister of defense in Tel Aviv. Instead they were flown to the Lebanese border and deported to Lebanon.

In a petition submitted on the deportees' behalf, the legality of the deportations was attacked on a number of grounds, including the argument that all deportations are illegal under international law.[37] However, the Court granted an order nisi on one question alone: whether the deportation orders should be cancelled since the deportees had not been given the opportunity to present their case before an advisory committee as required by regulation 112(8).

Counsel for the authorities admitted that the military authorities were aware of their duty to allow a hearing but, acting without legal advice, they had decided that immediate deportation was needed in order to prevent a "deterioration in the security situation in the area." He conceded that the authorities had acted improperly, but requested the Court to dismiss the petition. His main argument was that the regulations do not require that the advisory committee review the deportation before it is carried out. The deportees could request the committee to look into the matter after they had been deported.

The president of the Court, Justice Landau, and deputy-president, Justice Haim Cohn, both held that the authorities must enable a deportee to submit his or her case to the advisory committee before the deportation is carried out. They categorically rejected the argument that the military commander's assessment of the seriousness of the security situation could excuse him from allowing a hearing. The military commander was duty-bound to respect the law. As Justice Landau put it in summing up this point:

> Issuing a deportation order is indubitably a severe measure, which may not be used except in time of emergency. If the authorities are of the opinion, that they cannot at the present time possibly put up with the delay in carrying out a deportation order so as to enable application to the advisory committee, they can propose repeal or amendment of regulation 112 (8). However, as long as the regulation exists in its present form, it must be respected in practice. It is intolerable that a binding legal provision will be respected or violated at the whim of the executive branch.[38]

While Justice Landau adopted a positivist approach to the actual hearing requirement—it had to be respected because it had statutory backing, but could be abolished provided the proper legislative procedure were followed—his approach to interpretation of the statutory provision was far from formalistic. Even though regulation 112 does not expressly say so, it must be taken as requiring that the hearing be held before the deportation order is carried out. The dissenting judge, Justice Kahan, took a formalistic approach on the interpretation issue. Regulation 112 does not specifically state that the deportation may not be carried out until the deportee has been given a chance to present his case to the advisory committee; the hearing may therefore be held after the deportation. Justice Kahan agreed that, according to general principles established by the Court that oblige every administrative body to act fairly in its dealings with the individual, the authorities should generally enable a deportee to apply to the advisory committee before his or her deportation. However, the right to a prior hearing is not an absolute one, and in emergency situations, when immediate action is required to protect public security, the authorities may deviate from their duty to allow such a hearing.

This split between the majority and minority touches on a number of fundamental issues. In the first place, are there some rights, albeit procedural, that may not be subjected to the security considerations of the authorities? Or do the security interests of the state, as perceived by the authorities, always retain status as "trump cards" that may justify deviation from the law by the very authorities who are responsible for its enforcement? Second, assuming that an exception on security grounds exists, what weight should the Court attach to the subjective assessment of the authorities that the exception pertains in given circumstances? All three judges were prepared to assume that the authorities acted as they did because of a sincere assessment that their action was necessary to promote security in the area. The majority could afford to act on the basis of this assumption since they held that this assessment could not excuse deliberate flouting of the law. The blind assumption of Justice Kahan on this matter is far more problematic, since it allowed the authorities to violate the minimal procedural rights of a deportee meant to guarantee review over the authorities' security assessment. One would expect such a theory at least to require some kind of objective finding that the step taken was indeed imperative for security reasons. There is little in the judgment of the Court that would support such a finding. The authorities admitted that they did not connect the deportees directly with the murder. The assessment of the military, who were obviously under pressure to react, that by immediately deporting three leaders of the Palestinian community they were taking a step that was imperative for the security of the area, provided a very shaky basis for allowing them to ignore the procedural rights of the individual.[39] Justice Kahan was prepared to entrust protection of those rights to the authorities against whose arbitrariness they are supposed to afford protection.

Finally, the real fear of the authorities was not that an advisory committee would stop the deportations or delay them for a considerable period. As Justice Landau pointed out, the advisory committee could have been convened within hours. It seems that what they really feared was that the deportees would petition the Supreme Court and obtain a temporary stay of the deportation. This would certainly have held up the deportations and forced the authorities to defend their action in court. It would also have allowed time for domestic and international pressure to halt the deportations. The authorities probably hoped that by acting quickly they could avoid judicial review. Justice Landau saw this quite clearly and regarded the attempt of the authorities to circumvent the Court's jurisdiction as "especially serious" since it was not the first time that the authorities had acted with undue haste in order to avoid judicial review.[40] Justice Kahan conceded that if the deportations had not been carried out immediately, they would have been held up by the procedural constraints placed on proceedings before the advisory committee and especially by a petition to the Court itself.[41] In admitting that it was legitimate for the authorities to act hastily to avoid these delays, he was in effect delegitimizing the Court's policy of enabling judicial review in all cases.

Although Justices Landau and Cohn agreed that the authorities had violated their duty to enable review by the advisory committee before the deportations were carried out, they disagreed over the legal implications of that violation. Justice Cohn was of the opinion that even if the deportation orders were valid when issued, their continued validity depended on respect for the deportees' right under regulation 112 (8). The orders therefore became invalid when they were carried out without allowing the deportees to present their case to the advisory committee.[42] Justice Landau held that the duty to allow a hearing after the deportation order has been issued does not affect the order's validity. The remedy for breach of the duty to allow a hearing is to order the hearing to be held.[43] In the *Hamas Deportation* case a bench of seven judges adopted this view.

It seems that both Justice Landau and Justice Cohn ignored another possibility, which relies on a distinction between the legality of the deportation order and the legality of the deportation itself. Legality of the deportation order should be regarded as a necessary, but not sufficient, condition for a legal deportation. The legality of the deportation itself also depends on respect for the procedural aspects of the deportation process, including the hearing requirement. Thus, a deportation carried out in violation of the hearing requirement should be regarded as illegal, even if the deportation order was valid. The result should be that the deportee be allowed to return and the hearing procedure should then be followed.

The logical conclusion of Justice Landau's position should also have been that the deportees be allowed to return to present their case before the advisory committee. Although that is what the Court did in fact decide, Justice Landau was not prepared to order their return. The reason he gave was a formal one—the petitioners had sought only one remedy: invalidation of the deportation order. They had not requested to be allowed to present their case before the advisory committee. Nevertheless, Justice Landau held that if the deportees were to apply for review of the deportation orders by the advisory committee, the committee would have to consider their applications. He added that even though the grounds for intervention by the Court in a decision of the advisory committee were extremely narrow, if the petitioners were to state, in their applications for review, that they would respect the laws of the military government in their activities as public leaders, and to disassociate themselves unambiguously from the incitement that had been published in their names in the press, the committee should allow them to appear before it in person so that it could hear their explanations, according to the procedure that should have been followed from the outset.[44]

Justice Landau's directive, which amounted to a conditional order to allow the deportees to return in order to present their case before the advisory committee, clashed with the military's claim that the return of the deportees would seriously undermine security in the area. Justice Landau could not ignore this. He stated that he did not underestimate the danger to security, but added:

I don't know if account was taken of the alternative possibility of the danger of unrest in the Territories, if the population realizes that an act of the authorities that was not done in a legal manner remains in force without the fault being corrected, by allowing petitioners 1 and 2 to explain their case to the advisory committee in person. I am of the opinion that the respondents would do well to reconsider their stand on this matter.[45]

One has to be somewhat naive to believe that the situation of unrest in the Territories was really going to be affected by the population's perception of whether the military had acted according to the procedural formalities of the Defence Regulations. Deportations may conceivably have a deterrent impact on potential leaders; they certainly sometimes served as a catalyst for actions of protest, resistance, or violence. It is hard to believe, however, that the population would be more accepting of deportations if they perceived that procedural constraints were respected. One may assume that Justice Landau appreciated this point too. His remarks may therefore be taken as addressing a broader and more basic question: the legitimacy of the Court's role if it were to accept the illegal act of the authorities without providing a remedy. Was Justice Landau intimating that the legitimacy of the Court's function in review over acts in the Territories is an important component in reducing tensions there?

Justice Cohn, who took the view that the deportation orders became invalid when the authorities ignored the hearing requirement, also addressed the argument which he referred to as an argument *in terrorem*: that if the Court were to invalidate the deportation orders and allow the deportees to return to their homes, it would by its own hand endanger public security in the Territories. Justice Cohn was not prepared to dismiss the argument that the Court would not grant a discretionary remedy if it were proved that there were a real danger that the public would be harmed as a direct result of that remedy. He explained that he did not adhere to the view "that justice must be done at any price, even at the price of human life, such that *fiat iustitia et pereat mundus;* in a world that has been destroyed there is no longer any point in doing justice."[46]

Nevertheless, Justice Cohn was not prepared to accept the military commander's statement that he had "certain knowledge" that return of the deportees would seriously endanger public security as adequate evidence of such a danger. Justice Cohn himself was far from convinced that such a danger indeed existed. Furthermore, even if the commander's assessment were to prove accurate, he had legal means at his disposal to deal with the situation.

The final order given by the Court reflected Justice Landau's view. The Court refused to invalidate the deportation order. However, it specified that the advisory committee was bound to hear an application submitted by the petitioners, who should be allowed to appear in person if the conditions specified by Justice Landau were met.[47]

The hearing requirement was the main issue dealt with in the *Hamas Deportation* case. The authorities were aware that according to the *Kawasme I* precedent they were not entitled to ignore the requirement of a hearing before the deportation, even if they assessed that security requirements demanded immediate action. Relying on the remarks of Justices Landau and Cohn in the *Kawasme I* decision that this requirement knew no exception under prevailing law, an attempt was made to amend the law. The military commanders promulgated military orders according to which a deportation order under regulation 112 that is limited to a period of up to two years could be carried out immediately. In such a case, the hearing would be held after the deportation.[48] On the strength of these orders, the 415 suspected *Hamas* and *Islamic Jihad* activists were deported without a hearing.

When the matter came before the Supreme Court, it abandoned the position taken by the majority in the *Kawasme I* case. The Court held that the duty to allow a prior hearing is not an absolute duty. In concrete circumstances in which immediate action is demanded for security reasons, the authorities have the inherent power to take such action without allowing a prior hearing. The Court stressed, however, that the need to take immediate action must be based on an assessment of the specific circumstances of a case, and cannot rest on a general power to dispense with prior hearings in certain categories of cases (such as temporary deportation).[49]

Applying this principle to the case before it, the Court held that the military orders that allowed the authorities to dispense with a prior hearing merely on the basis of the temporary nature of the deportation were invalid.[50] The situation was therefore identical to the situation created in the *Kawasme I* case: the authorities had deported people without allowing a hearing. This did not make the deportation order invalid. The remedy was to order the authorities to facilitate full hearings in which the deportees themselves could be present and represented by lawyers. However, to make it quite clear that this did not mean that the deportees could return pending the hearing, the Court stated explicitly that the hearings could be held at any place where the IDF could ensure proper proceedings.[51] This, in effect, meant that the hearings could be held in the part of Southern Lebanon that was then under the effective control of the IDF.[52] This in itself was a highly questionable ruling, because holding hearings on the sovereign territory of another state would seem to be a violation of international law.[53]

Nature of the Hearing

While the right to review of a deportation order by an advisory committee is established by regulation 112 (8) of the Defence Regulations,
these regulations give no details as to the nature of the proceedings
before the advisory committee. Regulation 112 (8) simply states that the
committee, if asked to do so by the person against whom a deportation
order has been issued, may "consider and make recommendations to the
Government in respect of any such deportation order."

A number of issues concerning the procedure and scope of review by
the advisory committee have reached the Supreme Court. These questions relate first and foremost to the very nature of the advisory committee and its relationship with the military commander. Is the committee merely an adjunct body whose duty is to advise the commander
whether, on the strength of the evidence before him, the deportation
order should be carried out, or is it a quasi-judicial body that must
review the justification for deporting the deportee?

The general perception of the advisory committees themselves was
that their role is confined to examining the deportation order in light of
the evidence that the commander submits to them. While admitting
secret evidence that is not revealed to the deportee or his or her lawyer,
the committees refused both to allow the deportees to summon witnesses and to open proceedings to the public. In a series of decisions, the
Court somewhat eroded this perception of the committees' role and
transformed them into quasi-judicial bodies.

The first issue that reached the Court relates to the question of
secret evidence. In the *Na'azal* case,[54] the petitioners complained that the
advisory committee had refused them access to secret evidence that it
had seen. The Court drew a parallel between the powers of the advisory
committee and those of a judge reviewing an order for administrative
detention under Israeli law, who is empowered to examine secret evidence not made available to the detainee or his or her counsel. The
Court explained:

> This is the only reasonable arrangement that balances between two
> interests: on the one hand maintaining repeated supervision over the
> considerations and decisions of the military commander, and on the
> other hand preventing harm to the security of the state by revealing
> secret sources of information. Of course, this does not provide the
> opportunity to respond to *every* factual allegation and the advisory
> committee must take this into account when it examines the weight or
> credibility of the information.[55]

In two cases the petitioners argued that deportation proceedings
should be compared to a criminal trial.[56] If the evidence on which the

commander based his decision to deport remains privileged, the deportation order should be revoked, as the reasons for the order cannot be
proved in court. Justices Bach and Elon refused to accept the analogy
to a criminal trial. They explained that in a criminal trial the presumption of innocence applies, and it is incumbent on the prosecution
to prove the charge. If the evidence against the accused is privileged,
the prosecution cannot lift the burden of proof. However, "a deportation order under regulation 112 . . . is an act of an administrative
authority and not a criminal conviction by a court."[57] The commander
who issues the order must be convinced that there is clear, unambiguous, and convincing evidence against the deportee and his decision
may be examined by the advisory committee, whose decision is subject
to judicial review. However, the burden is on the petitioner to show
that the commander's decision was unjustified. Justice Elon explained
that accepting the petitioner's argument would "deprive regulation
112 of meaning."[58]

Like the Court's attitude on the administrative nature of house
demolitions, this reply reflects a highly formalistic approach to the distinction between administrative and criminal proceedings. It rests on the
procedure determined by the law, rather than on the substantive nature
of the matter. The Court itself has stated on more than one occasion that
deportation is a severe sanction. It is imposed on a person because of his
or her past activities. It is indeed true that the declared aim is not retribution, but securing public safety and maintaining public order. But
these are also aims of some criminal sanctions. It seems to me that the
severity of the sanction should determine the procedure. A severe sanction should not be allowed unless the person on whom it is imposed has
a proper chance of defending himself. And when the evidence against a
person is privileged, that person's chances of defending himself are seriously impeded.

The argument that demanding that deportations be based on open
evidence would make regulation 112 meaningless is not convincing. If
this demand were accepted, regulation 112 could be applied only in
those circumstances in which the authorities can produce open evidence
of the danger presented by the deportee. The concern of the judges lest
this interpretation make regulation 112 "meaningless" is telling.

The advisory committees initially took the view that their task was
to review the evidence presented by the military commander and not to
try the deportee. They therefore refused to subpoena witnesses at the
request of the deportee or to hear witnesses produced by him. In the *Afu*
case, Justice Shamgar agreed that the military commander does not have
to prove his allegations as he would before a judicial tribunal. Nevertheless, he held that

in a case in which the appellant raises a detailed and reasoned argument, that seems to be raised in good faith, according to which a given
witness is likely to provide the committee with relevant information,
that has direct relevance to the matter before the committee and that
is likely to shed light on the issue which the committee has to contend
with, the committee will act in a proper manner if it decides to hear
the witness.[59]

In reviewing the way the advisory committees interpreted this directive, the Court refused to recognize the right of the deportee to cross-
examine the military commander who issued the deportation order. In
the *Maslam* case it held that, as all the evidence on which the military
commander relied is presented to the committee, cross-examination of
the commander would not "contribute to the relevant information,
which is all before the committee, and would not shed light on the issue
the committee has to contend with, since the committee must reach its
conclusion independently on the basis of the same material, and without
being influenced by the commander's decision."[60]

Paradoxically, while the *Maslam* decision narrowed the directive
given in the *Afu* case concerning subpoena of witnesses by the deportees,
it is the strongest judicial statement on record regarding the independent
nature of the advisory committees' functions. The perception of the
Court is that the committees are not merely to examine whether there is
sufficient evidence to support the military commander's decision to
deport; they must also examine independently whether a deportation
order should have been issued and should be carried out. Unfortunately,
the fact that the advisory committees are appointed by the military commanders who issue the orders seriously weakens the minimal institutional independence required for the committees to fulfill such a role in
a credible manner.

In many cases the committees' commission signed by the military
commander who issues the deportation order includes the stipulation
that the committee's proceedings not be held in public. The advisory
committees regarded themselves as bound by this stipulation and
refused to allow opening of the hearings to the general public. While the
Court initially supported this approach,[61] it later modified its position,
holding that, unless secret evidence was being heard, opening the proceedings would "serve the public interest and weaken the fears
expressed by the petitioners . . . about the lack of independence of the
advisory committees, and slanderous talk about their considerations,
their manner of operation and the regularity of their proceedings."[62]

The Court revoked the military commander's directive that the proceedings not be held in public and left the matter for each committee to
decide "according to the circumstances and the constraints connected

with the conditions on the site and the security needs." This may be regarded as one more step in the direction of bolstering the image of the advisory committees as independent judicial bodies.

DECISIONS IN INDIVIDUAL CASES

As in the case of administrative detention, the law provides a special mechanism for review of the commander's decision to deport. The initial attitude of the Court was that review by the advisory committee barred review of the individual facts of the case by the Court itself.

In *Marar* v. *Minister of Defense* the petitioner had been under administrative detention for an extended period of time when an order was issued for his deportation. His main argument was that his deportation could not be required by one of the purposes set out in regulation 108, since the security of the state and the public peace were well protected while he was under detention. Justice Haim Cohn refused to entertain the argument. He held that only the advisory committee could look into the grounds for the deportation order. Justice Cohn added:

> This court does not know, nor should it know, what the security data were that required deportation of the petitioner from the country, rather than his continued detention. On the other hand, from the advisory committee's decision, which was laid before us, it transpires that the committee heard from one of the security staff all the (secret) matters that formed the basis for the minister of defense's considerations; and that after hearing this it was satisfied that there was no room to recommend reconsideration of the matter. As far as the material-security justification for the deportation order goes, from our point of view that is the end of the matter.[63]

The *Marar* decision may be seen as the paradigm of a judicial decision that takes a highly restrictive view of the Court's role in reviewing decisions made on security grounds. The Court is concerned solely with questions of formal power and even on these questions its view is highly formalistic. It bows to the discretion of the authorities, especially when an internal mechanism has been created to review the decision of a military commander. This approach was followed both in the *Awwad* case[64] and the *Kawasme II* case.

The turning point in the Court's attitude on the scope of judicial review over deportations came in a case that dealt with deportation of an infiltrator, rather than deportation of a resident of the Territories under regulation 112. In *Shahahin* v. *IDF Commander in Gaza*[65] the petitioner had entered the area illegally shortly after the 1967 War and had been arrested and charged with security offences. While he was still in prison an order was signed for his deportation after he had served his sentence. Just before his release, his family challenged this deportation order in court and, before their petition could be heard, the commander revoked the deportation order. Upon his release the petitioner was allowed to live in the area, but a short time later he was informed that his permit to reside in the area had expired and that he had to leave. If he failed to do so on his own accord, he would be deported. His petition related to this decision of the military commander, the legal basis of which was the power of the commander to deport any person who had infiltrated into the Territories after 1967.[66]

Having established the formal power to deport infiltrators, Justice Shamgar addressed the criteria that must be met to justify use of that power in an individual case. As the decision to deport is made by an administrative body, the evidence on which that body relies does not have to be admissible in a court of law. It must, however, be clear, unambiguous, and convincing.[67] The legal basis for the deportation in the instant case was infiltration into the area, and the Court could have rested its decision on its finding that the evidence of the petitioner's illegal entry to the Territories met this evidentiary test. Nevertheless, as the first deportation order had been repealed, the Court decided that "there is need for a separate, additional and independent examination of the justification for the authorities having shifted their ground and refusing to relate to the petitioner in the way they did after repeal of the previous deportation order."[68]

Justice Shamgar proceeded to review the evidence on which the military commander had relied in reaching his conclusion that the petitioner had, since his release, been involved in subversive activities. His decision not to interfere with the commander's decision was based on his conclusion that the evidence of this involvement was also clear, unambiguous, and convincing.[69]

The *Shahahin* decision related to deportation of an infiltrator. Even though the statement made by Justice Shamgar was obviously not restricted to this type of deportation, in applying the evidential test to deportations under regulation 112, two questions obviously arise. First, as opposed to deportation of infiltrators, deportations under regulation 112 are subject to review by the advisory committees. One of the main reasons given for the *Marar* approach was that this review obviates the need for judicial review. Second, to what must the evidence relate? Is it sufficient that it relate to the activities of the deportee, or must it also relate to the need to deport him?

The opportunity to test the Court's approach in a deportation case under regulation 112 arose in the *Na'azal* case.[70] Justice Shamgar made no mention of the *Marar* or *Awwad* decisions. Instead he stated that the parameters for judicial review in such cases were laid down in two other decisions that he himself had written: the *Baransa* decision,[71] which dealt with judicial review over restriction orders placed on individuals according to regulation 110 of the Defence Regulations, and the *Shahahin* decision, discussed previously.[72] In the first of these two decisions, Justice Shamgar had explicitly rejected the narrow approach to judicial review taken in the *Marar* case. In the second decision Justice Shamgar had adopted the evidential test previously mentioned. Making no mention of the statutory review by the advisory committee, he now stated explicitly that this test would apply to deportations under regulation 112.[73]

The *Shahahin* approach, which has been followed in subsequent deportation cases,[74] requires the Supreme Court itself to review the evidence relied on by the military commander in making his decision. The fact that an advisory committee has examined this evidence and supported the commander's decision does not preclude substantive judicial review. However, the scope of judicial review is still limited by the Court's perception of its jurisdiction as a High Court of Justice.

In the *Kawasme II* case Justice Landau stated that "questions relating to the efficacy and prudence of the decision taken [to deport—D.K.] exceed the field of judicial review and belong to the field of political decision-making."[75] Even after the Court abandoned the *Marar* approach, it quoted this statement with approval.[76] It stated repeatedly that it is not the Court's duty to decide whether deportation of the petitioners is a good idea and "whether the deportation is needed or justified"[77]

If the Court examines the facts of the case but does not decide whether the deportation is justified or not, what precisely does it review? According to the approach taken in the *Na'azal* decision, the issue reviewed by the Court is whether there was clear, unambiguous, and convincing evidence that the conditions laid down in regulation 108 applied, namely whether on the basis of this evidence the deportation order was "necessary or expedient . . . for securing the public safety, the defense of the area, the maintenance of public order or the suppression of mutiny, rebellion or riot."[78] The problem is, of course, that whether these conditions apply is a matter of assessment that relates to the future. This assessment is not simply a function of facts relating to the deportees' past activities.

The Court addressed this problem in the *Satiha* decision,[79] handed down soon after the *Na'azal* decision. The petitioner argued that all the evidence related to his past activities, whereas the aim of deportation under regulation 112 is to prevent a future danger. The Court replied by quoting from its leading precedent dealing with police supervision orders under regulation 110 of the Defense Regulations, in which the same issue was addressed.[80] The object of deportation is preventive and the measure may not be employed unless it is meant to prevent a future danger. However, the only basis for assessing whether a future danger exists is the past actions of the deportee. Thus, clear, unambiguous, and convincing evidence of past actions that the authorities regard as threatening is sufficient for the Court to accept the assessment of the military commander that the conditions in regulation 108 apply.[81]

HAMAS DEPORTATION CASE

In dealing with deportation cases, the Court followed a pattern similar to that in the house demolition cases. The main features of this pattern are ignoring or rejecting arguments that relate to the legality of the measure itself, coupled with an attempt to strengthen the procedural protections in individual cases. This pattern was evident in the *Hamas Deportation* decision, which deserves separate consideration.

The decision by the Cabinet to deport over 400 alleged activists of the *Hamas* and *Islamic Jihad* movements was made in direct response to the abduction and murder of a member of the Israeli border police and following a series of murders for which these movements had allegedly claimed responsibility. As explained, in order to pave the way for this deportation, new military legislation was promulgated and within a few hours the deportees were arrested, placed on buses, and driven in the direction of the Lebanese border. Before the buses reached the border, lawyers acting for some of the deportees and for the Association for Civil Rights in Israel (ACRI) petitioned the Court. Justice Barak, the Court's duty judge at the time, granted a temporary injunction in the middle of the night, and the buses were halted. The next day a bench of seven justices heard the government's request to revoke the temporary injunction. The chief-of-staff appeared before the Court and explained why he assessed that stopping the deportation would seriously undermine the security situation. By a majority of five to two, the Court revoked the temporary injunction, and the deportation went ahead.[82] The hearing on the merits of the case was held a month after the deportation had taken place, when the deportees were encamped in Lebanon north of the security zone, which was then controlled by the IDF.

The first striking feature of the decision in this case is the lack of any attempt by the Court to address arguments of principle raised by the petitioners against the deportation.[83] Arguments relating to the legality of deportations under international law, deporting non-Lebanese citizens to Lebanon against the will of the Lebanese government, and carrying out deportations from Israeli territory (as opposed to deportations

from the Occupied Territories) were simply ignored.[84] No explanation
was given by the Court for refraining to address these questions.[85]

The only general argument of principle that the Court did allude to
was that the deportation was a mass deportation, outlawed under international law, even according to the interpretation of article 49 of
Geneva Convention IV adopted by the Court itself. The Court stated:

> The orders that were given in this case were based on particular infor-
> mation in respect of each deportee, that is to say on individual consid-
> erations that pointed, in the respondents opinion, to a basis for every
> one of the deportees himself. In other words, we are not talking of a
> *collective* order but of a collection of *individual* orders, each one of
> which stands on its own feet, and meets the requirements of regulation
> 108 [of the Defense Regulations].[86]

Had the military commanders initiated the deportation on the basis
of security grounds related to each one of the deportees, the Court's
argument that the fact that there were many individual orders did not
make the deportation a collective one would have been more persuasive. However, in the *Hamas Deportation* case a political decision was
made to deport 400 activists, and the two military commanders
involved then filled their quotas by supplying the names of leading
activists. The very intention of the deportation was to create a dramatic
effect by its scope, rather than by the specific individuals included in the
lists of deportees. In these circumstances, the Court's reasoning must be
regarded as another case of formalism whose purpose is to legitimize
executive action.

Most of the Court's judgment in the *Hamas Deportation* case
related to the hearing issue.[87] As we saw earlier, the Court reversed the
principled stand taken in the *Kawasme I* case, according to which the
demand for a hearing prior to a deportation is not subject to an exception on grounds of security imperatives. Although it had not been shown
that this security exception applied, the Court once again held that violation of the prior hearing requirement did not make the deportations
invalid, and that the appropriate remedy was to hold the hearings after
the deportation had taken place. Once the Court had revoked the temporary injunction, thereby providing judicial approval for the deportation to go ahead without the required hearing, its decision that ignoring
the hearing requirement did not *per se* make the deportations illegal
became inevitable.[88]

The *Hamas Deportation* case was not a run-of-the-mill case. The
Cabinet had decided on a dramatic move in its attempt to counter terror, or at least to persuade the Israeli public that it was doing something
about terror; the case received worldwide attention and censure from all

quarters, including the UN Security Council;[89] and the chief-of-staff himself appeared before the Court at the initial stage in order to explain why security would be seriously undermined if the deportations were stopped. It is therefore not particularly surprising that the Court was unwilling to intervene in the deportation decision or to accept arguments that would have delegitimized it.[90] In fact it could be said that this case provides a dramatic illustration of the Court's general approach in cases relating to security measures or major policy decisions connected with the Occupied Territories.[91] I shall return to this point in the concluding chapter.

CONCLUSIONS

In its decisions relating to the Occupied Territories, the Court has ratio-nalized virtually all controversial actions of the Israeli authorities, espe-cially those most problematic under principles of international humani-tarian law. The text of article 49 of Geneva Convention IV is pellucid: it prohibits all deportations of protected persons from occupied territory. Yet, contrary to the view of most, if not all, objective commentators, the Supreme Court ruled that deportations carried out by military authori-ties on security grounds are not covered by this prohibition. Punitive house demolitions are incompatible with fundamental principles of international humanitarian law, human rights standards, and penal law. The Court consistently ignored these principles or refused to apply them on the basis of highly questionable arguments. Establishing Israeli set-tlements in occupied territory is not only controversial politically: it is widely regarded as incompatible with the international law of belliger-ent occupation. The Court did indeed strike a serious blow against establishment of settlements on private land requisitioned for military purposes. However, it refused to rule whether establishing settlements is compatible with the final paragraph of article 49 of Geneva Convention IV. It otherwise legitimized the settlement policy by accepting that estab-lishing civilian settlements may be regarded as a military need, by refus-ing to interfere with use of state land for settlements, and by including settlers as part of the local population for the purposes of article 43 of the Hague Regulations. The Court also allowed wide-scale changes in local law, thereby blunting the force of article 43 of the Hague Regula-tions. The Court's courageous 1999 judgment on the interrogation methods of the General Security Service was a victory for the rule of law and legal values. However, this judgment did not relate to policies or actions in the Occupied Territories themselves. Furthermore, the Court prevaricated for a long time before delivering its judgment, during which time the illegal practices were widely used against Palestinians.

In its jurisprudence relating to Israel itself, the Supreme Court of Israel has earned a well-deserved reputation as a rights-minded court. It created a judicial bill of rights before enactment of the Basic Law: Human Dignity and Liberty, and offered a fair degree of protection for the individual against governmental arbitrariness. One of the foundations of its jurisprudence has been a principle of interpretation in favor of human rights. According to this principle, when interpreting statutory instruments that grant governmental authorities power to restrict rights and liberties of the individual, the Court must adopt the interpretation that is least restrictive of those rights and freedoms.

This rights-minded approach is generally conspicuous by its absence in decisions relating to the Occupied Territories. The jurisprudence of these decisions is blatantly government-minded. As discussed in chapter 3, the Court stated that in interpreting Geneva Convention IV it would adopt the interpretation least invasive of state sovereignty. Application of this canon of interpretation to an international instrument dealing with humanitarian law epitomizes the government-minded approach of the Court. The manner in which the Court interpreted regulation 119 of the Defence Regulations (that permits punitive house demolitions) and the notion (reiterated on more than one occasion) that demolition of a terrorist's family home can be justified as a general deterrent measure are further examples of the Court's departure from accepted standards of human rights protection. Allowing the authorities to deny the right of West Bank and Gaza Palestinians who have taken up residence elsewhere to return to their own country, by citing "vital interests of the state" that are not spelled out, is another example of this mind-set.

In some cases the Court did indeed incorporate part of its "domestic philosophy" of human rights protection in cases relating to the Occupied Territories. Thus, in the *Morcous* case[1] the Court applied its principle of non-discrimination in ordering the authorities to supply the gasmasks supplied to Israeli settlers to Palestinian residents of the West Bank. In the *Electric Co. (2)* case[2] the Court was receptive to the argument that making the Palestinian residents of the West Bank dependent on an Israeli electricity supplier was not necessarily in their interests. However, these cases are the exception and do not reflect the Court's jurisprudence on substantive issues.

While the Court failed to intervene on substantive matters, it made a concerted effort to strengthen the procedural constraints on use of governmental powers. Thus, the Court "judicialized" the procedure before the appeals committees in deportation cases; it held that a hearing must be granted before a house is demolished; it set guidelines for military court judges who review administrative detention orders; it recommended establishment of a court of appeals against decisions of the military courts and of a special committee to monitor conditions in the Ketziot detention center. The significance of these decisions should not be denied. It should be recalled, however, that the Court has not always been prepared to support its own procedural demands. The Court backed down when its ruling that a hearing must be held before demolition of houses was put to the test. It refused to enjoin deportation of Palestinians who had been denied the hearing required by its own jurisprudence. It refrained from overturning the decision of a military judge who did not adhere to its procedural directives regarding review of administrative detention.

In its decision in the *Na'azal* case,[3] the Court was asked to intervene in the decision to demolish the family home of a suicide bomber who had placed a bomb on a bus that killed twenty-two people and wounded forty-eight. In referring to the Court's jurisprudence on house demolitions, Justice Matza stated:

> The binding ruling is that in applying the said sanction great care and reasonable proportionality are required, which are not a matter of competence but of discretion. . . . All the judges on this court are anxious about the existence of these criteria. On the background of this anxiety regarding the severity of the harm to innocent persons, who had no part in the acts of the terrorist, and who even could not have known of his involvement in terrorist activity, we did not hesitate, in every appropriate case, to express our view during the proceedings; and on more that one occasion our remarks motivated the security authorities to agree (without waiting for a judicial decision) to mitigate the damage to the living quarters of others which are in the building that is to be demolished.[4]

This statement is highly revealing. Justice Matza concedes that while the Court does not wish to take responsibility for interfering with government action, it will pressure the authorities to back down or modify their stand in some cases. This is a fair description of the Court's modus operandi. Both an early study of the Court's approach in petitions relating to the Occupied Territories[5] and recent research[6] have shown that the Court has often forced the authorities to reconsider planned action or to compromise with the petitioner. Sometimes pressure on the authorities is the direct result of remarks made by judges during a hearing, as Justice Matza intimated in the passage previously quoted. In other cases issuance of an interim injunction by the Court, pending a final decision in the case, has allowed time for public opinion to force the authorities to reconsider their opinion.[7] The authorities frequently back down or compromise before the matter reaches court.[8] This system of "settlement in the Court's shadow" has meant that the restraining influence of the Court has been far greater than can be gleaned from its actual decisions. In fact, when out-of-court settlement is taken into account, the rate of actual success of Palestinian petitioners from the Occupied Territories is higher than the overall success rate of petitioners to the Supreme Court.[9]

Using pressure on the authorities to back down or reconsider their decision, rather than ruling on the merits, is consistent with the distinction between the Court's attitude on questions of substance and procedure. Subjecting the authorities to procedural constraints, such as a hearing before house demolitions, may limit use of governmental powers. However, it leaves ultimate responsibility for employing those powers in the hands of the military authorities, rather than the Court.

In my introduction, I presented different perceptions of the Court's role in review over petitions relating to the Occupied Territories. I asked which function of the Court has been dominant: its legitimizing or restraining function.

I suggest that the answer rests on a distinction between the Court's decisions and the influence of its shadow. If we restrict our attention to actual Court decisions, the focus of this study, it is difficult to escape the conclusion that the Court's legitimizing function has dominated. But when the overall picture is considered, the conclusion is far less clear, since the Court's shadow has played a significant role in restraining the authorities.

How is it that the Court's shadow has had this restraining influence if its actual bite is so mild? In other words, given the fact that the authorities usually prevail when the matter is left for a final determination of the Court, why do they back down or compromise so often in the pre-decision stages? I suggest a number of conceivable answers.

The Supreme Court of Israel plays a unique role in the Israeli political system. Its judges enjoy enormous prestige and respect, especially among the political and legal elites. The judges are regarded not only as experts in matters of law, but also as guardians of society's moral fabric. It is therefore extremely difficult for government counsel and the authorities they represent to resist pressure by the judges to reconsider their position or to back down in a specific case. It is often far more convenient for the judges to force the authorities to resolve a case out of court than to allow the case to reach the decision stage. The judges have frequently forced the hand of the authorities in this way, thus obviating the need for judgment. In the second place, the chance of losing in court generally outweighs the gains likely to be made by the authorities in fighting a case. Thus, the general policy has been not to defend a case unless the legal advisors are convinced that the Court will rule in favor of the authorities, either because they have a strong legal and factual case or because the case raises a major question of principle in which the Court will be reluctant to delegitimize the stand taken by the government. The paucity of decisions against the authorities is a reflection of the accuracy of government lawyers in predicting the attitude of the Court in those cases that it has refused to settle out of court. These lawyers may also have allowed themselves a wide margin of error and settled many cases that they would have won, had they gone to court.

A further possible answer lies in the use made by government lawyers of the potential review by the Court. Within the corridors of power, lawyers have used the threat of judicial review as a way of restraining the military authorities. In contrast to the previous explanation, their threat is not based on a real assessment of the chances of winning or losing if the matter goes to court. On the contrary, many of these lawyers, familiar with the general trend of the Court to legitimize government actions, may be only too aware that if the matter goes to court, the authorities will prevail. They nevertheless use their professional prestige and status to persuade the military authorities that it would not be advisable to defend the action in court.

Even if we concede that the Court's shadow has fulfilled a significant restraining function, we must return to the issues raised by the Court's jurisprudence. One question in this regard relates to the clear disparity between the Court's general jurisprudence and its jurisprudence in cases relating to the Occupied Territories.[10] How can one explain the fact that a court that has played such a dominant role in forging a democratic and essentially liberal body of jurisprudence has consistently displayed a government-minded approach in decisions relating to the Occupied Territories?

It seems to me that part of the answer to this question lies in the very nature of domestic courts in situations of conflict. In democratic countries, courts enjoy varying degrees of independence. This independence ensures that the judges' decisions are based on their conscience and are not dictated by other branches of government. It should not conceal the fact, however, that courts "are part of the machinery of authority within the State and as such cannot avoid the making of political decisions."[11] Judges may be independent, but they are not neutral.[12]

In times of relative calm, the impact of the judges' role as political functionaries of the state may be subtle and may even pass undetected. Judges may be perceived as functionaries who can act as neutral arbitrators between authorities and individuals. However, this "stance of neutrality" can be maintained only when the dispute before the court is perceived to be a "domestic dispute" between a government agency and an individual. It cannot be maintained when the dispute is perceived to be an "external dispute" involving a challenge to the very authority of the state. In such a case, courts will inevitably act as institutions whose primary duty is to protect the perceived interests of the state, even when this involves serious incursions on individual liberties and basic human rights.[13] In some jurisdictions courts have avoided ruling in such situations, relying on doctrines of nonjusticiability or "act of state" to justify their passivity. The Supreme Court has refused to resort to such doctrines when individual rights are concerned. But, as Justice Cheshin intimated in the *Sabeach* case,[14] the refusal of a court to employ the "act of state" doctrine does not change the nature of the matter before it. When what is in essence an act of state is involved, the likelihood of a court intervening is extremely low, even if the legal doctrine is not employed.

Judges of the Supreme Court have occasionally conceded that courts are state institutions whose primary duty is to protect the state against its enemies. In the *Kawasme(1)* case,[15] three Palestinian leaders had been deported from the West Bank without the legally required hearing. While counsel for the authorities conceded that they had acted unlawfully, he argued that the Court should not grant a remedy to the deportees since they had incited the population in the Occupied Territories to violence "and more than that to the destruction of the State of Israel itself by use of arms."[16] Justice Landau noted that he had seriously considered this argument, and added:

> It seems to me that to the extent that we have unambiguous evidence, of the kind that is admissible in court, which proves from the words of the petitioners themselves, that they incited the population in the Territories to violent action and to the destruction of the State of Israel by violent means, as a "final solution" for their national aspirations, or that they would engage in such incitement if they were allowed to return to their homes, they are not worthy for any remedy from this court, which serves as one of the authorities of the state.[17]

Whether a particular case is perceived as a "domestic dispute" or a challenge to the very authority of the state is not always an easy question. The answer greatly depends on the political context and the perceptions of decision-makers and the public within a given society. In shaping these perceptions, one factor will always be dominant: whether the society perceives itself as subject to external or internal threat against its security or territorial integrity. In stressing the subjective element of "society's perception," I have no intention of intimating that this perception does not reflect objective reality. One reason why a society perceives itself as threatened is, of course, that a threat does in fact exist. However, the crucial issue is not whether an objective threat exists, but whether the given society perceives it to exist. This has been illustrated time and again in the reaction of the U.S. Supreme Court in times of perceived crisis.[18]

In the case of Israel, objective factors point to a potent threat to state security. The perception of the events that led to the occupation of the West Bank and Gaza (described in the Introduction) left an indelible impact on those who lived through this period. During the first ten years of the occupation a formal state of war existed between Israel and all its neighbors. Peace treaties have since been concluded with Egypt and Jordan, but a formal state of war still obtains between Israel and some Arab states such as Syria and Iraq. Important forces in the Muslim and Arab world constantly deny the very legitimacy of the state, and threats to use force against the state are an everyday occurrence. Chances of another war between Israel and one or more surrounding countries cloud any analysis of future developments in the area. Despite the Oslo Accords and subsequent agreements between Israel and the PLO, an end to the conflict with the Palestinians still seems far away. Events since the end of September 2000 provide a sad reminder of this harsh reality. At times terrorist attacks against civilian targets have resulted in many deaths and serious injuries. In this situation, disputes between Palestinians in the Occupied Territories and the military authorities there are likely to be perceived as "external disputes" between the state and its enemies, rather than "domestic disputes" between a governmental authority and an individual.

A second part of the answer to the question relating to the disparity between the Court's "regular" jurisprudence and its jurisprudence in cases from the Occupied Territories rests on the political dimensions of Israel's self-identity and the Zionist narrative of its conflict with the Palestinians. The State if Israel is constitutionally defined as the "state of the Jewish people." Actions perceived as contrary to the interests of the Jewish collective and its right to maintain such a state have always been regarded as threats to the security of the state.[19] Even before the 1967 War, nationalist tendencies of Arabs in Israel who found it difficult to identify with the Jewish state were perceived by the establishment as threatening the very existence of the state. The *Yeredor* case[20] dealt with the decision of the Central Elections Committee to disqualify a party list for *Knesset* elections. The reasons given were that most of the candidates had been members of the Arab movement *el-Ard*, which the Court had held in a previous case to be an unlawful association because it identified with Israel's enemies in the Arab world. I have elsewhere discussed the constitutional implications of the decision in this case.[21] For present purposes, the important point is the glaring discrepancy between the ways in which two of the judges viewed the danger presented by such a list participating in the elections. Justice Haim Cohn, who took the view that in the absence of statutory authority the Central Elections Committee lacked the power to disqualify lists, also held that no evidence had been produced to show what danger to state security would be created by allowing the list to run.[22] Justice Sussman, on the other hand, was so convinced of the danger involved that he invoked natural law principles of self-defense as the basis for disqualifying the list. The aim of the list was perceived as "destruction of the state, bringing a holocaust on the majority of its inhabitants for whom the state was established, and joining up with its enemies."[23]

Perceiving rejection of the Jewish state in terms of actual survival and "Holocaust," whether a reflection of political reality or not, has had an appreciable impact on the readiness of the Court to interfere in measures adopted by the executive on security grounds. Rejection of the Jewish state is a threat to survival and justifies countermeasures in self-defense. Furthermore, the struggle with the Palestinian people is an existential struggle. Thus, even when the Court has been prepared to extend the scope of its review over security matters, it has rarely been prepared to rule that insufficient weight has been given to basic individual rights in decisions relating to use of security measures against members of the Arab minority in Israel itself and against Palestinian residents of the Occupied Territories. It has only been prepared to intervene in such cases when it has held that the authorities lack the legal power to employ the challenged action,[24] that there were procedural irregularities,[25] that the power invoked was not one in which security considerations were a proper purpose,[26] or that the real reasons for use of the discretion were not security considerations.[27] The one case cited by all as an example of the readiness of the Court to intervene in the discretion of the authorities in security matters relates to an article in the Hebrew press.[28]

In the eye's of the Jewish citizens of Israel, the state's position in the Occupied Territories cannot be divorced from their perception of the events that led up to the 1967 War and from the wider context of the conflict between Israel and the Arab world. The commitment of some forces in Israeli society to continued control over the Occupied Territories is founded on religious or nationalistic grounds. However, as I noted in the Introduction, even those who reject these grounds generally share the perception that until a proper peace agreement has been reached, Israeli control must be maintained for reasons of security. Thus, most of the Jewish public in Israel regard challenges to the authority of the IDF in the Territories as acts of war that threaten the very security of the state itself, rather than as expressions of the desires of a people subject to military occupation to be free of the occupying army. Since continued domination of the Occupied Territories is regarded as essential to the security of the state, attempts to force Israel to relinquish control are perceived as being directed against state security.

Petitions relating to actions of the military in the Occupied Territories fit the pattern of decisions in cases in which parties to the Arab-Israel conflict are involved. It is indeed true that many of the petitions submitted by Palestinian residents of the Territories do not relate directly to measures taken on security grounds. However, *perceptions* of security remain in the background at all times. In the context of the Israel-Arab conflict, political measures taken as part of a policy of managing that conflict are perceived as intimately connected with state security.[29] This attitude is evident in cases relating to the Occupied Territories. Two cases will suffice to illustrate this point.

In the *Beth-El* case[30] discussed in detail in chapters 1, 2, and 5, the issue was the legality of requisitioning private land for the establishment of Jewish settlements. The authorities argued that the settlements were established for military needs that constitute legitimate grounds for requisitioning land in occupied territory according to international law. In explaining her decision to accept that argument, Justice Ben-Porat expressed her general perception of Israel's situation in the following words:

> Israel, a small state with its long and narrow territory inside the Green Line, is unfortunately surrounded by countries, which do not conceal their hostility towards it. I doubt whether this situation, which I will not examine in detail, has a parallel in the history of mankind. Hostility expresses itself not only in economic boycott as a means of warfare, but also in raids of members of the PLO from the territories of several of these countries for the purpose of committing violence in Israel. Above all, these inroads place Israel in constant danger of a *surprise war*, such as occurred in 1973 when attack came simultaneously from north and south. It is reasonable therefore that in this special situation, which calls for the utmost preparedness to withstand all possible trouble if, where and when it arises, unusual solutions become necessary. Against this background, the argument that in containing sudden trouble the time factor is of prime importance is good common sense. One of those solutions, which is the subject of the proceedings before us, is the creation of a civilian Jewish presence at *particularly* sensitive spots.[31]

In the *Shahin* case[32] the question was whether residents of the Occupied Territories have the right that immediate family members who are citizens of foreign countries be granted permanent residency status. The military government's policy was only to grant permission for permanent status in exceptional cases. It did not attempt to justify this policy on narrow security grounds, but relied merely on the general power of an occupying force to restrict freedom of movement to and from the occupied territory. The Court accepted the argument that an occupying power does not have the duty to allow free movement into occupied territory, especially from the territory of a country in a state of war with it. In concluding his judgment, Justice Shamgar saw fit to remark: "It is the hope of all that peace will solve all these problems, but their solution immediately at a time of war, by allowing the movement of many—and not of a few individuals—*into* the area occupied by IDF forces cannot serve as cause for the intervention of this court."[33] Thus. although there was no active war at the time, the Court's perception of the formal state of belligerency between Israel and its neighbors was that of *wartime*.

Given this perception of the political context, Israeli judges will not be neutral in judging the conflicting claims of the government and Palestinians subject to military rule. In the struggle between government policies and Palestinian arguments of rights based on justice, international legal standards, or lofty legal principles, the Court has shown a marked preference for "state arguments." The dominant narrative holds that the state is being attacked, the authorities are trying to protect it, and the ultimate duty of the Court is to assist them in this task.

The wide political context is one in which a dispute between "Palestinian outsiders" and the authorities may well be perceived as a dispute between the state and its enemies. This perspective may either be aggravated or mitigated in a specific case, depending on the type of action that is being challenged and the type of legal argument being made against that action. Arguments challenging policies in the Occupied Territories that are regarded as part of the government's conflict-management strategy or the very power of the authorities to use certain measures, and arguments based on international law, by implication challenge either the sovereignty or authority of the state. They are therefore likely to aggravate the general perception. Restricted arguments that relate only to the specific facts of a given case rather than to a wider general principle, those that focus on matters of procedural fairness, or that are based on the self-professed values of the society itself, rather than those of international law, might mitigate the perception.

Judicial review by the domestic courts of an occupying power over acts of the military in occupied territory is novel. The review by Israel's Supreme Court over acts in the Occupied Territories is the first, and only, precedent. The mere existence of this review has had a significant restraining influence on the authorities. However, in the actual decisions themselves, especially those dealing with substantive questions of principle or policy, the legitimizing function of the Court has been dominant.

The Israeli precedent exposes the inherent difficulties involved in such judicial review. Standards of international law are the main yardstick for reviewing actions of the military in occupied territory. How-ever, domestic courts are notoriously reluctant to enforce standards of international law against the executive branch of government, and find all kinds of mechanisms to avoid doing so.[34] The Israeli Supreme Court's attitude to application of the standards of international law seems to fit a general pattern. Second, military occupation is a function of conflict. Involving a domestic court in adjudicating disputes between military authorities and residents of the occupied territory assumes an element of neutrality between the parties that cannot exist in such a situation.

In the West Bank and Gaza, the inherent difficulties of military occupation have been aggravated by the ambiguous attitude of the Israeli authorities and large sections of Israeli society toward the very idea that these territories are occupied. As we saw chapter 1, there is a clear disparity between the political stance taken by the governments that have held power since 1967 and the stance taken by their lawyers when appearing before the Supreme Court. While representatives of the government continued to argue, both in international forums and in the *Knesset*, that the West Bank and Gaza are not occupied territory, its lawyers sought to justify actions in these areas on the basis of the inter-national law of belligerent occupation. In many ways, this provided the government with a convenient system of control. On the political level, the government relates to the Occupied Territories as colonies, with all that this entails: exploitation of their resources and markets for the ben-efit of the home country and its citizens and a clear distinction between the status of the "natives" and those of the settlers. But when challenged on the legal level, it resorts to the law of belligerent occupation, which provides it with the framework for restricting the rights and liberties of the local Palestinian residents on grounds of security and military needs. True, the law of belligerent occupation places serious constraints on the freedom of action of the occupying power, but the authorities generally enjoyed the support of the Court in circumventing these constraints.

When perceived in this context, review by the Supreme Court over actions of the authorities in the Occupied Territories loses some of it uniqueness. Most civilian institutions of government have had a hand in administering various aspects of life in the Territories. Thus, for exam-ple, the Israel Police have been in charge of criminal investigations; offi-cials of the Israel Lands Authority and the Water Commissioner have been involved in management of land and water resources. Furthermore, although review over military authorities in occupied territory may be unprecedented, review by courts of a colonial power over actions of colonial authorities is not without precedent.

In the chapter 1 we saw that there was some question whether the Court had jurisdiction over actions taken by the military in occupied territory. It is, of course, impossible to know what restraints would have been placed on the actions of the authorities had the Court declined to exercise jurisdiction over such actions. However critical one may be of many of the Court's decisions, the relevant question cannot only be what the position would have been if the Court had taken a more activist stand in petitions relating to the Occupied Territories. One must also consider what the position would have been if the Court had declined to assume jurisdiction in such petitions. The answer to this question is far from clear. In the short term, the lack of formal external constraints on the discretion of the military almost certainly would have resulted in more arbitrariness. However, the process of decolonization in other parts of the world generally began when elites in the mother country became aware of the disparity between the declared democratic values of their society and their country's actions in the colony. Is it possible that in the medium or long term, the very lack of restraint that would have resulted from the absence of judicial review would have made the occupation less palatable for Israeli elites, and that the pressure to end the occupation by political settlement, which began after the *Intifada* started in 1987, would have been felt much earlier? I leave the reader to speculate on this question.

NOTES

ABBREVIATIONS

Isr YHB   Israel Yearbook on Human Rights

PD   *Piskei Din* (official reports of Supreme Court decisions)

NOTES TO THE INTRODUCTION

1. See *The Rule of Law in the Areas Administered by Israel* (Tel Aviv: Israel National Section of the International Commission of Jurists, 1981). This book was written in response to R. Shehadeh, *The West Bank and the Rule of Law* (n.p.: International Commission of Jurists, 1980), a highly critical study of Israeli policies in the West Bank during the first decade of the occupation.

2. U. Amit-Kohn et al., *Israel, the "Intifada" and the Rule of Law* (Tel Aviv: Israel Ministry of Defense Publications, 1993) 17–18.

3. See *Dweikat v. Government of Israel* (1980) 34 (1) PD 1 (*Elon Moreh* case) [English summary: 9 *Isr YHR* (1979) 345]; *Electricity Company for Jerusalem District v. Minister of Energy and Infrastructure* (1980) 35 (2) PD 673 (*Electricity Co. [No. 2]* case); *Association for Civil Rights in Israel v. Officer Commanding Central Command* (1988) 43 (2) PD 529 (the *ACRI* case) [English summary: 23 *Isr YHR* (1993) 294]; *Morcous v. Minister of Defense* (1991) 45 (1) PD 467 [English summary: 23 *Isr YHR* (1993) 339]. All these cases are discussed in the text.

4. For an early discussion of the Court's jurisprudence, written soon after the *Elon Moreh* and *Electricity Co. (No. 2)* cases, in which the writer portrays the Court as the protector of the rule of law in the Occupied Territories, see M. Negbi, *Justice Under Occupation: The Israeli Supreme Court versus the Military Administration in the Occupied Territories* (in Hebrew) (Jerusalem: Cana Publishing House, 1981).

5. See *Yedioth Aharanot*, 3 September 1993, p. 4. *B'Tselem* is the Israeli Information Center for Human Rights in the Occupied Territories.

6. See R. Shamir, "'Landmark Cases' and the Reproduction of Legitimacy: The Case of Israel's High Court of Justice," 24 *Law and Soc Rev* (1990) 781, 795. Also see L. Shelef, "The Green Line is the Border of Judicial Activism: Queries about the Supreme Court Judgments in the Territories" (in Hebrew) 17 *Tel Aviv U L Rev* (1993) 757.

7. C. Black, *The People and the Court: Judicial Review in a Democracy* (New York: Macmillan, 1990) 223. Also see A. M. Bickel, *The Least Dangerous Branch: The Supreme Court at the Bar of Politics* (Indianapolis: Bobbs-Merrill, 1962) 30; T. L. Becker, *Comparative Judicial Politics: The Political Functionings of Courts* (Chicago: Rand McNally, 1970) 238–246.

8. This case is discussed at length by Negbi, *Justice Under Occupation*, 146–147.

9. See *Arjov v. IDF Commander of Judea and Samaria* (1985) 42 (1) PD 353.

10. See Y. Dotan, "Judicial Rhetoric, Government Lawyers and Human Rights: The Case of the Israel High Court of Justice during the *Intifada*," 33 *Law and Soc Rev* (1999) 319.

11. It must be stressed that the following description is not an attempt to present an objective view of the events that led to the war. As this study is concerned with the functioning of an Israeli institution what is relevant is not what really happened, but how events were perceived in Israeli eyes. The discussion is based on the following sources: G. Barzilai, *A Democracy in Wartime: Conflict and Consensus in Israel* (in Hebrew) (Tel Aviv: Sifriat Poalim, 1992); R. Pedatzur, *The Triumph of Embarrassment: Israel and the Territories After the Six-Day War* (in Hebrew) (Tel Aviv: Bitan, 1996); S. Gazit, *Trapped* (in Hebrew) (Tel Aviv: Zmora-Bitan, 1999).

12. Dayan was chief-of-staff at the time of the 1956 Sinai Campaign and had later served as minister of agriculture. In 1967 he was a member of *Knesset* on behalf of the activist Rafi party.

13. For a retrospective analysis of the events that led to the war see R. B. Parker, ed., *The Six-Day War: A Retrospective* (Gainesville: University Press of Florida, 1996).

14. The clearest manifestations of the anxiety, shared by the political leadership and the public, were the preparations made during the waiting period to cope with expected casualties. Fourteen thousand hospital beds and thousands of coffins were prepared and municipal parks were turned into potential burial grounds.

15. On the decisions relating to Jerusalem see M. Benvenisti, *Jerusalem, The Torn City* (Jerusalem: Isratypeset, 1976).

16. See section 1 of Law and Government Order (No. 1), 1967.

17. For a description of political developments in the Occupied Territories over the years see: M. Nisan, *Israel and the Territories: A Study in Control* (Jerusalem: Turtledove, 1978); M. Benvenisti, *The West Bank Data Project: A Survey of Israel's Policies* (Washington, DC: American Enterprise Institute, 1984); D. Peretz, *The West Bank: History, Politics, Society, and Economy* (Boul-

der: Westview, 1986); D. McDowall, *Palestine and Israel: The Uprising and Beyond* (Berkeley: University of California Press, 1989); Gazit, *Trapped*. For a discussion of legal developments see E. Playfair, ed., *International Law and the Administration of the Occupied Territories* (Oxford: Clarendon Press, 1992).

18. A new stage in the occupation started with the beginning of the *al-Aqsa Intifada* in September 2000. However, as stated in the Preface, this study does not deal with developments since this *Intifada* started. All references to the *Intifada* are to the *Intifada* that began in December 1987.

19. Since the beginning of the *al-Aqsa Intifada* a number of petitions relating to other security measures have been submitted. At the time of writing the Court had yet to deliver judgment in these petitions.

20. The exceptions were Haim Cohn, who served as attorney-general, and for a short period also as minister of justice, before being appointed directly to the Supreme Court and Zvi Berinson, who was director-general of a government ministry when he was appointed to the Supreme Court.

21. The High Court of Justice is not the highest court in England. However, the Mandate authorities were not prepared to entrust issue of prerogative writs to local Arab and Jewish judges. This jurisdiction was therefore placed in the hands of the Supreme Court in which the majority of judges were British.

22. See I. Zamir, "On Justice in the High Court of Justice," (in Hebrew) 26 *HaPraklit* (1970) 212.

23. This development has been discussed elsewhere by the present writer: see D. Kretzmer, "Judicial Review of *Knesset* Decisions," 8 *Tel Aviv U Studies in Law* (1988) 95.

24. See suggestions by the head of the main opposition party, who was later to become prime minister, to curtail the Court's jurisdiction to deal with certain petitions from the Territories: *The Jerusalem Post*, 9 April 1993, p. 2; *The Jerusalem Post*, 11 April 1993, p. 2.

25. See *Ha'aretz*, 26 October 1979, p. 1. Also see Negbi, *Justice Under Occupation*, 69–73.

26. See G. Barzilai, E. Yuchtman-Yaar, and Z. Segal, *The Israeli Supreme Court and the Israeli Public* (in Hebrew) (Tel Aviv: Papirus, 1994), 177. It should be noted that since the publication of this book there have been developments that suggest that the Court may have lost its legitimacy in the eyes of the ultra-Orthodox section of the Jewish public. This has largely been the result of the perception by members of this section of the public that the Court has taken an "antireligious" stand in matters of state and religion.

27. Ibid., 181.

28. Two partial basic laws on human rights were enacted in 1992. See Basic Law: Freedom of Occupation and Basic Law: Human Dignity and Liberty. See D. Kretzmer, "The New Basic Laws on Human Rights: A Mini-Revolution in Israeli Constitutional Law?" 14 *Netherlands Q HR* (1996) 173. Also see D. Barak-Erez, "From an Unwritten to a Written Constitution: The Israeli Challenge in American Perspective," 26 *Columbia HRL Rev* (1995) 309.

29. This was subject to one exception that relates to entrenched clauses in basic laws: see Kretzmer, "Judicial Review of *Knesset* Decisions." The Court has ruled that the Basic Law: Human Dignity and Liberty and the Basic Law: Free-

dom of Occupation, enacted in 1992, allow for judicial review of parliamentary legislation passed after those basic laws were enacted: *Mizrahi Bank v. Migdal, Cooperative Village* (1995) 49 (4) PD 221.

30. This approach is discussed in R. Gavison, M. Kremnitzer, and Y. Dotan, *Judicial Activism: For and Against—The Role of the High Court of Justice in Israeli Society* (in Hebrew) (Jerusalem: Magnus Press, 2000).

31. *Public Committee Against Torture in Israel v. Government of Israel,* 1999 (3) Takdin-Elyon 458.

32. *Plonim v. Minister of Defense* (1997) 44 (1) PD 721.

33. *Kaadan v. Israel Lands Administration* (1995) 44 (1) PD 264.

34. See *Jiryis v. District Commissioner for Haifa District* (1964) 18 (4) PD 673, 679.

35. See *Yeredor v. Central Elections Committee* (1965) 19 (3) PD 365, 389. For a discussion of the Weimar influence on this decision see E. Salzberger and F. Oz-Salzberger, "The German Tradition of the Israeli Supreme Court" (in Hebrew) 21 *Tel Aviv U L Rev* (1998) 259.

36. See *Neiman v. Chairman of Central Elections Committee* (1988) 42 (4) PD 177.

37. On the distinction between independence and neutrality of judges see J. A. G. Griffith, *The Politics of the Judiciary,* 4th ed. (London: Fontana, 1991) 269.

NOTES TO CHAPTER 1

1. But see R. Shehadeh, *Occupier's Law: Israel and the West Bank,* revised ed. (Washington: Institute for Palestine Studies, 1988) for a description of the far-reaching changes made in the legal system after 1967.

2. See *In re Societe Bonduelle et Cie,* June 29, 1951, in 18 International Law Reports, ed. H. Lauterpacht (1951) 573.

3. See M. Shamgar, "Legal Concepts and Problems of the Israeli Military Government—The Initial Stage" in *Military Government in the Territories Administered by Israel 1967–1980, The Legal Aspects,* ed. M. Shamgar (Jerusalem: Harry Sacher Institute for Legislative Research and Comparative Law, 1982) 13, 43 n. 56. Shamgar writes that the state *expressly agreed* to jurisdiction (emphasis in original). This approach had in fact been followed even before Mr. Shamgar became attorney-general. The first petition relating to the Occupied Territories was submitted on 20 June 1967, less than two weeks after the beginning of the occupation: see E. Nathan, "The Power of Supervision of the High Court of Justice over Military Government" in *Military Government in the Territories,* 109, 114, who cites a case in which the order *nisi* was set aside before the petition was actually heard.

4. Shamgar, "Legal Concepts." Also see M. Negbi, *Justice Under Occupation: The Israeli Supreme Court versus the Military Occupation in the Occupied Territories* (in Hebrew) (Jerusalem: Cana Publishing House, 1981) 12–18.

5. See *Kach Faction v. Knesset Speaker* (1985) 39 (3) PD 141, 157.

6. See U. Amit-Kohn et al., *Israel, the "Intifada" and the Rule of Law* (Tel

Aviv: Ministry of Defense Publications, 1993) 61. Shlomo Gazit, who served as the IDF Coordinator of Activities in the Territories from August 1967 until 1974, claims that another reason for accepting the Court's jurisdiction was the Israeli refusal to recognize the "Green Line" as the border between Israel and the West Bank. Gazit, *Trapped* (in Hebrew) (Tel Aviv: Zmora-Bitan, 1999) 42, n. 6.

   7. See *Christian Society for the Holy Places* v. *Minister of Defense* (1971) 26 (1) PD 574 [English summary: 2 *Isr YHR* (1972) 354].

   8. See *Electricity Corporation for Jerusalem District* v. *Minister of Defense* (1972) 27 (1) PD 124, 136 [English summary: 5 *Isr YHR* (1975) 381]; *Khelou* v. *Government of Israel* (1972) 27 (2) PD 169, 176 (*Rafiah Approach* case) [English summary: 5 *Isr YHR* (1975) 384].

   9. See *Electricity Corporation for Jerusalem District* v. *Minister of Defense*, 136.

   10. *Rafiah Approach* case, 176. Also see *Ayyub* v. *Minister of Defense* (1978) 33 (2) PD 113, 126 (*Beth El* case) [English summary: 9 *IsrYHR* (1979) 337]; *Dweikat* v. *Government of Israel* (1979) 34 (1) PD 1, 13 (*Elon Moreh* case) [English summary: 9 *Isr YHR* (1979) 345].

   11. *Ja'amait Ascan* v. *IDF Commander in Judea and Samaria* (1982) 37 (4) PD 785, 809.

   12. An "act of state" has been defined as "a prerogative act of policy in the field of foreign affairs performed by the Crown in the course of its relationship with another state or its subjects." 18 *Halsbury's Laws of England* (4th ed.) para. 1413. In England, detention of an enemy alien in time of war or his deportation have been held to be acts of state that may not be reviewed by a court: see *R.* v. *Vine Street Police Station Superintendent, ex parte Liebmann* [1916] 1 K.B.268; *Netz* v. *Secretary of State for Home Affairs* [1946] 1 Ch. 224; *R.* v. *Bottrill: ex parte Kuechenmeister* [1947] K.B. 41.

   13. See Y. S. Zemach, *Political Questions in the Courts: A Judicial Function in Democracies in Israel and the United States* (Detroit: Wayne University Press, 1976) 141–171; and cf. L. Henkin, "Is there a 'Political Question' Doctrine?" 85 *Yale LJ* (1976) 597.

   14. In a case relating to confiscation of property by the IDF during the 1982 campaign in Lebanon the "act of state" doctrine was raised at the initial stage only to be abandoned in the final hearing, probably because the authorities realized that the Court was not receptive to it. *El-Naawar* v. *Minister of Defense* (1982) 39 (3) PD 449, 454.

   15. See *Sabeach* v. *IDF Commander in Judea and Samaria* (1996) 50 (1) PD 353, 368.

   16. The U.S. government position questioning the legality of settlements is set out in "Memorandum of the State Department Legal Advisor Concerning Legality of Israeli Settlements in the Occupied Territories," 17 (1) *International Legal Materials* (1978) 777. Also see U.S. Statements with regard to Security Council Resolution 465, 19 *International Legal Materials* (1980) 540.

   17. *Beth El case*, 124.

   18. Ibid.

   19. Ibid., 122.

20. Ibid., 128–129.

21. *Elon Moreh* case, 14.

22. See *Morcous* v. *Minister of Defense* (1991) 45 (1) PD 467. Also see *Samara* v. *IDF Commander of Judea and Samaria* (1979) 34 (4) PD 1 [English summary: 11 *Isr YHR* (1981) 362], in which the Court dismissed the argument that refusal to allow family unification could be regarded as nonjusticiable because security considerations were involved,

23. See *Bargil* v. *Government of Israel* (1991) 47 (4) PD 210.

24. Ibid., 218. In two previous cases that had nothing to do with the Occupied Territories, Justice Shamgar advanced the view that the dominant nature of the question before the Court determines whether it is justiciable or not. Thus, even a question with legal aspects will be nonjusticiable if its dominant nature is political: see *Aloni* v. *Minister of Justice* (1986) 41 (2) PD 1; *Ressler* v. *Minister of Defense* (1988) 42 (2) PD 441. Also see *Kiryat Arba Local Council* v. *Prime Minister* (1994) 48 (5) PD 597. Relying on the *Bargil* decision, the Court refused to interfere in the policy of Prime Minister Yitzchak Rabin's government to halt all new building plans in Jewish settlements in the Occupied Territories.

25. *Bargil* v. *Government of Israel*, 220. A similar approach was adopted in *I'ad* v. *IDF Commander in Judea and Samaria*, 1999 (3) Takdin-Elyon 1771.

26. *Bargil* v. *Government of Israel*, 221.

27. 330 U.S. 763 (1950).

28. See Shamgar, "Legal Concepts," 43, n. 56.

29. *Shapira* v. *State of Israel* (1982) 36 (1) PD 337, 357.

30.See *Christian Society for the Holy Places* v. *Minister of Defense* (petition rested on article 43 of the Hague Regulations); *Rafiah Approach* case (petition based on international law of belligerent occupation); *Dahud* v. *Minister of Defense* (1978) 32 (3) PD 477 (question related to provision in Jordanian Municipalities Law).

31. See *Al-Taliya* v. *Minister of Defense* (1978) 33 (3) PD 505.

32. Ibid., 512.

33. In *Ja'amait Ascan* v. *IDF Commander*, 810 Justice Barak stated: "that every Israeli soldier carries with him in his knapsack the rules of customary public international law dealing with the rules of war and the fundamental rules of Israeli administrative law."

34. See the dictum of Justice Cheshin in *Sabeach* v. *IDF Commander*, 368, 369:

> We have in the past supervised the acts of the military commander who intends to demolish the houses of terrorists. We supervised these acts and subjected them to judicial review. We will continue to do so in the future. But the truth is that the review and supervision is not the same as the review and supervision, which we apply to ordinary administrative authorities. The different subject matter itself dictates different ways of intervention. An act of state and an act of war do not change their nature even if they are subject to judicial review.

35. See, e.g., *Morcous* v. *Minister of Defense*, 32; *Turkmahn* v. *Minister of Defense* (1992) 48 (1) PD 217 [English summary: 25 *Isr YHR.* (1995) 347].

36. See, e.g., *Shahin v. IDF Commander in Judea and Samaria* (1986) 41 (1) PD 197. Having ruled that the authorities do not have a duty to allow family unification on the West Bank, the Court did not examine whether their decision not to allow it in the specific case met the demands of reasonableness. See Y. Dinstein, "Unification of Families in the Occupied Territories" (in Hebrew) 13 *Tel Aviv U LR* (1988) 221.

37. The cases on house demolition are examined in detail in chapter 9.

38. See, e.g., *Al-Taliya v. Minister of Defense*.

39. See Shamgar, ed., *Military Government in the Territories*, 450.

40. *Rafiah Approach* case, 183–184. The third judge, Justice Landau, opined that military legislation in occupied territory should be compared to internal directives adopted by administrative authorities. As Justice Kister pointed out, this comparison is inadequate because internal directives only bind the administration itself, while military legislation is directed toward the public.

41. *Abu Itta v. IDF Commander in Judea and Samaria* (1981) 37 (2) PD 197 [English summary: 13 *Isr YHR* (1983) 348].

42. Ibid., 230–231.

43. See the remarks of the Court in *Ja'amait Ascan v. IDF Commander*, 792–793. And also see *Tahaa v. Minister of Defense* (1988) 45 (2) PD 45 in which the Court examined a military order that imposed a bond on parents for the good behavior of their children on the basis of both international law and Israeli administrative law; *Amar v. Minister of Defense* (1983) 38 (4) PD 645, dealing with military orders delaying municipal elections; *Tamimi v. Minister of Defense* (1985) 40 (2) PD 505, dealing with a military order setting up a Bar Association.

44. *Association for Civil Rights in Israel v. Minister of Defense* (1993) 47 (1) PD 267 (*Hamas Deportation* case)]English summary: 23 *Isr YHR* (1993) 353], 290.

45. *Ja'amait Ascan v. IDF Commander*, 793.

NOTES TO CHAPTER 2

1. This attitude to conventional law is a function of the British constitutional system under which treaty-making power is a royal prerogative. In modern times this means that this power is wielded by the executive branch of government. Recognition of rights and duties defined in treaties not incorporated in the law of the land by parliamentary legislation would place law-making power in the hands of the executive, thereby circumventing the legislative supremacy of parliament.

2. For a review of the Israeli approach see R. Lapidot, "Public International Law," in *Forty Years of Israeli Law* (Jerusalem: Harry Sacher Institute for Legislative Research and Comparative Law, 1990), 807.

3. See Proclamation Regarding the Taking of Power by the I.D.F (7.6.1967) in 1 *Proclamations, Orders and Appointments of the Judea and Samaria Command*, 3. A similar order was promulgated relating to Gaza and Northern Sinai, in Israeli hands until handed over to Egypt under the terms of the Peace Treaty between the two countries.

4. Security Provisions Order (West Bank—1967) art. 35, in 1 *Proclamations, Orders and Appointments of Judea and Samaria Command*, 5.

5. The procedure according to which this contingency file was prepared is described by M. Shamgar, "Legal Concepts and Problems of The Israeli Military Government—The Initial Stage," in *Military Government in the Territories Administered by Israel 1967–1980, The Legal Aspects*, ed. M. Shamgar (Jerusalem: Harry Sacher Institute for Legislative Research and Comparative Law, 1982), 13. The draft legislation was written so as to conform to Geneva Convention IV.

6. Speaking in the *Knesset* three weeks after issue of the said order, Minister of Justice Yaakov Shimshon Shapira spoke of the liberation of main parts of the Land of Israel from the burden of foreigners and the legal outlook of the State of Israel that the law, jurisdiction and administration of the state applies to parts of the Land of Israel that are in actual fact in its sphere of sovereignty: (27.6.67) 49 *Divrei Haknesset* 2420.

7. But see A. Roberts, "Prolonged Military Occupation: The Israeli-Occupied Territories Since 1967," 84 *Am J of Int L* (1990) 44, 62, n. 55. Roberts points out that the above provision was issued during the war, while the section repealing it was issued after the war.

8. See A. Rubinstein, "The Changing Status of the 'Territories' (West Bank and Gaza): From Escrow to Legal Mongrel," 8 *Tel Aviv Studies in Law* (1988) 59, 63.

9. See Y. Z. Blum, "The Missing Reversioner: Reflections on the Status of Judea and Samaria," 3 *Isr L Rev* (1968) 279. In a later article Blum argued that Israel had never regarded its status in any area of the Land of Israel as that of an occupier: see Y. Z. Blum, "The Redemption of Zion in International Law," (in Hebrew) 27 *HaPraklit* (1971) 315. Blum's approach was attacked by Y. Dinstein, "The Future Redemption of Zion in International Law," (in Hebrew) 27 *HaPraklit* (1971) 5 and 27 *HaPraklit* (1972) 519. It should be noted that Israel's status in the West Bank and Gaza has generated a great deal of discussion and controversy in academic and political circles. As most of this discussion played no part in Supreme Court decisions it is not reviewed here. For a summary of the divergent views expressed in the discussion see B. Dayanim, "The Israeli Supreme Court and the Deportations of Palestinians: The Interaction of Law and Legitimacy," 30 *Stanford J of Int L* (1994) 115, 143–150.

10. See M. Shamgar, "The Observance of International Law in the Administered Territories," 1 *Isr YHR* (1971) 262.

11. See Shamgar, "The Observance of International Law"; T. Meron, "West Bank and Gaza: Human Rights and Humanitarian Law in the Period of Transition," 9 *Isr YHR* (1979) 106.

12. See UN Doc. A/32/PV. 27 at 83–85, cited in Meron, "West Bank and Gaza," 109, n.6.

13. For a detailed exposition of the Government of Israel's stand on the applicability of the Geneva Convention see E. R. Cohen, *Human Rights in the Israeli-Occupied Territories* (Manchester: Manchester University Press, 1985) 43–56; N. Bar-Yaacov, "The Applicability of the Laws of War to Judea and Samaria (The West Bank) and to the Gaza Strip," 24 *Isr L Rev* (1988) 485.

14. See Shamgar, "Legal Concepts," 32.

15. See Y. Dinstein, "The International Law of Belligerent Occupation and Human Rights," 8 *Isr YHR* (1978) 104, 107; Meron, "West Bank and Gaza."

16. See, e.g., S. M. Boyd, "The Applicability of International Law to the Occupied Territories," 1 *Isr YHR* (1971) 258; A. Roberts, "What is a military occupation?" 54 *Brit Y Int L* (1984) 249, 281–283; R. A. Falk and B. H. Weston, "The Relevance of International Law to Palestinian Rights in the West Bank and Gaza: In Legal Defense of the Intifada," 32 *Harvard Int LJ* (1991) 129, 138–144; HansPeter Gesser, "Protection of the Civilian Population," in *The Handbook of Humanitarian Law in Armed Conflicts*, ed. D. Fleck (Oxford: Oxford University Press, 1995) 209, 244. For a succinct presentation of the Government of Israel's approach on applicability of Geneva Convention IV as well as that of its critics see B. Dayanim, "The Israeli Supreme Court," 143–150.

17. See *Report on the Work of the Conference of Government Experts for the Study of the Conventions for the Protection of War Victims* (Geneva: ICRC, 1947); *Commentary on IV Geneva Convention Relative to the Protection of Civilian Persons in Time of War*, ed. J. S.Pictet (Geneva: ICRC, 1958).

18. See D. Schindler, "The different types of armed conflicts according to the Geneva Conventions and Protocols," II *Recueil des Cours* (1979) 121, 132.

19. See *Commentary on IV Geneva Convention Relative to the Protection of Civilian Persons in Time of War*; Roberts, "What is a military occupation?"

20. See note of Red Cross quoted in 7 *Isr YHR* (1977) 169–170; Shamgar, "Legal Concepts," 32; Dayanim, "The Israeli Supreme Court," 146–148.

21. Roberts, "What is a military occupation?" 282.

22. See Shamgar, "Legal Concepts," 42–43; Bar-Yaacov, "The Applicability of the Laws of War."

23. See Cohen, *Human Rights in the Israeli-Occupied Territories*, 43. But cf. Bar-Yaacov, "The Applicability of the Laws of War," 492–493, who claims that the government's attitude to the applicability of the Hague Regulations is identical to its attitude toward applicability of Geneva Convention IV. The problem with this view is that the government has consistently relied on the Hague Regulations in its arguments before the Supreme Court in order to justify many of its actions.

24. (1971) 26 (1) PD 574 [English summary: 2 *Isr YHR* (1972) 354].

25. Ibid., 580.

26. Ibid., 581–582.

27. See, e.g., *Electricity Corporation for Jerusalem District Ltd.* v. *Minister of Defense* (1972) 27 (1) PD 124 (*Electricity Co. (No. 1)* case) [English summary: 5 *Isr YHR* (1975) 381].

28. *Khelou* v. *Government of Israel* (1972) 27 (2) PD 169, 177 (*Rafiah Approach* case) [English summary: 5 *Isr YHR* (1975) 384].

29. Ibid.

30. Ibid., 181. The third judge on the bench, Justice Kister, did not take a stand on this question, although he remarked that when in the course of a war a country enters territory not previously controlled by it, the military commander has the duty and power to enforce order and proper government in that territory, and that his power is recognized by international law (183–184).

31. *Rafiah Approach* case, 180.

32. See Y. Dinstein, "The Judgment in the *Rafiah Approach* Case" (in Hebrew) 3 *Tel Aviv UL Rev* (1974) 934.

33. *Ayyub* v. *Minister of Defense* (1978) 33 (2) P.D. 113 (*Beth El* case) [English summary: 9 *Isr YHR* (1979) 337].

34. Ibid., 117 (emphasis added).

35. Ibid., 121.

36. Ibid., 127.

37. Ibid.

38. *Dweikat* v. *Government of Israel* (1979) 34 (1) PD 1(*Elon Moreh* case) [English summary: 9 *Isr YHR* (1979) 345].

39. Ibid., 11.

40. Ibid., 13

41. Ibid., 12. Justice Landau went on to state that the scope of the hearing was also delimited by the basic legal principles followed by the IDF in the Territories, which were also according to the laws of war in international law.

42. Ibid., 29. The notion that in deciding on the legal status of a disputed area the Court should bow to the view of the executive was adopted after the Oslo Accords and subsequent agreements. Under these agreements the Occupied Territories were divided into different categories of areas, in each of which there is a different division of powers between Israel and the Palestinian Authority. In *Ali* v. *Minister of Defense* (1994) 50 (2) PD 845, the Court held that it would accept the military commander's statement regarding the demarcation line between the different areas.

43. *Elon Moreh* case, 29.

44. But see the remark of Justice Shamgar in *Shahin* v. *IDF Commander in Judea and Samaria* (1986) 41 (1) PD 197, in which he expressed support for the argument.

45. *Elon Moreh* case, 22.

46. This argument was based on the Area of Jurisdiction and Powers Ordinance, 1948 that provides that the law of the State of Israel shall apply to any part of Palestine which the minister of defense has defined by proclamation as being held by the IDF.

47. It held that the proclamation required by the Area of Jurisdiction and Powers Ordinance, 1948 had not been made.

48. *Haetzni* v. *Minister of Defense* (1980) 34 (3) PD 595, 597.

49. See, e.g., *Electricity Company for Jerusalem District Ltd.* v. *Minister of Energy and Infrastructure* (1980) 35 (2) PD 673, 688 (*Electricity Co. (No. 2)* case). But cf. the leading decision of the President of the Supreme Court, Justice Shamgar, in *Abu Itta* v. *IDF Commander in Judea and Samaria* (1981) 37 (2) PD 197 (*VAT* case) [English summary: 13 *Isr YHR* (1983) 348]. Justice Shamgar quotes the caveats in Justice Landau's decisions in the *Haetzni* and *Beth-El* decisions, although he later explains that the military commander derives his powers from his *de facto* effective control of the area and from the international law of war (228–230).

50. *Ja'amait Ascan* v. *IDF Commander in Judea and Samaria* (1982) 37 (4) PD 785, 792.

51. See *Satiha* v. *IDF Commander in Gaza,* 1985 (4) Takdin-Elyon 10; *Afu* v. *IDF Commander of West Bank* (1988) 42 (2) PD 4 [English summary: 23 *Isr YHR* (1993) 277]. Also see *Kiryat Arba Local Council* v. *Prime Minister* (1994) 48 (5) PD 597. For a forceful challenge to the notion that the regime of belligerent occupation persists after signing of peace agreements see Y. Dinstein, "The International Legal Status of the West Bank and the Gaza Strip—1998," 28 Isr YHR (1998) 37.

52. *Satiha* v. *IDF Commander,* 15.

53. See, e.g., the *Beth El* case, 44; *Mustafa* v. *Military Commander* (1983) 37 (1) PD 158; *Naasralla* v. *I.D.F. Commander of West Bank* (1988) 43 (2) PD 265 [English summary:23 *Isr YHR* (1993) 321]; *Matur* v. *IDF Commander in West Bank* (1989) 43 (3) PD 542; *Kawasme* v. *Minister of Defense* (1980) 35 (1) P.D. 617 (*Kawasme II* case) [English summary: 11 *Isr YHR* (1981) 349].

54. There is, however, the dictum of Justice Witkon regarding this matter that was previously cited from his decision in the *Elon Moreh* case.

55. See B. Rubin, "Adoption of International Treaties in Domestic Law by the Courts" (in Hebrew) 13 *Mishpatim* (1984) 210; H. Sommer, "Eppur si applica—the Geneva Convention (IV) and Israeli Law" (in Hebrew) 11 *Tel Aviv U L Rev* (1986) 263; Rubinstein, "The Changing Status of the 'Territories.'"

56. See D. Kretzmer, "The Application and Interpretation of Geneva Convention IV—Domestic Enforcement and Interpretation," (in Hebrew) 26 *Mishpatim* (1995) 49.

57. See *Afu* and *Ketziot* cases. Also see *Salam* v. *IDF Commander* (1992) 46 (5) PD 467.

58. *Kawasme II* case, 628.

59. See the decision of Justice Barak in *Ja'amait Ascan* case, 794.

60. See the decisions of Justice Bach in *Afu* and *Ketziot* cases.

61. *Ketziot* case, 832.

62. See Kretzmer, "The Application and Interpretation of Geneva Convention IV."

63. In both the *Afu* and *Ketziot* cases, counsel for the authorities expressly argued that the Convention was not enforceable.

NOTES TO CHAPTER 3

1. See *Christian Society for Holy Places* v. *Minister of Defense* (1971) 26 (1) PD 574 [English summary: 2 *Isr YHR* (1972) 354]; *Khelou* v. *Government of Israel* (1972) 27 (2) PD 169 (*Rafiah Approach* case) [English summary: 5 *Isr YHR* (1975) 384].

2. See *Kawasme* v. *Minister of Defense* (1980) 35 (1) PD 617, 636 (*Kawasme II* case) [English summary: 11 *Isr YHR* (1981) 344].

3. See *Ayyub* v. *Minister of Defense* (1978) 33 (2) PD 113 (*Beth El* case) [English summary: 9 *Isr YHR* (1979) 337]; *Dweikat* v. *Government of Israel* (1979) 34 (1) PD 1 (*Elon Moreh* case) [English summary: 9 *Isr YHR* (1979) 345].

4. *Beth El* case, 129.

5. *Elon Moreh* case, 29.

6. Ibid., 30.

7. See Y. Dinstein, "Deportations from Occupied Territories" (in Hebrew) 13 *Tel Aviv U L Rev* (1988) 403.

8. This distinction is supported by the Court's decision in the *Peace Now* case, *Bargil v. Government of Israel* (1991) 47 (4) PD 210, to dismiss the petition as nonjusticiable: see Chapter 1.

9. See *Kawasme II* case, discussed in a later section.

10. See *Kawasme II* case, 620; *Afu v. IDF Commander of West Bank* (1987) 42 (1) PD 4 [English summary: 23 *Isr YHR* (1993) 277]; *Naasralla v. IDF Commander of West Bank* (1988) 43 (2) PD 265 [English summary:23 *Isr YHR* (1993) 321]. This aspect of the Court's decisions in deportation cases will be discussed in detail in Chapter 10.

11. See *Afu* case.

12. See, e.g., Y. Dinstein, *The Laws of War* (in Hebrew) (Tel Aviv: Schocken, 1983), 225; G. von Glahn, *Law Among Nations,* 6th ed (New York: Macmillan, 1992), 782; E. R.Cohen, *Human Rights in the Israeli-Occupied Territories, 1967–1982* (Manchester: Manchester University Press, 1985), 110; T. Meron, *Human Rights and Humanitarian Norms as Customary Law* (Oxford: Clarendon Press, 1989), 48 n. 131; C. Greenwood, "The Administration of Occupied Territory in International Law" in *International Law and the Administration of the Occupied Territories: Two Decades of Israeli Occupation of the West Bank and Gaza Strip,* ed. E. Playfair (Oxford: Clarendon Press, 1992), 241, 294 n. 29. Also see B. Dayanim, "The Israeli Supreme Court and the Deportations of Palestinians: The Interaction of Law and Legitimacy," 30 *Stanford J of Int L* (1994) 115, 157–166. For views supporting that of the government see T. S. Kuttner, "Israel and the West Bank: Aspects of the Law of Belligerent Occupation," 7 *Isr YHR* (1977) 166, 214–217; C. V. Reicin, "Preventive Detention, Curfews, Demolitions of Houses, and Deportations: An Analysis of Measures Employed by Israel in the Administered Territories," 8 *Cardozo LR* (1987) 515, 528.

13. See *Commentary on IV Geneva Convention Relative to the Protection of Civilian Persons in Time of War,* ed. J. S.Pictet (Geneva: ICRC, 1958), 279.

14. *Awwad v. Commander of Judea and Samaria* (1979) 33 (3) PD 309 [English summary: 9 *Isr YHR* (1979) 343].

15. It should be noted, however, that Justice Shamgar concurred with Justice Sussman, but saw fit to state that by taking a stand on the substantive meaning of the Convention, the Court was not ruling on its *applicability* to the area because it had not heard argument on the question. No mention was made of the *domestic enforceability* of the Convention.

16. *Awwad* case, 316.

17. It would also seem that Pictet's emphasis was not on the prevention of arbitrariness as the guiding object of the Convention, but on the distinction between purposeful actions by the occupying power and dangers due to military operations. The relevant passage in Pictet's commentary states that "the main object of the Convention is to protect a strictly defined category of civilians from arbitrary action, and not from dangers due to the military operations them-

selves." *Commentary on IV Geneva Convention Relative to the Protection of Civilian Persons*, 10.

18. Article 78 states: "If the Occupying Power considers it necessary, for imperative reasons of security, to take safety measures concerning protected persons, it may, at the most, subject them to assigned residence or to internment."

19. In his decision in the *Afu* case, discussed later, Justice Shamgar suggested that the "evacuation" mentioned in the second paragraph is an exception to deportations that provides an indication of the meaning of the term "deportations."

20. *Kawasme II* case, 627.

21. (1985) 39 (3) PD 645 [English summary: 16 *Isr YHR* (1986) 329].

22. See M. Shamgar, "The Observance of International Law in the Administered Territories," 1 *Isr YHR* (1971) 262.

23. *Na'azal* case, 654. Surprising as it may seem, Justice Shamgar's view received support from Professor Yoram Dinstein, a harsh critic of the stand that the prohibition on deportations in article 49 is not absolute. Dinstein writes that "the word 'other' should be interpreted as a state which is not the the the deportees' state of citizenship." Y. Dinstein, "Deportation of the Mayors from Judea" (in Hebrew) 7 *Tel Aviv U. L. Rev* (1986) 158, 170–171. But see Kuttner, "Israel and the West Bank," 216, n. 158.

24. This point was apparently appreciated by D. Shefi, "The Reports of the U.N. Special Committees on Israeli Practices in the Territories—A Survey and Evaluation," in *Military Government in the Territories Administered by Israel,* 285. Shefi, who at the time of writing was advocate-general of the IDF, supported Shamgar's interpretation but explained it in the following way:

> It cannot be argued that deportation of agitators to the east bank of the Jordan constitutes deportation to "any other country" within the meaning of the art. 49, for *from the point of view of those who absorb the deportees on the east bank*, the place from which they were deported is not "a different country" (305, emphasis added).

Shefi fails to explain why the point of view should be that of the country receiving the deportees rather than the country deporting them.

25. See Vienna Convention of 23 May 1969 on the Law of Treaties.

26. *Afu* case, 27. Justice Shamgar overlooked the fact that in a previous case, which dealt with expulsion of infiltrators from the area after they had been released from prison, he had dismissed out of hand the argument that the expulsion was prohibited under article 49 of the Geneva Convention. He stated: "Whatever the interpretation of article 49, the thesis has never been advanced that it grants immunity from expulsion from the area to a person who entered illegally after the military rule began. There is no hint of this thesis in the accepted interpretation of the article, nor is there any logic in it." *Kasarawi* v. *Minister of Defense* (1985) 39 (3) PD 401, 410 [English summary: 16 *Isr YHR* (1986) 332].

27. And also see Dinstein, "Deportations from Occupied Territories," 411.

28. *Afu* case, 71.

29. See *Al-Teen* v. *Minister of Defense* (1972) 27 (1) PD 481. Also see

Arnon v. Attorney General (1972) 27 (1) PD 233 in which the Court held that only residents of the area are protected persons and that Israeli residents are therefore not entitled to protection under the convention.

30. See article 4 of Geneva Convention IV.

31. *Afu* case, 24.

32. See *Arjov v. IDF Commander of Judea and Samaria* (1985) 42 (1) PD 353, 366, 368.

33. See Dinstein, "Deportations from Occupied Territories," 410.

34. J. Stone, *No Peace, No Law in the Middle East* (Sidney: Maitland Publications PTY, 1969), 17.

35. See Dayanim, "The Israeli Supreme Court," 120–124. It should be noted that after Stone's lecture was published, individuals against whom a deportation order had been issued argued that they should be interned rather than deported. Their argument was not accepted. *Marer v. Minister of Defence* (1971) 25 (1) PD 141.

36. *Afu* case, 75.

37. Pictet's commentary refers to the mass deportations carried out by the Nazis and adds: "The thought of the physical and mental suffering endured by these 'displaced persons', among whom there were a great many women, children, old people and sick, can only lead to thankfulness for the prohibition embodied in this paragraph, which is intended to forbid such hateful practices for all time." *Commentary on IV Geneva Convention Relative to the Protection of Civilian Persons*, 279. This text in no way intimates that outlawing the type of deportations carried out by the Nazis was the *purpose* of article 49.

38. According to article 6 of the Nuremburg Charter, war crimes include "deportations to slave labor or for any other purpose of civilian population of or in occupied territory"; crimes against humanity include "deportation or other inhumane acts committed against any civilian population before or during the war." Office of US Chief Counsel for Prosecution of Axis Criminality, *Nazi Conspiring and Aggression* (Vol. I, 1946), 5.

39. For the drafting history of Geneva Convention IV see: *Commentary on IV Geneva Convention Relative to the Protection of Civilian Persons*, 3–9; D. Schindler and J. Toman, eds., *The Laws of Armed Conflicts—A Collection of Conventions, Resolutions and Other Documents* (Leiden: Sijthoff, 1973), 417; *Report on the Work of the Preliminary Conference of National Red Cross Societies for the Study of the Conventions and of Various Problems Relative to the Red Cross* (Geneva: ICRC, July 26–August 3, 1946); *Report on the Work of the Conference of Government Experts for the Study of the Conventions for the Protection of War Victims* (Geneva: ICRC, April 14–26, 1947).

40. See *Report on the Work of the Conference of Government Experts for the Study of the Conventions for the Protection of War Victims*.

41. The full text of the Tokyo Draft can be found at http://www.icrc.org/ihl. nsf/.

42. *Report on the Work of the Conference of Government Experts for the Study of the Conventions for the Protection of War Victims*, 289.

43. Article 27 of the Committee's draft states as follows: "Individual or collective deportations or transfers, carried out under physical or moral constraint,

to places outside occupied territories, and for whatever motives, are prohibited."

44. See Dinstein, "Deportations from Occupied Territories."

45. See *Shachshir* v. *IDF Commander on West Bank* (1988) 43 (2) PD 242; *Naasralla* v. *IDF Commander*; *Matur* v. *IDF Commander on West Bank* (1988) 43 (3) PD 542.

46. See *Naasralla* v. *IDF Commander*. Justice Bach pointed out that if his view of article 49 is accepted, the part of article 49 that deals with individual deportations is not part of customary law and it may therefore not be enforced by the Court. On the other hand, if the view of the majority that article 49 applies only to Nazi-type deportations is accepted, individual deportations on security grounds are not prohibited under the Convention. Also see *Matur* v. *IDF Commander*.

47. See *Sajedia* v. *Minister of Defense* (1988) 42 (3) PD 801 (*Ketziot* case) [English summary: 23 *Isr YHR* (1993) 288].

48. The statutory provision is to be found in the Emergency Regulations (Judea, Samaria, and Gaza—Jurisdiction over Offences and Legal Assistance), 1967. As these regulations were extended by *Knesset* legislation, they have the status of a *Knesset* statute.

49. *Ketziot* case, 812.

50. Ibid.

51. He also stated that the view he had taken in the *Afu* case, according to which deportation of an individual from the occupied territory is absolutely prohibited, must hold even more strongly "when we are dealing with the transfer of thousands of people." *Ketziot* case, 827.

52. *Ketziot* case, 830.

53. See *Commentary on IV Geneva Convention Relative to the Protection of Civilian Persons in Time of War*, 18.

54. Ibid., 21.

55. Shamgar, "Legal Concepts," 39. The emphasis is not in the original text.

56. See *Shahin* v. *IDF Commander in Judea and Samaria* (1986) 41 (1) PD 197 [English summary: 18 *Isr YHR* (1988) 241]. The emphasis is not in the original text.

57. See, e.g., *Ha'aretz* v. *Israel Electricity Company* (1977) 31 (2) PD 281 [English summary: 12 *Isr YHR* (1982) 290]; *Hilron Ltd.* v. *Fruit Council* (1976) 30 (3) PD 645.

58. See J. G. Merrills, *Development of International Law by the European Court of Human Rights* (Manchester: Manchester University Press, 1988), 70–71. Also see L. Henkin, "Introduction" in *The International Bill of Rights*, ed. L. Henkin (New York: Columbia University Press, 1981) 24.

NOTES TO CHAPTER 4

1. See Y. Dinstein, "Power of Legislation in the Occupied Territories" (in Hebrew) 2 *Tel Aviv U L Rev* (1972/3) 505, 509; "The Israel Supreme Court and the Law of Belligerent Occupation: Article 43 of the Hague Regulations," 25 *Isr YHR* (1996) 1. Dinstein's explanation that article 43 deals with two separate

principles was accepted by the Court in *Tamimi v. Minister of Defense* (1985) 41 (4) PD 57, 62. For a detailed discussion of the background and subsequent development of article 43 see E. Benvenisti, *The International Law of Occupation* (Princeton N.J.: Princeton University Press, 1993), 32–58.

2. See Benvenisti, *The International Law of Occupation*, 10.

3. *Christian Society for Holy Places v. Minister of Defense* (1971) 26 (1) PD 574 [English summary: 2 *Isr YHR* (1972) 354].

4. Under the Jordanian Labor Law, 1960, if mediation attempts fail, a labor dispute is to be referred to an arbitration council. It was discovered, however, that the arbitration council could not be appointed, as under the law, two of its members were to be appointed by associations of employers and employees that simply did not exist. The amendment in the Jordanian Labor Law provided that in the absence of representative employers' and employees' associations, council members would be appointed by the employer and employees involved in the particular dispute.

5. This is the view of E. H. Schwenk, "Legislative Power of the Military Occupant under Article 43, Hague Regulations," 54 *Yale LJ* (1945) 393.

6. Ibid., 398–399.

7. See *Tabeeb v. Minister of Defense* (1981) 36 (2) PD 622, 629 [English summary: 13 *Isr YHR* (1983) 364].

8. This view is criticized by Dinstein, who argues that Justice Cohn wrongly superimposed the first part of article 43 (the duty to ensure and restore) on the second part (the duty to respect the law in force). Dinstein, "The Israel Supreme Court and the Law of Belligerent Occupation."

9. *Christian Society for Holy Places v. Minister of Defense*, 587.

10. Dinstein, "Power of Legislation in the Occupied Territories."

11. See *Tabeeb v. Minister of Defense*; *Ja'amait Ascan v. IDF Commander in Judea and Samaria* (1982) 37 (4) PD 785, 798; *Abu Itta v. IDF Commander in Judea and Samaria* (1981) 37 (2) PD 197, 309 (VAT case) [English summary: 13 *Isr YHR* (1983) 348].

12. See, e.g., *Tag v. Minister of Defense* (1991) 46 (5) PD 467, 474 [English summary: 25 *Isr YHR* (1995) 330].

13. *Awwad v. Military Commander in Judea and Samaria* (1979) 33 (3) PD 309 [English summary: 9 *Isr YHR* (1979) 343].

14. Ibid., 316. This view was repeated by Justice Ben Porat in *Afu v. IDF Commander of West Bank* (1987) 42 (1) PD 4 [English summary: 23 Isr YHR (1993) 277].

15. See *Al-Taliya v. Minister of Defense* (1978) 33 (3) PD 505.

16. See *Amar v. Minister of Defense* (1983) 38 (4) PD 645.

17. See *Tahaa v. Minister of Defense* (1988) 45 (2) PD 45.

18. *VAT* case, 310.

19. *Tamimi v. Minister of Defense*, 59.

20. Another exception is *Insh el-Usra Society v. IDF Commander in Judea and Samaria* (1988) 43 (3) PD 673.

21. See Proclamation Regarding Government and Law (Area of West Bank) (No. 2), 1967 issued on 7 June 1967 and Proclamation Regarding Government and Law (Gaza Strip and Northern Sinai) (No. 2), 1967 issued on 8 June 1967.

22. For a review of these changes see R. Shehadeh, *Occupier's Law: Israel and the West Bank*, 2nd ed. (Washington: Institute for Palestine Studies, 1988) and E. Benvenisti, *Legal Dualism: The Absorption of the Occupied Territories into Israel* (Boulder: Westview, 1990).

23. *Christian Society for Holy Places* v. *Minister of Defense*, 582.

24. Ibid., 584.

25. See Dinstein, "Power of Legislation in the Occupied Territories," and *VAT* case, 309.

26. *Christian Society for Holy Places* v. *Minister of Defense*, 588.

27. See *Tabeeb* v. *Minister of Defense*, 631–630; *VAT* case, 309; *Tamimi* v. *Minister of Defense*, 62.

28. See Schwenk, "Legislative Power of the Military Occupant," 393.

29. *Tabeeb* v. *Minister of Defense*, 632

30. *VAT* case, 310.

31. See *Dudin* v. *IDF Commander in West Bank Area* (1991) 46 (1) PD 89.

32. See Schwenk, "Legislative Power of the Military Occupant," 400–401; M. S. McDougal and F. P. Feliciano, *The International Law of War* (Dordrecht: Martinus Nijhoff, 1994), 757; Dinstein, "The International Law of Belligerent Occupation and Human Rights," 8 *Isr YHR* (1978) 104, 122. It would seem that the original intention was that the necessity to change the law must be based on the military needs of the occupying power, but it was later recognized that ensuring and promoting public order and public life could also create the necessity. Benvenisti, *The International Law of Occupation*, 12–16.

33. *Electricity Company for Jerusalem District* v. *Minister of Defense* (1972) 27 (1) PD 124 (*Electricity Co. (No. 1)* case) [English summary: 5 Isr YHR (1975) 381].

34. Ibid., 138–139.

35. The political background to the commander's decision, which involved a clash between the integrationist policies of Minister of Defense Moshe Dayan, and anti-integrationist views of other leading members of the ruling Labor Party, is discussed by M. Negbi, *Justice Under Occupation: The Israeli Supreme Court versus the Military Administration in the Occupied Territories* (Jerusalem: Cana Publishing House, 1981), 123–129.

36. See E. Playfair, "Playing on Principle? Israel's Justification for its Administrative Acts in the Occupied West Bank," in *International Law and the Administration of Occupied Territories*, ed. E. Playfair (Oxford: Clarendon Press, 1992) 205, 216–220.

37. *Electricity Co. (No. 1)* case, 138. Also see *Economic Corporation for Jerusalem Ltd.* v. *IDF Commander in Judea and Samaria* (1993) 49 (1) PD 89, in which the Court held that article 43 is a general provision that must be interpreted so as to take into account changing conditions in the occupied territory. These include the establishment of Israeli settlements. (The Court upheld the power given to the local council of Israeli settlements to impose municipal rates similar to those imposed in Israel.)

38. See A. Pellet, "The Destruction of Troy Will Not Take Place," in *International Law and the Administration of Occupied Territories*, 169.

39. See Playfair, "Playing on Principle?"

40. *Electricity Company for Jerusalem District* v. *Minister of Energy and Infrastructure* (1980) 35 (2) PD 673 (*Electricity Co. (No. 2)* case) [English summary: 11 *Isr YHR* (1981) 354].

41. For a full discussion of the background to this case see Negbi, *Justice Under Occupation*, 129–142.

42. *Electricity Co. (No. 2)* case, 688. It would seem that in making this assumption Justice Kahan ignored the fact that, as previously pointed out, article 43 deals with two questions: the governmental duties of the occupant and the restrictions on his power to change local law.

43. Ibid., 689.

44. Ibid., 690.

45. Ibid.

46. The Court held, however, that the minister could not implement the acquisition of the East Jerusalem Company unless he made sure that it would not affect the company's operations on the West Bank, and even ordered him to consult with the company's directors before making a final decision. As Negbi shows, at the time these conditions made acquisition almost impossible. Negbi, *Justice Under Occupation*, 141.

47. *Ja'amait Ascan* v. *IDF Commander*, 794–795.

48. Ibid., 800.

49. Ibid., 812.

50. Ibid., 813.

51. Also see *Hebron Municipality* v. *Minister of Defense* (1994) 50 (2) PD 617, in which the Court upheld the reasonableness of a highway plan that involved expropriation of agricultural land.

52. These amendments to the Jordanian law were upheld in *Dudin* v. *IDF Commander in West Bank Area*. For a description of the Jordanian planning laws and the changes introduced by military legislation see A. Coon, *Town Planning under Military Occupation, An Examination of the Law and Practice of Town Planning in the Occupied West Bank* (Aldershot: Dartmouth, 1992) 39–62.

53. This point is developed by A. Cassese, "Powers and Duties of an Occupant in Relation to Land and Natural Resourses," in *International Law and the Administration of Occupied Territories*, 419, 440–441. Also see Playfair, "Playing on Principle?"

54. *Dweikat* v. *Government of Israel* (1979) 34 (1) PD 1 (*Elon Moreh* case) [English summary: 9 *Isr YHR* (1979) 345].

55. It should be stressed that even after the Oslo Accords and subsequent agreements there remained a great deal of ambiguity in the government's approach to the status of the West Bank and Gaza.

56. At the time the new tax was imposed, there were open borders and free flow of labor, goods and services between Israel and the Occupied Territories. There was a well-founded fear that if the tax were to be imposed in Israel only, Israeli consumers and producers would flock to purchase goods and services in the Occupied Territories, where they would not have to pay VAT.

57. The argument is discussed at length by Y. Dinstein, "VAT (value added tax) in the Occupied Territories" (in Hebrew) 10 *Tel Aviv U L Rev* (1984) 159.

58. *VAT* case, 310

59. Ibid., 327–328.

60. See G. von Glahn, "Taxation under Belligerent Occupation," in *International Law and the Administration of Occupied Territories*, 341, 372. Von Glahn was not persuaded that there was convincing evidence that the new tax served to improve, or even maintain, civil life of the population or the needs of the IDF.

NOTES TO CHAPTER 5

1. Soon after the settlement policy in the Territories was initiated the minister of defense, Moshe Dayan, stated:

> I regard settlement as the most important thing and the factor that has the greatest weight in creating political facts, on the basis of the assumption—as the Prime Minister has also stated—that we will not leave a place in which we have established a settlement or outpost. Therefore, in determining the map and in determining our desire for a new map, I see settlement as the most symbolic factor and the one that will most bind us ourselves.

Statement of Moshe Dayan of December 1968 cited in R. Pedatzur, *The Triumph of Embarrassment, Israel and the Territories After the Six-Day War* (in Hebrew) (Tel Aviv: Bitan, 1996) 161. Also see M. Benvenisti, *The West Bank Data Project, A Survey of Israel's Policies* (Washington: American Enterprise Institute, 1984) 49–63; S. Gazit, *Trapped* (in Hebrew) (Tel Aviv: Zmora-Bitan, 1999) 217–219.

2. For discussion of the background to the settlement policy see Benvenisti, *The West Bank Data Project*; D. Peretz, *The West Bank, History, Politics, Society and Economy* (Boulder: Westview, 1986) 59–78; N. Aruri, ed., *Occupation: Israel over Palestine* (London: Zed Books, 1984) 117–164; I. Peleg, *Human Rights in the West Bank and Gaza: Legacy and Politics* (Syracuse, N.Y: Syracuse University Press, 1995) 22–28; Pedatzur, *The Triumph of Embarrassment*, 160–255; I. Lustick, *Unsettled States, Disputed Lands: Britain and Ireland, France and Algeria, Israel and the West Bank-Gaza* (Cornell: Cornell University Press, 1993) 7–25, 351–384; Gazit, *Trapped*, 217–249.

3. M. Drobles, *Settlement in Judea and Samaria: Strategy, Policy and Planning* (in Hebrew) (Jerusalem: WZO Settlement Division, 1980) 3.

4. Ibid.

5. For a description of the views of the religious/nationalistic supporters of settlements see R. I. Friedman, *Zealots for Zion, Inside Israel's West Bank Settlement Movement* (New York: Random House, 1992); D. Hiro, *Sharing the Promised Land* (London: Coronet Books, 1996), ch. 8.

6. On the various arguments made in support of settlements see Gazit, *Trapped*, 218.

7. See Y. Dinstein, "Settlement and Expulsion in the Occupied Territories," (in Hebrew) 6 *Tel Aviv U L Rev* (1979) 188; E. Benvenisti, *The International Law of Occupation* (Princeton: Princeton University Press, 1993) 140; G.

von Glahn, *Law Among Nations*, 6th ed. (New York: Macmillan, 1992); A. Roberts, "Prolonged Military Occupation: The Israeli-Occupied Territories 1967–1988," in *International Law and the Administration of Occupied Territories*, ed. E. Playfair (Oxford: Clarendon Press, 1992) 25, 65–68. The Israeli government's reply to this argument has been twofold: (1) that article 49 only applies to forced transfers and (2) that the object of article 49 is to prevent displacement of the local population: *The Rule of Law in the Areas Administered by Israel* (Tel Aviv: Israel National Section of the International Commission of Jurists, 1981) 54–55; D. Shefi, "The Reports of the U.N. Special Committees on Israeli Practices in the Territories—A Survey and Evaluation," in *Military Government in the Territories Administered by Israel 1967–1980, The Legal Aspects*, ed. M. Shamgar (Jerusalem: Harry Sacher Institute for Legislative Research and Comparative Law, 1982) 285, 313–317.

8. See *Ja'amait Ascan v. IDF Commander in Judea and Samaria* (1982) 37 (4) PD 787.

9. See A. Cassese, "Powers and Duties of an Occupant in Relation to Land and Natural Resources" in *International Law and the Administration of Occupied Territories*, 419, 431. Cassese argues that the final paragraph of article 49 of Geneva Convention IV is "the logical conclusion of the requirement of customary international law whereby the occupant is not allowed to use the property of the occupied country, or of its inhabitants, for the furtherance of its own economic or other interests."

10. See article 46 of the Hague Regulations.

11. See article 52 of the Hague Regulations.

12. See I. Lustick, "Israel and the West Bank After Elon Moreh: The Mechanics of De Facto Annexation," 35 *Middle East Journal* (1981) 557, 564. Lustick describes the proposals considered in government circles following the Court's decision in the *Elon Moreh* case (discussed later) that ordered dismantling a settlement established on private land requisitioned for military needs. These proposals included legislation to restrict the Court's jurisdiction in cases relating to land use on the West Bank. Also see Gazit, *Trapped*, 243–244. Gazit claims that the settlers who joined the *Elon Moreh* case wanted the government to lose the case so that the *Knesset* would enact legislation restricting the Court's jurisdiction over actions in the Occupied Territories and giving the government unrestricted powers to establish new settlements there.

13. See chapter 1.

14. See *Ayreib v. Appeals Committee* (1984) 40 (2) PD 57.

15. See *Bargil v. Government of Israel* (1991) 47 (4) PD 210 (*Peace Now* case). Also see *I'ad v. IDF Commander in Judea and Samaria*, 1999 (3) Takdin-Elyon 1771, in which the Court held that a petition relating to a regional land use plan that would link the civilian settlement of Ma'ale Adumim to Jerusalem was nonjusticiable.

16. See *Ayyub v. Minister of Defense* (1978) 33 (2) PD 113, 124 (*Beth El* case) [English summary: 9 *Isr YHR* (1979) 337]; *Dweikat v. Government of Israel* (1979) 34 (1) PD 1 (*Elon Moreh* case) [English summary: 9 *Isr YHR* (1979) 345].

17. *Khelou v. Government of Israel* (1972) 27 (2) PD 169 (*Rafiah Approach* case) [English summary: 5 *Isr YHR* (1975) 384].

18. For the detailed background to the case see M. Negbi, *Justice Under Occupation: The Israeli Supreme Court Versus the Military Administration in the Occupied Territories* (in Hebrew) (Jerusalem: Cana Publishing House, 1981) 29–33; S. Gazit, *Trapped*, 73–75.

19. *Rafiah Approach* case, 175.

20. *Nachal* is an army unit whose members combine military service with service in agricultural settlements (usually kibbutzim). A *Nachal* outpost is manned by soldiers who also engage in cultivating the land. After some time many of these outposts are converted into civilian settlements.

21. See chapters 1 and 2.

22. *Rafiah Approach* case, 176. Writing in response to the *Rafiah Approach* case, Professor Yoram Dinstein was critical of the way the Court sidestepped the settlement question entirely. Dinstein's view was that establishment of a *Nachal* outpost manned by soldiers is no different from establishing an army camp that may be removed when conditions no longer require its presence in the area on security grounds. "One who reads the judgment by itself cannot know if Israel adhered or not to the demands of article 49 [of the Geneva Convention]." Y. Dinstein, "The Judgment in the *Rafiah Approach* Case," (in Hebrew) 3 *Tel Aviv U L Rev* (1973) 934, 941

23. *Rafiah Approach* case, 177.

24. Ibid., 181. The third justice on the bench, Justice Kister, did not refer to the question of settlement. He agreed that the Court would not hasten to intervene in the "actions of a military commander or those acting on his behalf, when he acts to protect the security of the areas under his control" and that given the facts set out in the decision of Justice Landau, there was no place for intervention in the present case (185). He did, however, stress that the residents had only been moved 3 kilometers from their places of residence, that they were allowed to work their fields during the day, and that they had been compensated (185).

25. See B. Geva, "The Question of the Balance between Security Considerations and the Protection of Human and Civil Rights" (in Hebrew) 5 *Mishpatim* (1973/4) 685.

26. This attitude was manifest in another land case decided some time after the *Rafiah Approach* case. Landowners in the village of Anata, who claimed that an area including houses and cultivated land had been closed for the purpose of establishing a civilian settlement, obtained a temporary injunction to stop work on the land. In reply the government submitted evidence that the area of land closed was much smaller than claimed by the petitioners, that there were no houses on it, and that most of it was fallow. More important, however, the government declared that the purpose of the closure was not to establish a settlement but to construct important military installations. Counsel for the petitioners conceded the power of the army to requisition land for military installations, but argued that there was no need to requisition that particular land as the installations could be placed elsewhere. The Court was not impressed with the argument. Justice Sussman stated that the "decision where the camp has to be is a pure military decision, in which this court cannot interfere, as long as it hasn't been proven that it was influenced by improper considerations or from bad faith." *Salame* v. *Minister of Defense* (1978) 33 (1) PD 471, 473]English summary: 10 *Isr YHR* (1980) 330].

27. The *Beth El* case was not the first attempt by Palestinians to challenge use of requisitioned private land for the establishment of a civilian settlement. Shortly after the Likud government came to power it was decided to establish the settlement of Neve Tsuf. Part of the land on which the settlement was to be established was private land. When the landowners challenged requisition of their land for the settlement the government decided not to defend its action. The orders for the requisition of the private land were cancelled and the settlement was confined to the public lands. The case of the private landowners therefore became moot. Gazit, *Trapped*, 240–241.

28. *Ayyub* v. *Minister of Defense.*

29. See *Davar*, 20 May 1977, 3.

30. This agreement was not formally included in the Accords as Mr. Begin claimed that he did not have the political authority to make such an agreement. However, in a letter to President Carter that was part of the Camp David deal, Mr. Begin promised to put a free vote to Israel's *Knesset* regarding "removal of Israeli settlers from the northern and southern Sinai areas." See 15 *Isr LR* (1980) 293.

31. *Beth El* case, 116–117.

32. Article 52 of the Hague Regulations states: "Requisitions in kind and services shall not be demanded from local authorities or inhabitants except for the needs of the army of occupation." Justice Landau pointed out in his opinion that this article has been interpreted as referring also to requisition of land.

33. Referring to his opinion in the *Rafiah Approach* case Justice Witkon said:

> One does not have to be an expert in military and security matters in order to appreciate that it is easier for terrorist elements to act in territory inhabited only by a population that is either indifferent or sympathetic towards the enemy than in territory in which there are also people who are likely to keep a watch over them and to inform the authorities of any suspicious movement. The terrorists will not find refuge among them, nor be provided with assistance and equipment. The matter is simple and there is no need to go into details. We will merely mention that according to the respondents' affidavits, the settlers are subject to the authority of the army, whether formally or by virtue of the circumstances. They are there because of the army and with its permission. I therefore still hold by the view that appealed to me in the *Rafiah Approach* case, that Jewish settlement in occupied territory—as long as the state of belligerency continues—fulfils real security needs. *Beth El* case, 119.

Also see the view of Justice Landau (ibid., 124) and of Justice Ben Porat (ibid., 132).

34. As the Court demanded positive proof that the specific settlements involved in the case fulfilled a security function, one commentator, writing a few years after the decision was handed down, claimed that while the government won the battle in the *Beth El* case, in fact it lost the war: see Negbi, *Justice Under Occupation*, 46.

35. On this fundamental duty see Benvenisti, *The International Law of Belligerent Occupation*, 3; C. Greenwood, "The Administration of Occupied Territory in International Law" in *International Law and the Administration of Occupied Territories*, 241.

36. *Beth El* case, 123.

37. Ibid., 131. Also see the concurring opinion of Justice Ben Porat who stressed the relativity of the term "permanent."

38. *Amira v. Minister of Defense* (1979) 34 (1) PD 90 [English summary: 10 *Isr YHR* (1980) 331].

39. General Peled had been a member of the General Staff during the 1967 War. Soon after the War he retired and began taking a radical stand in favor of establishing an independent Palestinian state in the West Bank and Gaza. During the 1970s he was one of the first prominent Israelis who held talks with members of the PLO. In 1984 he was elected to the *Knesset* on behalf of the joint Jewish-Arab Progressive List for Peace.

40. Ibid.

41. Ibid., 95.

42. *Dweikat v. Government of Israel.*

43. *Elon Moreh* case, 16.

44. Ibid., 17.

45. Ibid., 18.

46. Ibid., 19.

47. In the *Beth El* case the settlers' application to join the proceedings was rejected by the Court's president. Negbi, *Justice Under Occupation*, 40.

48. Dagania was the first *kevutza* (communal settlement) founded by Zionist settlers near the Sea of Galilee in 1910; Netanya is a coastal town founded as a village by settlers from the Galilee in 1929.

49. *Elon Moreh* case, 22.

50. The petitioners submitted affidavits by two retired generals (one of whom was a former chief-of-staff) who negated the security arguments. Justice Witkon, who had written the main opinion in the *Beth El* case, stressed that the government had not lifted the onus of proving that the requisition was required for military needs.

51. The responses to the decision are discussed by Lustick, "Israel and the West Bank After Elon Moreh" and Gazit, *Trapped*, 244–248.

52. It should be noted that Plia Albeck, who at the time headed the civil division in the State Attorney's office, claims that the Likud government instituted the policy of establishing settlements on government land before the *Elon Moreh* case. She explains that this was a function of the capitalist approach of the Likud government, which objected to taking private property for public use. P. Albeck, *Lands in Judea and Samaria* (in Hebrew) (Tel Aviv-Jaffa District Committee of Israel Chamber of Advocates, lecture given on 28.5.85 at Beit Hapraklit).

53. For a detailed analysis of the land issue see E. Zamir, *State Lands in Judea and Samaria—Legal Survey* (in Hebrew) (Jerusalem: Jerusalem Institute for Israel Studies, 1985); R. Shehadeh, *Occupier's Law, Israel and the West Bank*, Revised edition (Washington: Institute for Palestine Studies, 1988), chapter I; Albeck, *Lands in Judea and Samaria.*

54. See Order Regarding Settlement of Land and Water (Judea and Samaria) (No. 291), 1968.

55. See Zamir, *State Lands in Judea and Samaria,* 27.

56. Order Relating to Government Property (Area of Judea and Samaria) (No. 59), 1967.

57. Government property is defined in the order and includes any property that belongs to the Hashemite Kingdom of Jordan or to any corporation in which the said kingdom has rights.

58. See M. Benvenisti, *The West Bank Data Project,* 34.

59. Ibid. The Ottoman land law that was in force on the West Bank when the IDF entered in 1967 distinguishes between five categories of land: *mulk, miri, mukafa, mawat,* and *matrouk.* Rights by prescription can only be acquired in *miri* land, in which the nominal ownership remains in perpetuity in the hands of the sultan. Thus, all land in which there was no proof of ownership by a *koushan* or registration was to be regarded as state land, unless it was *miri* land in which rights had been acquired through prescription. Albeck, *Lands in Judea and Samaria,* 8.

60. The requirement of possession and cultivation for ten years is based on article 78 of the Ottoman Land Law that was still in force when the IDF entered the area in 1967. According to this provision, if a person has been in possession of and has cultivated *miri* land for a period of ten years, he or she is entitled to demand that the land be registered in his or her name.

61. Albeck, Lands *in Judea and Samaria,* 8.

62. Drobles, *Settlement in Judea and Samaria,* 3.

63. (1981) 36 (1) PD 701.

64. This presumption is criticized by Cassese, ""Powers and Duties of an Occupant," 437–438.

65. On the categories of land recognized by Ottoman law see note 59. The most common form of land is *miri,* in which the sultan nominally holds ownership, but private individuals may gain right of use. In practice, once a private person has gained right of use, his or her right is equivalent to title. Some restrictions do, however, apply to such land. Thus, for instance, a person may not decide on the disposition of the land by will; it passes to all the heirs of the owner.

66. Justice Matza adopted a similar approach in *I'ad* v. *IDF Commander.* The case related to a regional land use plan prepared by the Government of Israel and the municipality of Ma'ale Adumim, a civilian settlement east of Jerusalem. The plan had two objectives: development of Ma'ale Adumim and creating an urban area that would unite this settlement with Jerusalem. Palestinian villagers in the area objected to the plan. They argued that it was drawn up in order to further Israeli interests and not the interests of the local West Bank population. In replying to this argument Justice Matza emphasized that the plan applied to state lands. The only question in his mind was therefore whether the plan affected legitimate interests of the villagers from the petitioners' villages. Because they had not proved that the plan harmed their interests their petition could not succeed. (The other two judges on the bench rejected the petition on grounds of nonjusticiability.)

67. *Ayreib* v. *Appeals Committee*, 69.

68. *Bargil* v. *Government of Israel.*

69. These were the Jericho–Ein Gedi highway, the Jordan Valley highway, and the Alon Highway. Benvenisti, *The West Bank Data Project*, 23.

70. Introduction to the "Development Plan for Highways" that is part of the *Master Plan for Settlement in Judea and Samaria and Development Plan for the Area for the years 1983–1986*, prepared by the Planning Team for Judea and Samaria of the Settlement Division of the WZO in association with the Ministry of Agriculture (1983), 27.

71. *Tabeeb* v. *Minister of Defense* (1981) 36 (2) PD 622 [English summary: 13 *Isr YHR* (1983) 364].

72. Ibid., 636.

73. Ibid., 637.

74. *Ja'amait Ascan* v. *IDF Commander in Judea and Samaria.*

75. *Tabeeb* v. *Minister of Defense*, 636.

76. For a description of the links between government ministries and the military government in the field of land use see Peretz, *The West Bank, History, Politics, Society and Economy*, 60–61.

77. *Ja'amait Ascan* v. *Minister of Defense* (1980) 35 (2) PD 285.

78. Ibid., 302.

79. *Ja'amait Ascan* v. *IDF Commander in Judea and Samaria.*

80. Ibid., 795.

81. See the statement from the WZO *Master Plan for Settlement,* cited in text accompanying note 70.

82. *Elon Moreh* case, 22.

NOTES TO CHAPTER 6

1. The decisions on deportation under article 112 of the Defence Regulations are discussed in chapter 10.

2. *La'afi* v. *Minister of Interior* (1973) 28 (1) PD 13.

3. Until 1967 Beit Tzefafa was divided. Half the village was on the Israeli side of the armistice line; the other half was on the Jordanian side. After 1967 the village was united and because it is regarded as part of Jerusalem, Israeli law applies to the whole village.

4. *La'afi* v. *Minister of Interior*, 16.

5. At this stage "family unification" was regarded only as covering cases of minor children joining their parents or spouse joining spouse.

6. *La'afi* v. *Minister of Interior*, 17.

7. Ibid., 18.

8. See *Aljera* v. *Head of Civil Administration*, 1987 (2) Takdin-Elyon 1.

9. *Al-Teen* v. *Minister of Defense* (1972) 27 (1) PD 481.

10. Ibid., 484.

11. Ibid., 486.

12. Almost all the decisions on this question are short unpublished decisions. See, e.g., *Taga* v. *Minister of Defense* (H.C. 489/76 of 14.3.77); *Yassin* v.

Minister of Interior (H.C. 147/81 of 25.10.81); *Khalad Tatzavia* v. *Minister of Interior* (H.C. 45/85 of 14.7.85); *Tatzaphari* v. *Minister of Defense* (H.C. 710/85 of 8.5.86); *Algezuna* v. *Head of Civil Administration* (H.C. 212/86 of 21.5.86); *Yassin* v. *Military Commander in Ramalla Area* (H.C. 377/86 of 1.10.86); *Sabana* v. *IDF Commander in Judea and Samaria* (H.C. 42/88 of 16.3.88). This policy has also been followed in East Jerusalem, in which Israeli law applies. See *Awwad* v. *Minister of Interior* (1988) 42 (2) PD 424.

13. See *Yassin* v. *Minister of Interior*; *Sabana* v. *IDF Commander*; *Yassin* v. *Military Commander*.

14. See *La'afi* v. *Minister of Interior*; *Al-Teen* v. *Minister of Defense*.

15. See *Yassin* v. *Minister of Interior*; *Yassin* v. *Military Commander*.

16. *Taiah* v. *Minister of Defense* (H.C. 489/76 of 21.3.77). See also *Al-Teen* v. *Minister of Defense*, 484–485.

17. *Khalil* v. *IDF Commander in Judea and Samaria*, 1986 (2) Takdin Elyon 84.

18. This policy was mentioned in *La'afi* v. *Minister of Interior* and *Garbia v. Minister of Interior* (H.C. 466/73 of 25.3.74). The decisions in both these cases referred to applications by residents of East Jerusalem, but it seems the policy was the same in the West Bank and Gaza.

19. See *Khalil* v. *IDF Commander*; *Sharab* v. *Head of Civil Administration in Gaza* (1987) 41(4) P.D. 670 [English summary: 18 *Isr. YHR* (1988) 247–248].

20. Unreported decision of 10.3.74 in H.C. 7/74.

21. *Samara* v. *IDF Commander in Judea and Samaria* (1979) 34(4) P.D. 1 [English summary: 11 *Isr YHR* (1981) 362].

22. Ibid., 3.

23. Ibid., 4.

24. Ibid., 5.

25. Ibid.

26. See Y. Dinstein, "Family Unification in the Occupied Territories" (in Hebrew) 13 *Tel Aviv U. L. Rev.* (1988) 221.

27. *Taiah* v. *Minister of Defense*.

28. *Khalil* v. *IDF Commander*.

29. (1985) 40 (2) PD 281.

30. Ibid., 284–285.

31. (1986) 41(1) P.D. 197 [English summary: 18 *Isr YHR* (1988) 241].

32. Ibid., 211.

33. Ibid., 216.

34. Ibid., 209.

35. Ibid., 217.

36. Ibid. This approach was reaffirmed in *Saudi* v. *Head of Civil Administration* (1983) 41(3) PD 138.

37. See Dinstein, "Family Unification."

38. Ibid. In *Ouashra* v. *Commander of IDF Forces in Judea and Samaria*, 1990 (2) Takdin Elyon 358 a further attempt was made to attack the family unification policy. In reply to the petition the authorities stated that immediate family members of West Bank residents would be granted visitor's permits that would be renewed periodically. Although the petitioners refused to accept this

solution, the Court declined to deal with the matter. It stated that time should be given to see how the new policy would be implemented and that the petitioners would retain the right to petition the Court again if this approach did not solve the family unification issue.

NOTES TO CHAPTER 7

1. *Dweikat* v. *Government of Israel* (1979) 34 (1) PD 1 (*Elon Moreh* case) [English summary: 9 *Isr YHR* (1979) 345].

2. *Abu Itta* v. *IDF Commander in Judea and Samaria* (1981) 37 (2) PD 179 (*VAT* case) [English summary: 13 *Isr YHR* (1983) 348].

3. Obviously, after the "*al-Aqsa Intifada*" began in September 2000 the security concerns of the authorities took on major proportions. As stated in the preface, this study was completed before that *Intifada* began and its implications are not discussed here.

4. See M. Benvenisti, *The Sling and the Club* (in Hebrew) (Jerusalem: Keter, 1988).

5. *Zalum* v. *Commander of Judea and Samaria* (1986) 41 (1) PD 528.

6. *Natshe* v. *Minister of Defense* (1981) 35 (3) PD 361.

7. *Zalum* v. *Commander of Judea and Samaria*, 531. The Court conceded that the measures taken did indeed affect the livelihood of the petitioners but, because they were offered compensation, their rights were protected.

8. See G. J. Alexander, "The Illusory Protection of Human Rights by National Courts During Periods of Emergency," 5 *HRJ* (1984) 1. I stress that the question is whether the society *perceives* itself as threatened, and not whether a real, objective threat to its security does indeed exist. This does not mean, of course, that the perception of a threat is necessarily purely subjective.

9. See W. Brennan, "The Quest to Develop a Jurisprudence of Civil Liberties in Times of Security Crises," 18 *Isr YHR* (1988) 11.

10. For a discussion of the "consensus attitudes" of judges see W. Mishler and R. S. Sheehan, "The Supreme Court as a Countermajoritarian Institution? The Impact of Public Opinion on Supreme Court Decisions," 87 *American Political Science Review* (1993) 87.

11. See I. Ritov and J. Baron, "Status -Quo and Omission Biases," 5 *J of Risk and Uncertainty* (1992) 49; I. Ritov and J. Baron, "Reluctance to Vaccinate—Omission Bias and Ambiguity," 3 *J of Behavioral Decision Making* (1990) 263.

12. *Public Committee Against Torture in Israel* v. *State of Israel*, 1999 (3) Takdin-Elyon 458.

13. See *Abu Ghosh* v. *Minister of Defense* (1953) 7 PD 941; *Ayubi* v. *Minister of Defense* (1950) 4 PD 222; *Asslan* v. *Military Governor of Galilee* (1951) 9 PD 689; *Kaufman v. Minister of Defense* (1953) 7 PD 534. This approach is described in M. Hofnung, *Israel—Security Needs vs. The Rule of Law, 1948–1991* (in Hebrew) (Jerusalem: Nevo, 1991) 93–100.

14. *Ayyub* v. *Minister of Defense* (1978) 33(2) PD 113, 126 (*Beth El* case) [English summary: 9 *Isr YHR* (1979) 337].

15. See S. Shetreet, "The Scope of Judicial Review of National Security Considerations in Free Speech and other Areas: the Israeli Perspective," 18 *Isr YHR* (1988) 35.

16. This trend has been described elsewhere by the present writer: see D. Kretzmer, "Judicial Review of Attorney General's Prosecutorial Decisions" (in Hebrew) 5 *Plilim* (1996) 121; D. Kretzmer, "Judicial Review of *Knesset* Decisions," 8 *Tel Aviv Studies In Law* (1988) 95.

17. See, e.g., *Shalelam* v. *Fire-Arms Licensing Officer* (1980) 36 (1) PD 317; *Schnitzer* v. *Chief Military Censor* (1988) 42 (4) PD 617; *Samara* v. *IDF Commander of Judea and Samaria* (1979) 34 (4) PD 1 [English summary: 11 *Isr YHR* (1981) 362].

18. *Schnitzer* v. *Chief Military Censor*, 639–640.

19. See I. Zamir, "Human Rights and National Security" (in Hebrew) 19 *Mishpatim* (1989) 19, 33, who points out that there is a disparity between theory and practice. Also see G. Barzilai, "The Argument of 'National Security' in Politics and Jurisprudence," in *Security Concerns—Insights from the Israeli Experience,* ed. A. Kleiman, D. Bar-Tal, and D. Yaacobson (Stamford and London: JAI Press, 1999) 243.

20. See B. Bracha, "Restrictions of Personal Freedom Without Due Process of Law According to the Defence (Emergency) Regulations, 1945," 8 *Isr YHR* (1976) 296.

21. The minutes of a special protest meeting held by the Jewish Lawyers' Association on 7 February 1946 appear in 3 *HaPraklit* (1947) 62.

22. See The Palestine (Revocations) Order in Council, 1948, 1948 *Statutory Instruments,* Vol. 1, Part I, 1350–1351.

23. *Na'azal* v. *IDF Commander in Judea and Samaria* (1985) 39 (3) PD 645, 652 [English summary: 16 *Isr YHR* (1986) 329].

24. A "hidden law" is defined as any act of legislation, which the authorities purported to legislate between 29.11.47 and 15.5.48, and which was not published in the official gazette, even though it was one of those acts of legislation whose publication in the gazette was, at the time, either obligatory or customary.

25. In an affidavit submitted to the Court in the case of *Kawasme* v. *Minister of Defense* (1980) 35 (1) PD 617 (*Kawasme II* case) [English summary: 11 *Isr YHR* (1981) 349], a leading Palestinian lawyer, Aziz Shehadeh, stated that in the light of this Order-in-Council, the Defence Regulations were not valid in 1967. R. Shehadeh, *Occupier's Law, Israel and the West Bank,* revised edition (Washington: Institute for Palestine Studies, 1985), xiv–xv. Also see B. Dayanim, "The Israeli Supreme Court and the Deportations of Palestinians: The Interaction of Law and Legitimacy," 30 *Stanford J of Int L* (1994) 115, 131–139.

26. *Awwad* v. *Military Commander of Judea and Samaria* (1979) 33 (3) PD 309 [English summary: 9 *Isr YHR* (1979) 343].

27. This conclusion was supported by an affidavit given by a Ministry of Justice official who served as an advisor on the law of Arab countries and had gained "expertise in Jordanian law and its sources." *Awwad* v. *Military Commander of Judea and Samaria,* 313. In the *Kawasme II* case, a number of affidavits were submitted by leading Palestinian lawyers, who argued that even if

the regulations were still in force in 1948, they were repealed when the 1935 Defence of Transjordan Law was applied to the West Bank in 1952. This argument was rejected. For a review of the arguments on this issue see D. Shefi, "The Reports of the U.N. Special Committees on Israeli Practices in the Territories— A Survey and Evaluation" in *Military Government in the Territories Administered by Israel, 1967–1980, The Legal Aspects,* ed. M. Shamgar (Jerusalem: Harry Sacher Institute for Legislative Research and Comparative Law, 1982) 285, 294–299. The ruling that the Defence Regulations were not repealed by regulations issued under the Transjordanian Defence Law is attacked by Shehadeh, *Occupier's Law, Israel and the West Bank,* xiv–xv, and supported by M. B. Carroll, "The Israeli Demolition of Palestinian Houses in the Occupied Territories: An Analysis of its Legality in International Law," 11 *Michigan J of Int L* (1990) 1195, 1204–1205. And see Dayanim, "The Israeli Supreme Court," 136–139.

28. *Awwad* v. *Military Commander of Judea and Samaria,* 314. Article 128 of the Constitution declares: "All laws, regulations and other statutory instruments in force in the Hashemite Kingdom of Jordan at the time this constitution comes into force shall remain valid until they are repealed or amended under a statute that is issued pursuant to it." In support of its view that this provision left regulation 112 intact, the Court cited a Jordanian court decision of 1954 that Jordanian emergency legislation that preceded the Constitution remained in force unless it had been expressly repealed (315). However, that decision dealt with administrative detention and did not expressly relate to the argument that the power to deport a citizen is inconsistent with an express provision in the Constitution.

29. *Kawasme II* case, 623.

30. The full title of this order is Interpretation Order (Further Provisions) (No. 5) (Judea and Samaria) (No. 224), 1968.

31. *Kawasme II* case, 626. A similar argument had been raised by Justice Sussman in *Awwad* v. *Military Commander of Judea and Samaria,* 313. However, as he rejected the argument that the Jordanian Constitution repealed article 112, he saw no need to voice a final opinion on the effect of the Interpretation Order.

32. The third judge on the bench in the *Kawasme II* case, Justice Kahan, saw no need to express an opinion on the effect of the Jordanian constitution on regulation 112. He held that this question was of purely academic value, since "even if it were abrogated, the regulation was valid in the occupied territories by virtue of the [Interpretation Order]" (647).

33. Ibid., 636.

34. This rule and its interpretation by the Court are discussed in chapter 4.

35. See Justice Cohn's opinion in the *Kawasme II* case.

36. *Maslam v. IDF Commander in Gaza* (1991) 45 (3) PD 444.

37. The petitioners submitted opinions of two Gaza lawyers in support of their interpretation.

38. See *Maslam v. IDF Commander in Gaza,* 455.

39. *Sakhwill* v. *IDF Commander in Judea and Samaria* (1979) 34 (1) PD 464 [English summary: 10 *Isr YHR* (1980) 345].

40. Ibid., 466.

41. *Jabar* v. *Officer Commanding Central Command* (1986) 41 (2) PD 522 [English summary: 18 *Isr YHR* (1988) 252].

42. Article 53 of the Convention prohibits destruction of real or personal property "except where such destruction is rendered absolutely necessary by military operations."

43. *Jabar* v. *Officer Commanding Central Command*, 525–526.

44. See *Commentary on the IV Geneva Convention Relative to the Protection of Civilian Persons in Time of War*, ed. Jean S. Pictet (Geneva: ICRC, 1958) 336: "when the penal legislation of the occupied territory conflicts with the provisions of the Convention, the Convention must prevail." Also see Hans-Peter Gasser, "Protection of the Civilian Population" in *The Handbook of Humanitarian Law in Armed Conflicts*, ed. D. Fleck (Oxford: Oxford University Press, 1995) 209, 255; C. Greenwood, "The Administration of Occupied Territory in International Law" in *International Law and the Administration of the Occupied Territories*, ed. E. Playfair (Oxford: Clarendon Press, 1992) 241, 249.

45. See R. T. Yingling and R. W. Ginnane, "The Geneva Conventions of 1949," 46 *Am J of Int L* (1952) 393, 421. Citing article 64, the writers state that "the criminal law and courts of the occupied territory must be continued in effect for ordinary criminal offences committed by the local inhabitants and which do not involve the occupation forces."

NOTES TO CHAPTER 8

1. *Shawe* v. *IDF Commander in Gaza* (1990) 44 (4) PD 590.

2. The curfew, which applied from 22:00 until 03:00, had been in force for over two years by the time the petition was submitted and heard by the Court.

3. Ibid., 592.

4. *Father Samuel Panous* v. *Commander of Central Command*, 1992 (1) Takdin-Elyon 270.

5. The nature of the specific operation is not mentioned in the Court's decision, but it seems that the authorities wanted to conduct a house-to-house search for people who had carried out an attack on Israeli civilians.

6. The Court mentioned that counsel for the authorities had agreed that the matter should be reconsidered at the end of two weeks, but stated that this should be given formal expression. *Father Samuel Panous* v. *Commander of Central Command*, 270.

7. Ibid., 271.

8. *Insh el-Usra Society* v. *IDF Commander* (1988) 43 (3) PD 673. The authorities had ordered two-years' closure of a charitable association that ran activities to further the welfare of Palestinian women and families. The Court was convinced that the military commander had acted on strong evidence that the activities of the association served as a vehicle for "political activity that is hostile to the State of Israel, including hostile propaganda and incitement to violence against the State of Israel and IDF forces" (675). However, it held that, given the nature and importance of the association's activities, the length of the

closure order should not have exceeded one year. Although the Court's decision was handed down sixteen months after the closure order had been issued, it held that, given the security situation on the West Bank (at the height of the *Intifada*), the closure order would remain valid for a further period of two and a half months, during which time the commander could gather all necessary information and make a decision. In other words, while the Court held that the original closure order should not have been made for a period exceeding one year, it left the door open for the commander to issue a new order when the first order expired.

9. *Barcat* v. *Officer Commanding Central Command* (1992) 46 (5) PD 1 [English summary: 25 *Isr YHR* (1995) 341].

10. Ibid., 8.

11. See *L.S.M. Law in the Service of Man* v. *IDF Commander in Judea and Samaria* (1988) 42(3) PD 260 [English summary: 23 *Isr YHR* (1993) 293] (refusal of Court to interfere in blocking of international telephone calls); *Khouri* v. *Minister of Defense,* 1989 (3) Takdin-Elyon 102 (refusal to interfere in the confiscation of a car, after the owner's son had been convicted of carrying "nationalistic songs" in the car); *Khamdan* v. *IDF Commander in Judea and Samaria* (1985) 40 (2) PD 614 [English summary: 17 *Isr YHR* (1987) 316] (refusal to interfere in an order closing a sports club that the authorities claimed had served as a base for nationalistic activities and incitement); *Nazaal* v. *IDF Commander in Judea and Samaria* (1988) 42 (3) PD 641 [English summary: 19 *Isr YHR* (1989) 376] (refusal to interfere in decision to order closure of premises that had been leased to a pharmacist who used it as a base for preparing terrorist attacks).

12. See *57 Divrei HaKnesset,* 1471, 1867.

13. See Hofnung, *Israel—State Security Versus Rule of Law, 1948–1991* (Jerusalem: Nevo, 1991) 318, n.8.

14. See *Prisoners of Peace: Administrative Detention during the Oslo Process* (Jerusalem: B'Tselem, The Israeli Information Center for Human Rights in the Occupied Territories, June, 1997) 73.

15. See *B'Tselem* Administrative Detention Statistics at http://www.btselem.org.

16. See Order Concerning Security Provisions (Military Order 378), 1970.

17. For a detailed description of the Israeli law see S. Shetreet, "A Contemporary Model of Emergency Detention Law: An Assessment of the Israeli Law," 14 *Isr YHR* (1984) 182.

18. See Order Concerning Security Provisions (Amendment 18) (Military Order 815), 1980.

19. See Order Concerning Administrative Detention (Provisional Regulations) (Military Order 1229), 1988.

20. See Order Concerning Administrative Detention (Provisional Instructions) (Military Order 1236), 1988. In 1989 this order was amended to allow for a detention order for one year: see Order Concerning Administrative Detention (Provisional Regulations) (Amendment 4) (Military Order 1281), 1989. As a result of public pressure, this amendment was subsequently revoked and the maximum period for a detention order was reduced to six months (although the

order can always be extended at the end of this period). Order Concerning Administrative Detention (Provisional Instructions) (Amendment 9) (Military Order 1361), 1991.

21. See article 87D (c) of Order Concerning Security Provisions (Military Order 378), 1970.

22. See M. Rishmawi, "Administrative Detention in International Law: The Case of the Israeli Occupied West Bank and Gaza," 5 *Palestine Y Int L* (1989) 83, 93. Under Protocol I to Geneva Convention IV the one-year rule is abolished and the Convention and Protocol cease to apply upon termination of the occupation. This does not affect Israel's obligations because it has not ratified Protocol I.

23. Ibid.

24. See article 78 of Geneva Convention IV.

25. For a full discussion of administrative detention in international law see Rishmawi, "Administrative Detention in International Law"; Playfair, "Administrative Detention in the Israeli-Occupied West Bank"; A. Pacheco, "Occupying an Uprising: The Geneva Law and Israeli Administrative Detention Policy During the First Year of the Palestinian General Uprising," 21 *Columbia HRL Rev* (1990) 515.

26. See *Abu Bakar* v. *Judge of Shechem Military Court* (1988) 40 (3) PD 649.

27. See *Delaisha* v. *IDF Commander on West Bank*, 1995 (3) Takdin-Elyon 1231; *Al-Akhmar* v. *Minister of Defense*, 1996 (3) Takdin-Elyon 1328; *Al-Akhmar* v. *IDF Commander on West Bank*, 1997 (2) Takdin-Elyon 94.

28. See *Abu Obeid* v. *IDF Commander in Judea and Samaria* (1988) 42 (4) PD 566 [English summary: 23 *Isr YHR* (1993) 315].

29. *Sajedia* v. *Minister of Defense* (1988) 42 (3) PD 801, 822 (*Ketziot* case) [English summary: 23 *Isr YHR* (1993) 288].

30. See *Rakhman* v. *IDF Commander* (1989) 43 (3) PD 78; *Khamed* v. *IDF Commander*, 1989 (3) Takdin-Elyon 84.

31. See *Baryush* v. *IDF Commander in Judea and Samaria*, 1989 (3) Takdin-Elyon 142. The petitioner claimed that the detention order had been issued in bad faith and that there was no evidence that he had continued with his hostile activities after being released from a previous term of administrative detention. With the consent of the parties the Court examined the classified evidence and held that there was concrete, credible, and serious evidence that justified the military judge's decision not to interfere in the detention order. And cf. *Tahabub* v. *IDF Commander on West Bank* (1989) 43 (1) PD 757, 760. The authorities had renewed a detention order. The petitioner claimed that the authorities had no evidence that he had continued his hostile activities from the detention center, and that they had renewed the detention order against him because he had spoken to the judges who visited the center in the *Ketziot* case. The Court refused to examine the evidence, but it sent the matter back to the reviewing military judge with instructions to examine whether there was any basis to the petitioner's claim.

32. See *Shaar* v. *IDF Commander in Judea and Samaria* (1994) 48 (3) PD 675.

33. See *Abu Obeid* v. *IDF Commander in Judea and Samaria*, 569. In this case the Court held that the military judge had not examined whether the detainee could have been charged with a criminal offence. With the consent of both parties the Court itself looked at all the evidence, including the classified evidence, and held that criminal charges could not have been brought and that the administrative detention was justified. The reason a person cannot be charged in a criminal court is that much of the evidence could not be produced in a criminal case. *Katamash* v. *IDF Commander in Judea and Samaria*, 1994 (2) Takdin-Elyon 2084. Presumably the reason is that the evidence is provided by informers who, for obvious reasons, cannot be produced as witnesses in court. As presented to the military authorities and the reviewing judge, the evidence of informers is hearsay evidence that would not be admitted in a criminal trial.

34. See *Rakhman* v. *IDF Commander*.

35. See *Delaisha* v. *IDF Commander on West Bank*; *Federman* v. *IDF Commander in Judea and Samaria*, 1994 (2) Takdin-Elyon 2298, 2301.

36. *Delaisha* v. *IDF Commander on West Bank*. But see *Citrin* v. *IDF Commander in Judea and Samaria*, 1996 (1) Takdin-Elyon 76, 78 in which the Court spoke of "a fear that shows it to be highly probable that the petitioner will commit a violent act," and *Association for Protecting the Rights of the Jewish Citizen* v. *IDF Commander in Judea and Samaria*, 1996 (4) Takdin-Elyon 45, 46 in which the Court spoke of "preventing occurrences in which there is a real danger to the public peace and perhaps even, in the end, to human life."

37. See *El-Amla* v. *IDF Commander in Judea and Samaria* (1998) 52 (3) PD 346.

38. 1990 (2) Takdin-Elyon 187.

39. See chapter 3.

40. An appeal is wholly successful if the judge orders immediate release of the detainee. It is partially successful if the judge shortens the period of detention.

41. *Ketziot* case, 820–821.

42. Ibid., 822.

43. See *Abu Obeid* v. *IDF Commander in Judea and Samaria*.

44. *Ketziot* case, 823.

45. Ibid., 823–827.

46. For a longer discussion of the issues and the earlier cases see Yuval Ginbar, *The Face and the Mirror: Israel's View of its Interrogation Techniques Examined* (LL.M diss., University of Essex, 1996); M. Kremnitzer and R. Segev, "Using Force During Investigations" (in Hebrew) 4 *Mishpat Umimshal* (1998) 667, 672–673; E. Benvenisti, "The Role of National Courts in Preventing Torture of Suspected Terrorists," 8 *European J of Int L* (1997) 596.

47. See *Report of Commission of Inquiry into the Methods of Investigation of the GSS Regarding Hostile Terrorist Activities* (the *Landau Report*) October 1987. Parts of the Report were published in 23 *Isr L Rev* (1989) 146.

48. For a series of articles criticizing the *Landau Report* see 23 *Isr L Rev* (1989) 192–406. Also see A. Enker, "The Use of Force in Interrogations and the Necessity Defense," in *Israel and International Human Rights Law: The Issue of Torture* (Jerusalem: Center for Human Rights, Hebrew University of Jerusalem, 1995) 55.

49. *The Interrogation of Palestinians During the Intifada: Ill-treatment, "Moderate Physical Pressure" or Torture?* (Jerusalem: *B'Tselem*, The Israeli Information Center for Human Rights in the Occupied Territories, March 1991).

50. *Salkhaht* v. *Government of Israel* (1991) 47 PD IV 837.

51. For another decision in the same vein see *Hassan* v. *General Security Service* (1995) 42 Dinim-Elyon 83. When the case came up for hearing the interrogation had been completed and the petitioner had submitted a complaint to the Department for Investigation of Police and Security Personnel. The Court held that in these circumstances it did not have to continue with the case.

52. See, e.g., *Kamal* v. *Minister of Defense* (1997), unreported decision of 23 June 1997 in H.C.3802/97; *Korahn* v. *Minister of Defense* (1997), unreported decision of 8 January 1998 in H.C. 7628/97. (Both decisions can be found on the home page of the Supreme Court: www.court.gov.il). In the latter case the authorities declared that they were not using the methods mentioned by the petitioner "at this stage." And see Kremnitzer and Segal, "Using Force During Interrogations," 671–675.

53. *Balebisi* v. *General Security Service*, 1995 (1) Takdin-Elyon 1634.

54. "Shaking" was described by an expert in one case as the interrogatee being "shaken a number of times while being held by the collar or lapel of his shirt in a forward then backward motion." Ginbar, *The Face and the Mirror*, 46. In at least one case this resulted in the death of an interrogatee (47).

55. 1996 (3) Takdin-Elyon 1018.

56. *Mubarak* v. *General Security Service*, 1996 (3) Takdin-Elyon 1013.

57. See Kremnitzer and Segev, "Using Force in Interrogations."

58. Also see *Ghanimat* v. *Minister of Defense,* unreported decision of 1 January 1998 in H.C. 7563/97, in which the Court, by a majority of two to one, refused to grant an interim injunction after having heard explanations by the General Security Service *in camera.* The Court demanded that it be provided with a report on the progress of the interrogation ten days later.

59. See, for example, the *Report of the UN Special Rapporteur on Torture*, E/CN.4/1999/61, para. 394, in which the Special Rapporteur refers to the Court's positions and states that he "is also bound to note that administration of justice in these formally authorized practices can only tend to corrode the integrity of those organs, whose traditional commitment to the rule of law and human rights have in the past been internationally respected." Also see *Conclusions and Recommendations of the Committee against Torture,* A/53/44, paras. 232–242; *Concluding Observations of the Human Rights Committee,* CCPR/C/79/Add. 93, para. 19.

60. See *Public Committee Against Torture in Israel* v. *Government of Israel,* 1999 (3) Takdin-Elyon 458. The decision deals with two petitions submitted by the NGO's and five petitions submitted by individual interrogatees.

61. For a strong criticism of the Court's failure to deliver a decision on the merits of the issue, written before the 1999 judgment, see Kremitzer and Segev, "Using Force in Interrogations."

62. For a report showing that the "special" methods were widely used in interrogation of Palestinians see *Routine Torture: Interrogation Methods of the*

General Security Service (Jerusalem: *B'Tselem*, The Israeli Information Center for Human Rights in the Occupied Territories, January 1998).

63. For a fascinating discussion of this feature in the decision-making of the U.S. Supreme Court see W. Brennan, "The Quest to Develop a Jurisprudence of Civil Liberties in Times of Security Crises," 18 *Isr YHR* (1988) 11.

64. *Korematsu v. United States,* 323 US 214, 65 S Ct 193, 89 L Ed 194 (1944).

65. It should also be noted that having conceded that in an individual case an interrogator who used "special" methods could possibly raise the necessity defense against criminal liability, the Court stated that the attorney general, who heads the prosecution service, could "guide himself as to the circumstances in which interrogators who claimed to have acted in an isolated case on strength of the feeling of 'necessity' would not be prosecuted."

NOTES TO CHAPTER 9

1. *Jerusalem Post,* 23 November 1981.

2. See E. Playfair, *Demolition and Sealing of Houses as a Punitive Measure in the Israeli-Occupied West Bank* (Ramallah: Al-Haq/Law in the Service of Man, 1987) citing records kept by *Al-Haq.*

3. See *Violations of Human Rights in the Territories, 1990/1991* (Jerusalem: *B'Tselem*, The Israeli Information Center for Human Rights in the Occupied Territories, 1991) 32–33.

4. *Sakhwill v. Commander of Judea and Samaria* (1979) 34 (1) PD 464 [English summary: 10 *Isr YHR* (1980) 345].

5. In H.C. 515/75 the petition against a demolition was withdrawn by consent of both parties after counsel for the government declared that there was no intention to demolish the house. In H.C. 71/79 and 123/79 the petitions were dismissed when counsel for the government informed the Court that the houses would not be demolished.

6. The Court has mentioned this "restraint" of the authorities on a number of occasions. The Court intimated that were the authorities to depart from their practice, it would intervene. *Nazaal v. IDF Commander in Judea and Samaria* (1994) 48 (5) PD 338, 345 [English summary: 19 *Isr YHR* (1989) 376]; *Natshe v. Minister of Defense* 1994 (3) Takdin Elyon 1277, 1279.

7. See the statement of Defense Minister Dayan in *Knesset* (29/10/1968) 53 *Divrei HaKnesset* 100. Also see M. Shamgar, "The Observance of International Law in the Administered Territories," 1 *Isr YHR* (1971) 262, 275.

8. See, e.g., *Jabri v. Minister of Defense*, H.C. 1786/90 (5.7.90), unreported.

9. It is therefore difficult to understand the argument made by Alan Dershowitz that house demolitions are preferable to imprisonment. A. Dershowitz, "Symposium: Human Rights in Times of War; Part 2—Compliance with International Conventions, Destruction of Houses, and Administrative Detentions;" 1 *Isr YHR* (1970) 376–377.

10. See, e.g., *Abu Mir v. IDF Commander of Gaza*, H.C. 830/88 (5.3.89), unreported, in which the Court upheld the decision to demolish the house of a person who had fled the area.

11. *Nazaal* v. *IDF Commander*; *Natshe* v. *Minister of Defense*; *Ghanimat* v. *Officer Commanding Central Command*, 1997 (1) Takdin-Elyon 182; *Yassin* v. *IDF Commander in Judea and Samaria* (1997) 53 Dinim Elyon 148.

12. See M. B. Carroll, "The Israeli Demolition of Palestinian Houses in the Occupied Territories: An Analysis of its Legality in International Law," 11 *Mich J Int L* (1990) 1195; D. Simon, "The Demolition of Homes in the Israeli Occupied Territories," 19 *Yale J Int L* (1994) 1; Y. Dinstein, "The Israel Supreme Court and the Law of Belligerent Occupation: Demolitions and Sealing Off of Houses," 29 *Isr YHR* (2000) 285. Besides the specific prohibitions mentioned in the text, Dinstein cites article 78 of Geneva Convention IV according to which the most serious security measures that an occupying power may adopt are assigned residence and internment. He argues that as demolitions and sealing of houses go beyond such measures they are implicitly proscribed.

13. See *Akvidar* v. *Turkey* (1997) 23 EHRR 143, in which the European Court of Human Rights held that destruction of homes by Turkish security forces amounted to a violation of article 8 of the European Convention on Fundamental Rights and Freedoms, which protects the right to one's private and family life and one's home. The Court stated that because it had found a violation of article 8, it did not have to decide whether the right against cruel and inhuman treatment and punishment had been violated too.

14. Property may be *requisitioned* "for the needs of the army of occupation" (article 52). However, requisition is of a temporary nature.

15. This article appears in section II of the Regulations that deals with "Hostilities" and not in section III, "Military Authority over the Territory of the Hostile State." But restrictions that apply to armies during actual combat must surely also apply after the hostilities have ceased.

16. See Shamgar, "The Observance of International Law," 275. Also see D. Shefi, "The Reports of the U. N. Committees on Israeli Practices in the Territories—A Survey and Evaluation," in *Military Government in the Territories Administered by Israel, 1967–1980, The Legal Aspects,* ed. M. Shamgar (Jerusalem: Harry Sacher Institute for Legislative Research and Comparative Law, 1982) 285, 301–303. (At the time of writing this article Shefi was advocate-general of the IDF). The argument also appears in *The Rule of Law in the Areas Administered by Israel* (Tel Aviv: Israel National Section of International Commission of Jurists, 1981) 69–70.

17. Compare articles 30, 49 (2), 62, 64, and 78 of Geneva Convention IV.

18. See Carroll, "The Israeli Demolition," 1210, who quotes a letter by the Director of the Department of Principles and Law at the ICRC dated 25 November 1961. The emphasis appears in the original text of the letter.

19. See article 50 of the Hague Regulations and article 33 of Geneva Convention IV.

20. The authorities have no control over the *submission* of petitions to the Court, though before the hearing requirement was institutionalized they could, in effect, avoid judicial review by demolishing the house immediately after they had informed the owner or tenant of the demolition order. Once a petition has been submitted the authorities can prevent substantive review by stepping down

before the Court decides the case, or by negotiating an agreed settlement that involves modifying the original order.

21. *Sakhwill v. IDF Commander in Judea and Samaria.*

22. *Khamed v. IDF Commander in Judea and Samaria* (1981) 35 (3) PD 223.

23. *Khamamara v. Minister of Defense* (1982) 36 (2) PD 755.

24. See *Khamri v. Commander in Judea and Samaria* (1982) 36 (3) PD 439 [English summary: 17 *Isr YHR* (1987) 314].

25. Ibid., 444.

26. See *Muzlakh v. Minister of Defense* (1982) 36 (4) PD 610.

27. See *Sakhwill v. IDF Commander; Jabar v. Officer Commanding Central Command* (1987) 41 (2) PD 522 [English summary: 18 *Isr YHR* (1988) 252]. And see chapter 7.

28. See *Dujlas v. IDF Commander in Judea and Samaria* (1985) 40 (2) PD 42 [English summary: 17 *Isr YHR* (1987) 315]. Also see *Kaus v. IDF Commander in Judea and Samaria,* 1986 (2) Takdin-Elyon 146; *Bakhari v. IDF Commander in Judea and Samaria* (1989) 44 (1) PD 92 [English summary: 23 *Isr YHR* (1993) 325]; *Tag v. Minister of Defense* (1991) 46 (5) PD 467 [English summary: 25 *Isr YHR* (1995) 330]; *Abu Khalawah v. Officer Commanding Home Front,* 1997 (3) Takdin-Elyon 111.

29. *Dujlas v. IDF Commander.*

30. Ibid., 44.

31. See *Bakhari v. IDF Commander; Sanuar v. IDF Commander in Gaza* (1989) 43 (2) PD 821 [English summary: 25 *Isr YHR* (1995) 324].

32. See Dinstein, "The Israel Supreme Court and the Law of Belligerent Occupation: Demolitions and Sealing Off of Houses," 298, who terms the comparison between imprisonment of a breadwinner and destruction of a house "spurious."

33. Justice Cheshin was appointed to the bench in 1991 and was not a party to any of the decisions handed down before this time.

34. See *Hizrahn v. IDF Commander in Judea and Samaria* (1991) 46 (2) PD 150 [English summary: 23 *Isr YHR* (1993) 349]; *Elamarin v. IDF Commander in Gaza* (1992) 46 (3) PD 693. As will be seen later, this approach was adopted by the Court in *Turkmahn v. Minister of Defense* (1991) 48 (1) PD 217 [English summary: 25 *Isr YHR* (1995) 347].

35. See *Nazaal v. IDF Commander,* in which Justice Cheshin was of the opinion that the demolition order had to be restricted to the room in which the bomber himself had lived; *Ghanimat v. Officer Commanding Central Command.*

36. See *Ghanimat v. Officer Commanding Central Command.* This case dealt with the decision of the military commander to demolish part of a house in which a suicide bomber, whose bomb in a Tel Aviv cafe had killed three people and wounded tens of others, had lived with his wife and four children. The decision of the military commander, which was upheld by the majority, was consistent with Justice Cheshin's initial approach, because the commander declared that every effort would be made not to cause damage to part of the house in which the bomber's sister-in-law and family lived.

37. See dictum of the Court in *Shukeri* v. *Minister of Defense*, 1990 (1) Takdin Elyon 75.

38. *Sabeach* v. *IDF Commander in Judea and Samaria* (1996) 50 (1) PD 353.

39. Ibid., 363.

40. See article 33 of Geneva Convention IV: "No protected person may be punished for an offense he or she has not personally committed. Collective penalties and likewise all measures of intimidation or of terrorism are prohibited."

41. See G. von Glahn, "The Protection of Human Rights in Time of Armed Conflicts," 1 *Isr YHR* (1971) 208, 225–227; F. Kalshoven, *Belligerent Reprisals* (Leyden: A.W.Sijthoff, 1971) 315–321.

42. See Shamgar, "The Observance of International Law," 262, 275; "Compliance with International Conventions, Destruction of Houses, and Administrative Detention," 1 *Isr YHR.* (1971) 376, 380.

43. See *Jabar* v. *Officer Commanding Central Command*. Also see J. Stone, "Behind the Cease-Fire Lines: Israel's Administration in Gaza and the West Bank," in *Of Law and Man: Essays in Honor of Haim H. Cohn*, ed. S. Shoham (Tel Aviv: Sabra Books, 1997).

44. *Sakhwill* v. *IDF Commander*, 466.

45. *Khamamara* v. *Minister of Defense*, 756. Also see Shamgar, "The Observance of International Law," 275.

46. *Abu Alahn* v. *Minister of Defense* (1983) 37 (2) PD 169.

47. *Shukeri* v. *Minister of Defense*.

48. Ibid., 76.

49. *Abu Kabita* v. *Minister of Defense*, 1991 (2) Takdin-Elyon 378 (emphasis added).

50. See *Nazaal* v. *IDF Commander*, 346. Also see *Sabeach* v. *IDF Commander*.

51. Besides the decisions cited in the text see *Natshe* v. *Minister of Defense*; *Tag* v. *Minister of Defense*.

52. The attempt to distinguish between the punitive and deterrent character of security measures is discussed and rejected by Kalshoven, *Belligerent Reprisals*, 38–39.

53. "General deterrence" means deterring others, while deterring the offender from repeating his offense is referred to as "special deterrence." J. Andenaes, *Punishment and Deterrence* (Ann Arbor: University of Michigan Press, 1974) 175–181.

54. For analyses of the accepted definition of legal punishment see I. Primoratz, *Justifying Legal Punishment* (Atlantic Highlands, N.J: Humanities Press International, 1990) 1; G. Newman, *The Punishment Response* (New York: Lippincott, 1978) 7–11.

55. See, e.g., *Timraz* v. *IDF Commander in Gaza* (1991) 45 (2) PD 325 [English summary: 23 *Isr Y HR* (1993) 337]. In this case the Court upheld an order to destroy a building that was adjacent to an army post, after evidence was presented showing a long list of attacks on soldiers in the post. In many of the attacks, the attackers had used the building as cover or a place of refuge.

56. The notion that the object of house demolition is general deterrence appears in numerous decisions: see, e.g., *Ragabi* v. *IDF Commander in Judea and Samaria* (1989) 43 (3) PD 177 [English summary: 23 *Isr YHR* (1993) 324]; *Abu Daka* v. *IDF Commander in Gaza* (1989) 44 (3) PD 452 [English summary: 23 *Isr YHR* (1993) 322]; *Nasman* v. *IDF Commander in Gaza* (1989) 43 (4) PD 461 [English summary: 23 *Isr YHR* (1993) 327]; *Avida* v. *IDF Commander in Gaza*, 1990 (1) Takdin-Elyon 91; *Mashal* v. *Officer Commanding Central Command*, 1990 (2) Takdin-Elyon 189. From an historical point of view it is highly doubtful whether the original aim of the sanction was indeed deterrence. The British institutionalized the sanction in Ireland in an attempt to create a legal framework for reprisal actions carried out by British soldiers in response to attacks by the Irish fighters. C. Townshend, *The British Campaign in Ireland, 1919–1921* (London: Oxford University Press, 1975) 148–151; C. Campbell, *Emergency Law in Ireland, 1918–1925* (Oxford: Clarendon Press, 1994). It has been argued that house demolitions as a form of punishment or reprisal were first used by the British in the Anglo-Boer War. D. Shalem, *Justifying Demolition: The Rhetoric of Israel's Policy of Punitive House Demolition in the Occupied Territories 1967–1997* (M.A. diss., Hebrew University of Jerusalem, n.d.).

57. *Shukeri* v. *Minister of Defense.*

58. Justice Barak repeated this idea in *Radakha* v. *IDF Commander on West Bank*, 1992 (2) Takdin-Elyon 1769, in which he stated that measures taken under regulation 119 are not punitive. They are an administrative reaction that is designed to protect order and security.

59. See Kalshoven, *Belligerent Reprisals*, 320.

60. Kalshoven coined the term "quasi reprisal" to describe an action aimed against the civilian population in occupied territory, in order to persuade it to refrain from resisting the occupation. Ibid., 36–40. Kalshoven rejects the attempt to distinguish between punitive and deterrent retaliatory measures.

61. See, e.g., *Elfasfus* v. *Minister of Defense* (1988) 43 (1) PD 576, 578 [English summary: 23 *Isr YHR* (1993) 316]; *Ali Daoud* v. *Commander in Judea and Samaria*, 1989 (2) Takdin-Elyon 181; *Abu Khalawah* v. *Officer Commanding Home Front*; *Abu Daka* v. *IDF Commander in Gaza*; *Tag* v. *Minister of Defense.*

62. *Khamri* v. *IDF Commander in Judea and Samaria*, 439.

63. Ibid., 442.

64. Ibid.

65. Also see *Tamimi* v. *Military Commander of the West Bank*, 1986 (3) Takdin-Elyon 84 [English summary: 18 *Isr YHR* (1988) 248].

66. *Jabar* v. *Officer Commanding Central Command*, 525.

67. *Alzak* v. *Military Commander of West Bank*, 1987 (1) Takdin-Elyon 1.

68. See *Tamimi* v. *Military Commander.*

69. See *Khamri* v. *IDF Commander*; *Jabar* v. *Officer Commanding Central Command*; *Nasman* v. *IDF Commander*; *Al-Radouan* v. *IDF Commander in Judea and Samaria*, HC 681,703,714,716/82 (22.8.83), unreported. In the last-mentioned case the Court stated that it "doesn't see that there is room for this court to take a position on the timing of exercise of the military commander's powers under regulation 119."

70. *Nasman* v. *IDF Commander*, 465.

71. *Cf. Lubin* v. *Tel Aviv-Jaffa Municipality* (1957) 12 PD 1041. In this case the Court dealt with a statutory provision that authorized a municipality to include in by-laws "provisions regarding examination, attachment and confiscation of pork." The question was whether the municipality was authorized to make a by-law according to which pork could be confiscated without judicial proceedings. The Supreme Court interpreted the enabling legislation according to "the principle of not harming the citizen's property without resort to a judicial authority" (1059). It held that the municipality was not authorized to confiscate and destroy pork without a judicial order.

72. It does mean, however, that the sanction may be imposed on the strength of evidence that would not be admissible in court. In the *Khamri* v. *IDF Commander*, the evidence was based on confessions of the two sons. Their counsel submitted affidavits that these confessions had been obtained illegally. The Court held that because the sons did not claim in their affidavits that they did not commit the act attributed to them "these affidavits do not affect the evidentiary basis that was before the military commander" (442). Although Israeli law does not adopt a general exclusionary rule, a confession may not be admitted in a criminal trial unless it was given of free will. Thus, if the accuseds' argument had been accepted in their criminal trial, they could not have been convicted on the strength of their confessions. Their parents' house could, however, be demolished.

73. The Basic Law states expressly that it does not affect the validity of any law that was in force before the Basic Law was enacted.

74. Section 8 of the Basic Law states that a protected right may not be limited, except for a worthy purpose and provided the limitation does not exceed what is necessary. This proviso has been interpreted as incorporating a proportionality test similar to the test adopted both in German and Canadian constitutional law.

75. See *Abu Khalawah* v. *Officer Commanding Home Front; Sharif* v. *Officer Commanding Home Front* (1996) 50 (4) PD 491.

76. See *Sakhwill* v. *IDF Commander; Khamed* v. *IDF Commander; Al-Jamal* v. *Minister of Defense* (1989) 43 (2) PD 66.

77. 1987 (2) Takdin-Elyon 53.

78. *Association for Civil Rights in Israel* v. *Officer Commanding Central Command* (1988) 43 (2) PD 529 (*ACRI* case) [English summary: 23 *Isr YHR* (1993) 294].

79. Ibid., 540–541. It should be noted that the exception referred to is not relevant in cases of demolitions under regulation 119, which are of a punitive nature. Demolition of a house in the operational circumstances described by Justice Shamgar is carried out under the military commander's power to destroy property when it is rendered absolutely necessary by military operations. It is therefore not clear why Justice Shamgar saw fit to mention this exception in relation to demolitions under regulation 119. See Dinstein, "The Israel Supreme Court and the Law of Belligerent Occupation: Demolitions and Sealing Off of Houses," 288–289.

80. *Association for Civil Rights in Israel* v. *Officer Commanding Southern*

Command (1990) 44 (4) PD 626 (*al-Boureij* case) [English summary: 23 *Isr YHR* (1993) 333].

81. The sense that this was an excuse in order to avoid compliance with the hearing requirement and other principles relating to use of regulation 119 is reinforced when one reads the description of events by the military advocate-general at the time. A. Straschnov, *Justice Under Fire* (in Hebrew) (Tel Aviv: Yedioth Ahronoth, 1994), 122–136.

82. *Association for Civil Rights in Israel v. Officer Commanding Southern Command*, 639

83. Ibid.

84. *ACRI* case, 536.

85. *Nimar v. IDF Commander in West Bank* (1991) 45 (3) PD 625 [English summary: 23 *Isr YHR* (1993) 331].

86. *Nasman v. IDF Commander* (1989) 44 (2) PD 601.

87. *Jabrin v. Minister of Defense*, HC 443/86, 515/86 (11.1.87), unreported.

88. *Hodli v. IDF Commander in Judea and Samaria* (1991) 47 (1) PD 612 [English summary: 25 *Isr YHR* (1995) 327].

89. *Turkmahn v. Minister of Defense*.

90. See *Sakhwill v. IDF Commander*; *Khamed v. IDF Commander*; *Khamamara v. Minister of Defense*; *Shweiki v. Minister of Defense*, HC 760/80 (5.1.81), unreported.

91. See e.g., *Khamri v. IDF Commander*; *Muzlakh v. Minister of Defense*; *Aga v. IDF Commander in Gaza* (1989) 44 (1) PD 536 [English summary: 23 *Isr YHR* (1993) 330]; *Craakara v. IDF Commander in Judea and Samaria*, 1991 (1) Takdin-Elyon 210.

92. *Kahavagi v. IDF Commander in Gaza* (1989) 44 (2) PD 227 [English summary: 23 *Isr YHR* (1993) 329]; *Elamarin v. IDF Commander*. In the latter case Justice Bach laid out the factors that the commander must consider in making his decision: (a) the severity of the act committed by the culprit; (b) whether the members of the household were aware of the culprit's activities; (c) the possibility of separating the culprit's apartment from other parts of the house; (d) the possibility of demolishing the culprit's apartment without harming the rest of the building; (e) the severity of the harm caused to others who were not aware of the culprit's activities (700–701). However, in reviewing the commander's decision Justice Bach ignored factors (b) and (c).

93. See, e.g., *Khamed v. IDF Commander*, 1990 (3) Takdin-Elyon 115; *Ghanimat v. Officer Commanding Central Command*.

94. See *Muzlakh v. Minister of Defense*; *Khamri v. IDF Commander*; *Zid v. IDF Commander in Judea and Samaria*, 1987 (1) Takdin-Elyon 30; *Shaahin v. Minister of Defense*, HC 970/89 (31.12.89), unreported; *Wahadan v. Minister of Defense*, 1990 (2) Takdin-Elyon 192; *Nakhla v. Officer Commanding Central Command*, 1990 (2) Takdin-Elyon 195.

95. In many decisions, the Court gives a detailed account of the acts by way of explanation for its conclusion that the severity of the acts justifies the harsh sanction: see, e.g., *Khamri v. IDF Commander*; *Abu Alaan v. Minister of Defense*; *Al-Radouan v. IDF Commander*; *Alzac v. Military Commander*; *Ahlil*

v. *Minister of Defense,* 43 (1) PD 568 [English summary: 23 *Isr YHR* (1993) 320]; *Al-Jamal* v. *Minister of Defense; Batash* v. *Military Governor of Gaza,* 1989 (2) Takdin-Elyon 276; *Samla* v. *IDF Commander in Judea and Samaria,* 1989 (2) Takdin-Elyon 120; *Kalbaani* v. *Officer Commanding Central Command,* HC 986/89 (25.2.90); *Wahadan* v. *Minister of Defense.*

96. See *Nazaal* v. *IDF Commander; Sabeach* v. *IDF Commander; Ghanimat* v. *Officer Commanding Central Command; Abu Khalawah* v. *Officer Commanding Home Front; Yassin* v. *IDF Commander.*

97. See, e.g., *Samla* v. *IDF Commander.*

98. Besides the decisions previously reviewed see *Sanuar* v. *IDF Commander,* 824; *Bakhari* v. *IDF Commander,* 95.

99. See *Al-Ajourme* v. *IDF Commander.* Also see *Ragabi* v. *IDF Commander,* 179.

100. See *Samla* v. *IDF Commander; Samaane* v. *Military Commander of Judea and Samaria,* HC 834/88 (5.3.89), unreported; *Abu Daka* v. *IDF Commander.*

101. *Khamamara* v. *Minister of Defense.*

102. Ibid., 756.

103. See *Khamri* v. *IDF Commander; Al-Radouan* v. *IDF Commander; Al-Jamal* v. *Minister of Defense.*

104. *Al-Jamal* v. *IDF Commander in Judea and Samaria,* 1989 (2) Takdin-Elyon 163. See also *Al-Sheekh* v. *Minister of Defense,* HC 1056/89 (27.3.90), unreported, in which the Court cited the *Al-Jamal* precedent adding that "as we are talking about sealing alone and not demolition, the owner of the apartment is not harmed."

105. *Al-Jamal* v. *IDF Commander,* 163.

106. See *Craakara* v. *IDF Commander.*

107. *Turkmahn* v. *Minister of Defense.*

108. Ibid., 220–221. Also see *Jabrin* v. *Minister of Defense,* in which the Court confirmed the decision to seal two rooms in a house, but overruled the decision to seal the kitchen that served all the remaining inhabitants.

109. See Tz. Kahane, "On Architecture, on Proper Norms and on the Quiet Overturn of a Juridical Rule" (in Hebrew) 41 *HaPraklit* (1994) 385, 399.

110. See *Abu Khalawah* v. *Officer Commanding Home Front; Yassin* v. *IDF Commander.*

111. See *Abu Khalawah* v. *Officer Commanding Home Front; Nazaal* v. *IDF Commander; Sabeach* v. *IDF Commander; Yassin* v. *IDF Commander.*

112. See, e.g., *Elkatzahf* v. *IDF Commander in Judea and Samaria* (1990) 44 (1) PD 614; *Shuahin* v. *IDF Commander in Judea and Samaria* (1990) 44 (3) PD 875 [English summary: 25 *Isr YHR* (1995) 325]; *Nazaal* v. *IDF Commander; Abu Khalawah* v. *Officer Commanding Home Front.*

113. See *Alrakab* v. *IDF Commander in Gaza,* HC 878/89 (4.1.90), unreported.

114. *Aga* v. *IDF Commander,* 539. Also see *Kahavagi* v. *IDF Commander,* 232; *Elkatzahf* v. *IDF Commander; Shuahin* v. *IDF Commander.*

115. But *cf.* A. Shalev, *The Intifada, Causes and Effects* (in Hebrew) (Tel Aviv: Papyrus, 1990), 127–129. Shalev attempts to examine the general deter-

rent effect of house demolitions after the beginning of the *Intifada* by compar-
ing the number of incidents of violence to the number of house demolitions in
the previous month. Shalev admits that his examination is not complete, but
maintains that his results "do point out the direction of matters." The results of
Shalev's work show that demolition did not have "an immediate effect on reducing the level of violence but, possibly the opposite effect." Also see S. Gazit,
Hamakel Vehagezer (Tel Aviv: Zmora-Bitan, 1985) 300, who presents opposing
views as to the efficacy of the measure as a deterrent.

116. This certainly has often been the Court's approach in cases relating to
civil rights in Israel. See, e.g., *Sa'ar v. Minister of Interior and Police* (1980) 34
(2) PD 169.

117. *Oijian v. IDF Commander; Alrakab v. IDF Commander; Abu Daka v.
IDF Commander in Gaza* (1989) 44 (3) PD 452; *Avida v. IDF Commander; Abu
Khalawah v. Officer Commanding Home Front; Ghanimat v. Officer Com-
manding Central Command.*

118. *Muzlakh v. Minister of Defense; Abu Khalawah v. Officer Command-
ing Home Front; Al-Jamal v. IDF Commander in Judea and Samaria,* 1989 (2)
Takdin-Elyon 163; *Sammane v. Military Commander; Wahadan v. Minister of
Defense; Laprukh v. IDF Commander in Judea and Samaria,* 1990 (2) Takdin-
Elyon 1122.

119. *Nazaal v. IDF Commander,* 347.

120. Ibid., 349. Also see the similar remarks of Justices Barak and Goldberg
in *Ghanimat v. Officer Commanding Central Command,* 74 and 75, and of Justice Barak in *Abu Khalawah v. Officer Commanding Home Front.*

NOTES TO CHAPTER 10

1. See E. R. Cohen, *Human Rights in the Israeli-Occupied Territories
1967–1982* (Manchester: Manchester University Press, 1985) 106.

2. A. Dayan, "We're programmed to deport" *Ha'aretz* Supplement, 17
January 1992, p. 19.

3. See *Violations of Human Rights in the Territories, 1990/91* (Jerusalem:
B'Tselem, The Israeli Information Center for Human Rights in the Occupied
Territories, 1991) 90. Also see A. Straschnov, *Justice Under Fire* (in Hebrew)
(Tel Aviv: Yedioth Ahronoth, 1994), 104 who states that sixty deportation
orders were issued from the beginning of the *Intifada* until 31.1.91. One of these
was cancelled on the recommendation of the advisory committee.

4. This is obviously also connected with the transferal of authority over
most of Gaza and parts of the West Bank to the Palestinian Authority under the
Oslo Accords and subsequent agreements.

5. *Marar v. Minister of Defense* (1971) 25 (1) PD 141. Although from the
Israeli political and legal perspective East Jerusalem is not regarded as part of
the Occupied Territories, until 1979 the law regarding deportations on security
grounds was identical to that in the Occupied Territories.

6. The original version of the regulation placed the power in the hands of
the High Commissioner. All his powers were taken over in 1948 by the respec-

tive governments of the areas that had been part of the British Mandate. The powers of the government in the West Bank and Gaza were assumed in 1967 by the IDF military commanders. Thus, instead of "government" in regulation 112, one must read "military commander of the area." *Na'azal v. IDF Commander in Judea and Samaria* (1985) 39 (3) PD 645, 648 [English summary: 16 *Isr YHR* (1986) 329].

7. See *Kawasme v. Minister of Defense* (1982) 36 (1) PD 617 (*Kawasme II* case) [English summary: 11 *Isr YHR* (1981) 349].

8. *Afu v. IDF Commander of the West Bank* (1987) 42 (1) PD 4 [English summary: 23 *Isr YHR* (1993) 277]. An English translation of this decision appears in 29 *International Legal Materials* (1990) 139.

9. *Kawasme II* case, 636.

10. Ibid., 646–647. As seen earlier, Justice Cohn held that regulation 112 had been repealed by the Jordanian Constitution and was only valid under the Interpretation Ordinance. Thus, the basis for the power of deportation was military legislation that was subject to the restrictions of customary international law.

11. *Kawasme II* case, 648.

12. Ibid., 649.

13. Ibid., 650.

14. *Na'azal v. IDF Commander in Judea and Samaria.*

15. Ibid., 653. See Dinstein, "Deportation of the Mayors from Judea" (in Hebrew) 8 *Tel Aviv U L Rev* (1981) 158. Justice Shamgar failed to mention that in the very same article Dinstein repeated the accepted view that article 49 of the Geneva Convention places an absolute prohibition on deportations from occupied territory. Dinstein argued that only deportations to slave labor or murder are outlawed by customary international law, while the prohibition against other types of deportations was an innovation of the Geneva Convention. Support for the view that customary international law prohibits deportation of protected persons from occupied territory is provided by T. Meron, *Human Rights and Humanitarian Norms as Customary Law* (Oxford: Clarendon Press, 1989) 48–49.

16. 1985 (4) Takdin-Elyon 10.

17. *Satiha v. IDF Commander in Gaza*, 12.

18. The Court also categorically rejected the argument that Gaza was no longer subject to a regime of belligerent occupation: ibid., 11.

19. See *Afu v. IDF Commander of the West Bank.*

20. See *Naasralla v. IDF Commander of West Bank* (1988) 43 (2) PD 265 [English summary: 23 *Isr YHR* (1993) 321].

21. *Marar v. Minister of Defense*, 143.

22. Ibid. The reference to "the state from which he arrived in Israel" seems to indicate that the Court confused the different types of deportation. The deportation order with which the Court was dealing was an order against a *resident* of East Jerusalem and there was no evidence that he had arrived from any other country.

23. This is an interesting argument. As we have seen, in decisions handed down some time after the *Marar* decision, the Court held that customary inter-

national law does not place an *absolute* obligation on a state to accept its own citizens (and therefore not to deport them). The only obligation is against *arbitrary* refusal to accept a citizen. Would the refusal of Jordan to accept a citizen who was being deported from the Occupied Territories be regarded as arbitrary?

24. *Marar* v. *Minister of Defense*, 144.

25. Ibid.

26. Ibid.

27. It should be noted that one of the two other judges on the bench, Justice Kister, declared that if the petitioner's life were in danger in Jordan, he should have openly informed the security authorities of the danger that awaited him in Jordan, and from what was hesitantly stated in the petition it was apparent that so far he had not done so.

28. (1985) 39 (1) PD 798 [English summary: 16 *Isr YHR* (1986) 330].

29. Ibid., 800.

30. *Maslam* v. *IDF Commander in Gaza* (1991) 45 (3) PD 444. As opposed to the *Shahahin* case the deportation orders in the *Maslam* case were based on regulation 112.

31. Ibid., 458.

32. Ibid., 459.

33. See Regulation 112 (8) of the Defence Regulations, 1945.

34. *Association for Civil Rights in Israel* v. *Minister of Defense* (1992) 47 (1) PD 267 (*Hamas Deportation* case) [English summary: 23 *Isr YHR* (1993) 353].

35. *Kawasme II* case.

36. See *Kawasme* v. *Minister of Defense* (1980) 35 (3) PD 113 (*Kawasme I* case) [English summary: 11 *Isr YHR* (1981) 344]; *Kawasme II* case.

37. See Kawa*sme I* case

38. Ibid., 120.

39. In a newspaper interview eleven years after the deportation, General (Res.) Benjamin Ben-Eliezer, who signed the deportation orders, explained that he had in fact acted to pacify the settlers. He conceded that Kawasme was a moderate and pragmatic leader who had been deported only because he was the mayor of the city in which the murder took place. Dayan, "We're programmed to deport," p. 23.

40. *Kawasme I* case, 119. Justice Landau was referring to the case of Dr. Ahmed Hamzi el-Natshe, a leading candidate in the pending elections for the mayoral post in Hebron, who was deported in March 1976. El-Natshe's lawyer submitted a petition to the Supreme Court challenging the legality of the deportation, but failed to request a temporary stay. The duty judge set the hearing for the afternoon, but before the petition could be heard the deportation was carried out. The judge who was to hear the motion, Justice Etzioni, wrote a decision severely criticizing the way the authorities acted to avoid judicial review: see HC 159/76 (20.3.76) unreported. A few years after his deportation Dr. el-Natshe was allowed to return to the West Bank. The case is discussed at length by M. Negbi, *Justice Under Occupation: The Israeli Supreme Court Versus the Military Administration in the Occupied Territories* (Jerusalem: Cana Publishing House, 1981) 82–88.

41. *Kawasme I* case, 139.

42. Ibid., 133.

43. Ibid., 123.

44. Ibid., 124–126.

45. Ibid., 125.

46. Ibid., 131.

47. The authorities acted according to the directive of Justice Landau. Two of the deportees were allowed to return to the West Bank in order to present their case before the advisory committee. On crossing the bridge between Jordan and the West Bank they were detained and the advisory committee convened in the vicinity of the bridge. After the committee recommended that the deportation orders be carried out the deportees submitted another petition to the court. *Kawasme II* case.

48. The deportee would be represented before the advisory committee by a lawyer or family member. In a further attempt to "sweeten" the temporary deportations, the military orders stated that the decision of the committee would be binding on the military commanders.

49. *Hamas Deportation* case, 289–290.

50. Ibid., 291.

51. Ibid., 292.

52. See H. Cohn, "Deportation According to Law" (in Hebrew) 1 *Mishpat Umimshal* (1993) 471. And cf. E. Benvenisti, "Judicial Review of Deportation Orders" (in Hebrew) 1 *Mishpat Umimshal* (1993) 441, 469. Benvenisti argues that as holding the hearings in Southern Lebanon would be a contravention of international law, the only way of interpreting the Court's ruling was to say that the hearings had to be held in Israel or the Occupied Territories.

53. N. Lerner, "Deportations from the Occupied Territories and the International Law" (in Hebrew) 4 *Plilim* (1994) 39, 44.

54. *Na'azal v. IDF Commander in Judea and Samaria*.

55. Ibid., 658.

56. See *Sachshir v. IDF Commander in Judea and Samaria* (1988) 43 (1) PD 529 [English summary: 23 *Isr YHR* (1993) 311]; *Matur v. IDF Commander in Judea and Samaria* (1989) 43 (2) PD 221 [English summary: 23 *Isr YHR* (1993) 316].

57. See *Matur v. IDF Commander in Judea and Samaria*, 224.

58. Ibid.

59. *Afu v. IDF Commander of the West Bank*, 65.

60. *Maslam v. IDF Commander in Gaza*.

61. Ibid. The Court added that the military commander's decision to close the proceedings was subject to the ordinary rules that apply to use of administrative discretion.

62. See *Boulus v. Advisory Committee* (1992) 46 (1) PD 466 [English summary: 25 *Isr YHR* (1995) 336].

63. *Marar v. Minister of Defense*, 142.

64. See *Awwad v. IDF Commander in Judea and Samaria* (1979) 33 (3) PD 309 [English summary: 9 *Isr YHR* (1979) 343].

65. *Shahabin v. IDF Commander in Gaza* (1984) 39 (1) PD 309 [English summary: 15 *Isr YHR* (1985) 277].

66. The petitioner contested the finding that he should be regarded as an infiltrator, but the Court found that since he had entered the Territories without permission after 1967 his claim was unfounded. The Court held that even if the petitioner had been a resident of the Territories before 1967, if he entered the area illegally after the IDF took control he met the legal definition of an infiltrator. Ibid., 321.

67. Ibid., 327.

68. Ibid., 328.

69. Ibid., 331.

70. *Na'azal* v. *IDF Commander in Judea and Samaria.*

71. *Baransa* v. *Officer Commanding Central Region* (1981) 36 (4) PD 247 [English summary: 17 *Isr YHR* (1987) 300].

72. *Shahahin* v. *IDF Commander in Gaza.*

73. *Na'azal* v. *IDF Commander in Judea and Samaria,* 655.

74. See *Afu* v. *IDF Commander of the West Bank; Lavadi* v. *IDF Commander on West Bank* (1988) 43 (2) PD 227, 237, 240 [English summary: 23 *Isr YHR* (1993) 309]. In a number of other cases the Court examined the evidence in detail and confirmed that the decision of the military commander was based on strong evidence without specifically mentioning the test laid down in the *Shahahin* case. *Matur* v. *IDF Commander on West Bank* (1988) 43 (3) PD 542; *Naasralla* v. *IDF Commander of West Bank; Shachshir* v. *IDF Commander on West Bank* (1988) 43 (2) PD 242.

75. *Kawasme II* case, 635.

76. *Maslam* v. *IDF Commander in Gaza.*

77. Ibid. Also see *Satiha* v. *IDF Commander in Gaza.*

78. See *Na'azal* v. *IDF Commander in Judea and Samaria,* 659.

79. *Satiha* v. *IDF Commander in Gaza.*

80. Ibid., 16.

81. Generally the evidence relates to actual terrorist activities or a senior leadership position in one of the Palestinian organizations that have been outlawed.

82. The two dissenting justices were Justices Barak and Orr. The Court never delivered a reasoned decision on the revocation of the temporary injunction.

83. See E. Benvenisti, "Judicial Review of Deportation Orders," 451. Also see B. Dayanim, "The Israeli Supreme Court and the Deportations of Palestinians: The Interaction of Law and Legitimacy," 30 *Stanford J of Int L* (1994) 115, 165.

84. The Court also refused to deal with arguments made against the specific orders that had been issued against each one of the deportees. It explained that these arguments should be addressed by the advisory committees that would deal with appeals. As Benvenisti points out (ibid.), this explanation does not cover general arguments that go to the very legality of the deportation, as the advisory committees are only empowered to deal with arguments against a specific deportation order, on the assumption that the military commander has the legal power to make such an order.

85. See Lerner, "Deportations from the Occupied Territories."

86. *Hamas Deportation case*, 281. (Emphasis in original).

87. For an excellent discussion of the way the Court dealt with this issue see E. Benvenisti, "Judicial Review of Deportation Orders."

88. It will be recalled that in the *Kawasme I* case, the deportation had already taken place before the matter reached the Court.

89. Resolution no. 799 (1992).

90. M. Kremnitzer, "Deport the Deportation—Some Comments on the Deportation Case, the High Court of Justice, Law, Politics and Morality" (in Hebrew) 4 *Plilim* (1994) 17.

91. This point is developed by G. Barzilai, E. Y. Yortman, and Z. Segal, "The Deportees Case, the Rule and the Rule of Law" (in Hebrew) 4 *Plilim* (1994) 9, 11, 14.

NOTES TO CONCLUSIONS

1. See *Morcous* v. *Minister of Defense* (1991) 45 (1) PD 467 [English summary: 23 *Isr YHR* (1993) 339].

2. *Electricity Company for Jerusalem District* v. *Minister of Energy and Infrastructure* (1980) 35 (2) PD 673.

3. See *Naazal* v. *IDF Commander in Judea and Samaria* (1994) 48 (5) PD 338.

4. Ibid., 347.

5. See M. Negbi, *Justice Under Occupation: The Israeli Supreme Court versus the Military Administration in the Occupied Territories* (Jerusalem: Cana Publishing House, 1981).

6. See Dotan, "Judicial Rhetoric, Government Lawyers and Human Rights: The Case of the Israel High Court of Justice during the *Intifada*," 33 *Law and Soc Review* (1999) 319.

7. Possibly the most dramatic example was the planned deportation of the mayor of Nablus, Bassam Shaka. Following a newspaper report on a conversation between Shaka and the Coordinator of Government Activities in the Territories, in which Shaka reportedly expressed support for a horrific terrorist attack on Israel's coastal road, an order for his deportation was issued. Shaka's wife petitioned the Supreme Court, which immediately issued an interim injunction against the deportation. Following this injunction, public pressure built up. At the Court's direction Shaka's case was brought before the advisory committee on deportations, and after Shaka declared that his views had been misrepresented the committee recommended revocation of the deportation order. The military commander acted on this recommendation. S. Gazit, *Trapped* (in Hebrew) (Tel Aviv: Zmora-Bitan, 1999) 94–95.

8. In many cases, the authorities backed down after a petition was submitted but before a hearing had been held. However, a practice also evolved under which the attorney for the potential petitioner, or for a human rights NGO, sends a copy of a petition to the state attorney's office before submitting it to court and the matter is subsequently settled without submission of the petition to court. Dotan, "Judicial Rhetoric, Government Lawyers and Human Rights."

9. Ibid. The reasons for this are not clear. One possible explanation is, of course, that there is far more arbitrariness in decisions of the military authorities in the Occupied Territories, thus forcing persons who are wronged to petition the Court more often than persons in Israel itself.

10. This point is developed by L. Shelef (Shaskolsy), *The Rule of Law and the Nature of Politics* (in Hebrew) (Tel Aviv: Papirus, 1996).

11. See J.A.G. Griffith, *The Politics of the Judiciary*, 4th ed. (London: Fontana, 1991) 272.

12. Ibid.

13. See R. Cotterrel, *The Sociology of Law*, 2nd ed. (London: Butterworths, 1992), 235: "Judges . . . as state functionaries, *cannot* neglect considerations of state interests and these may, on occasion, demand that doctrinal niceties be given short thrift in order to meet particular government emergencies."

14. *Sabeach* v. *IDF Commander in Judea and Samaria* (1996) 50 (1) PD 353.

15. *Kawasme* v. *Minister of Defense* (1980) 35 (3) PD 113 [English version: 11 *Isr YHR* (1981) 344].

16. Ibid., 121.

17. Ibid., 122.

18. See W. Brennan, "The Quest to Develop a Jurisprudence of Civil Liberties in Times of Security Crises," 18 *Isr YHR* (1988) 11.

19. I have developed this point elsewhere. D. Kretzmer, *The Legal Status of the Arabs in Israel* (Boulder: Westview Press, 1990) 136–139.

20. *Yeredor* v. *Central Elections Committee* (1965) 19 (3) PD 365.

21. See Kretzmer, *The Legal Status of the Arabs in Israel*, 24–26.

22. See *Yeredor* v. *Central Elections Committee*.

23. Ibid., 389.

24. See *Public Committee Against Torture in Israel* v. *State of Israel*, 1999 (3) Takdin-Elyon 458.

25. See, e.g., *Al-Karbutli* v. *Minister of Defense* (1948) 2 PD 5; *Al-Khouri* v. *Chief of Staff* (1949) 4 PD 34; *El-Rakhman* v. *Minister of Interior* (1951) 6 PD 364; *Ploni* v. *Minister of Defense* (1988) 42 (3) PD 133.

26. See *Kardosh* v. *Registrar of Companies* (1960) 15 PD 1151, upheld in further hearing in *Registrar of Companies* v. *Kardosh* (1961) 16 PD 1209.

27. See *Dweikat v. Government of Israel* (1980) 34 (1) PD 1 (*Elon Moreh* case) [English version: 9 *Isr YHR* (1979) 345]; *Kawasme* v. *Minister of Defense* (1982) 36 (1) PD 666.

28. *Schnitzer* v. *Chief Military Censor* (1988) 42 (4) PD 617.

29. See Kretzmer, *The Legal Status of the Arabs in Israel*, 136–139.

30. *Ayyub* v. *Minister of Defense* (1978) 33 (2) P.D. 113 (*Beth El* case) [English version: 9 *Isr YHR* (1979) 337].

31. Ibid., 132–133.

32. *Shahin* v. *IDF Commander in Judea and Samaria* (1986) 41 (1) PD 197 [English version: 18 *Isr YHR* (1988) 241].

33. Ibid., 216.

34. See E. Benvenisti, "Judicial Misgivings Regarding the Application of International Law: An Analysis of Attitudes of National Courts," 4 *European Journal of International Law* (1993) 159.

SELECT BIBLIOGRAPHY

BOOKS AND ARTICLES

Albeck, P. *Lands in Judea and Samaria.* Tel Aviv-Jaffa: District Committee of Israel Chamber of Advocates, 1985.

Alexander, G. J. "The Illusory Protection of Human Rights by National Courts During Periods of Emergency." 5 *HRJ* (1984) 1.

Amit-Kohn, U. et al. *Israel, the "Intifada" and the Rule of Law.* Tel Aviv: Israel Ministry of Defense Publications, 1993.

Aruri, N., ed. *Occupation: Israel over Palestine.* London: Zed Books, 1984.

Bar-Yaacov, N. "The Applicability of the Laws of War to Judea and Samaria (The West Bank) and to the Gaza Strip." 24 *Isr L Rev* (1988) 485.

Barzilai, G. *A Democracy in Wartime: Conflict and Consensus in Israel.* Tel Aviv: Sifriat Poalim, 1992.

———. "The Argument of 'National Security' in Politics and Jurisprudence." In *Security Concerns—Insights from the Israeli Experience,* ed. A. Kleiman, D. Bar-Tal, and D. Yaacobson, 243. Stamford and London: JAI Press, 1999.

———, Yortman, E. Y., and Z. Segal. "The Deportees Case, the Rule and the Rule of Law." 4 *Plilim* (1994) 9.

———. *The Israeli Supreme Court and the Israeli Public.* Tel Aviv: Papirus, 1994.

Benvenisti, E. "Judicial Misgivings Regarding the Application of International Law: An Analysis of Attitudes of National Courts." *European J of Int L* (1993) 159.

———. "Judicial Review of Deportation Orders." 1 *Mishpat Umimshal* (1993) 441.

———. *Legal Dualism: The Absorption of the Occupied Territories into Israel.* Boulder: Westview, 1990.

———. *The International Law of Occupation.* Princeton: Princeton University Press, 1993.

——. "The Role of National Courts in Preventing Torture of Suspected Terrorists." 8 *European J of Int L* (1997) 596.

——. "The Status of the Palestinian Authority." In *The Arab-Israeli Accords: Legal Perspectives*, edited by E. Cotran, and C. Mallat, 47. London: Kluwer, 1996.

Benvenisti, M. *Jerusalem, The Torn City.* Jerusalem: Isratypeset, 1976.

——. *The Sling and the Club.* Jerusalem: Keter, 1988.

——. *The West Bank Data Project, A Survey of Israel's Policies.* Washington: American Enterprise Institute, 1984.

Blum, Y. Z. "The Missing Reversioner: Reflections on the Status of Judea and Samaria." 3 *Isr L Rev* (1968) 279.

——. "The Redemption of Zion in International Law." 27 *HaPraklit* (1971) 315.

Boyd, S. M. "The Applicability of International Law to the Occupied Territories." 1 *Isr YHR* (1971) 258.

Bracha, B. "Restrictions of Personal Freedom Without Due Process of Law According to the Defence (Emergency) Regulations, 1945." 8 *Isr YHR* (1976) 296.

Brennan, W. "The Quest to Develop a Jurisprudence of Civil Liberties in Times of Security Crises." 18 *Isr YHR* (1988) 11.

Campbell, C. *Emergency Law in Ireland, 1918–1925.* Oxford: Clarendon Press, 1994.

Carroll, M. B. "The Israeli Demolition of Palestinian Houses in the Occupied Territories: An Analysis of its Legality in International Law." 11 *Mich J Int L* (1990) 1195.

Cassese, A. "Powers and Duties of an Occupant in Relation to Land and Natural Resources." In *International Law and the Administration of Occupied Territories*, edited by E. Playfair, 419. Oxford: Clarendon Press, 1992.

Cohen, E. R. *Human Rights in the Israeli-Occupied Territories, 1967–1982.* Manchester: Manchester University Press, 1985.

Cohn, H. "Deportation According to Law." 1 *Mishpat Umimshal* (1993) 471.

Commentary on IV Geneva Convention Relative to the Protection of Civilian Persons in Time of War, under the general editorship of J.S. Pictet. Geneva: ICRC, 1958.

Coon, A. *Town Planning under Military Occupation, An Examination of the Law and Practice of Town Planning in the Occupied West Bank.* Aldershot: Dartmouth, 1992.

Dayan, A. "We're programmed to deport." *Ha'aretz*, 17 January, 1992.

Dayanim, B. "The Israeli Supreme Court and the Deportations of Palestinians: The Interaction of Law and Legitimacy." 30 *Stanford J of Int L* (1994) 115.

Dershowitz, A. "Symposium: Human Rights in Times of War; Part 2—Compliance with International Conventions, Destruction of Houses, and Administrative Detentions." 1 *Isr YHR* (1970) 376.

Dinstein, Y. "Deportations from Occupied Territories." 13 *Tel Aviv U L Rev* (1988) 403.

——. "Deportation of the Mayors from Judea." 8 *Tel Aviv U L Rev* (1981) 158.

———. "Family Unification in the Occupied Territories." 13 *Tel Aviv U L Rev* (1988) 221.

———. "The Future Redemption of Zion in International Law." 27 *HaPraklit* (1971) 5.

———. "The International Law of Belligerent Occupation and Human Rights." 8 *Isr YHR* (1978) 104.

———. "The International Legal Status of the West Bank and the Gaza Strip—1998." 28 Isr YHR (1998) 37.

———. "The Israel Supreme Court and the Law of Belligerent Occupation: Article 43 of the Hague Regulations." 25 *Isr YHR* (1996) 1.

———. "The Israel Supreme Court and the Law of Belligerent Occupation: Demolitions and Sealing Off of Houses." 29 *Isr YHR* (2000) 285.

———. "The Judgment in the *Rafiah Approach* Case." 3 *Tel Aviv U L Rev* (1974) 934.

———. *The Laws of War*. Tel Aviv: Schocken, 1983.

———. "Power of Legislation in the Occupied Territories." 2 *Tel Aviv U L Rev* (1972/3) 505.

———. "Settlement and Expulsion in the Occupied Territories." 6 *Tel Aviv U L Rev* (1979) 188.

———. "VAT (value added tax) in the Occupied Territories." 10 *Tel Aviv U L Rev* (1984) 159.

Dotan, Y. "Judicial Rhetoric, Government Lawyers and Human Rights: The Case of the Israel High Court of Justice during the *Intifada*." 33 *Law and Soc Rev* (1999) 319.

Enker, A. "The Use of Force in Interrogations and the Necessity Defense." In *Israel and International Human Rights Law: The Issue of Torture*. Jerusalem: Center for Human Rights, Hebrew University of Jerusalem (1995) 55.

Falk, R. A., and Weston, B. H. "The Relevance of International Law to Palestinian Rights in the West Bank and Gaza: In Legal Defense of the Intifada." 32 *Harvard Int LJ* (1991) 129.

Friedman, R.I. *Zealots for Zion, Inside Israel's West Bank Settlement Movement*. New York: Random House, 1992.

Gasser, H. P. "Protection of the Civilian Population." In *The Handbook of Humanitarian Law in Armed Conflicts*, edited by D. Fleck, 209. Oxford: Oxford University Press, 1995.

Gazit, S. *Hamakel Vehagezer*. Tel Aviv: Zmora-Bitan, 1985.

———. *Trapped*. Tel Aviv: Zmora-Bitan, 1999.

Geva, B. "The Question of the Balance between Security Considerations and the Protection of Human and Civil Rights." 5 *Mishpatim* (1973/4) 685.

Ginbar, Y. *The Face and the Mirror: Israel's View of its Interrogation Techniques Examined*. (LL.M diss.) University of Essex, 1996.

Greenwood, C. "The Administration of Occupied Territory in International Law." In *International Law and the Administration of the Occupied Territories: Two Decades of Israeli Occupation of the West Bank and Gaza Strip*, edited by E. Playfair. Oxford: Clarendon Press, 1992.

Griffith, J. A. G. *The Politics of the Judiciary*. 4th ed. London: Fontana, 1991.

Henkin, L. "Is there a 'Political Question' Doctrine?" 85 *Yale L J* (1976) 597.

Hiro, D. *Sharing the Promised Land.* London: Coronet Books, 1996.

Hofnung, M. *Israel—Security Needs vs. The Rule of Law, 1948–1991.* Jerusalem: Nevo, 1991.

Kahane, Tz. "On Architecture, on Proper Norms and on the Quiet Overturn of a Juridical Rule." 41 *HaPraklit* (1994) 385.

Kalshoven, F. *Belligerent Reprisals.* Leyden: A.W. Sijthoff, 1971.

Kremnitzer, M. "Deport the Deportation—Some Comments on the Deportation Case, the High Court of Justice, Law, Politics and Morality." 4 *Plilim* (1994) 17.

———, and Segev, R. "Using Force During Investigations." 4 *Mishpat Umimshal* (1998) 667.

Kretzmer, D. "Judicial Review of Attorney General's Prosecutorial Decisions." 5 *Plilim* (1996) 121.

———. "Judicial Review of *Knesset* Decisions." 8 *Tel Aviv Studies In Law* (1988) 95.

———. "The Application and Interpretation of Geneva Convention IV—Domestic Enforcement and Interpretation." 26 (1) *Mishpatim* (1995) 49.

———. *The Legal Status of the Arabs in Israel.* Boulder: Westview Press, 1990.

———. "The New Basic Laws on Human Rights: A Mini-Revolution in Israeli Constitutional Law?." 14 *Netherlands Q HR* (1996) 173.

Kuttner, T. S. "Israel and the West Bank: Aspects of the Law of Belligerent Occupation." 7 *Isr YHR* (1977) 166.

Lapidot, R. "Public International Law." In *Forty Years of Israeli Law.* Jerusalem: Harry Sacher Institute for Legislative Research and Comparative Law (1990) 807.

Lerner, N. "Deportations from the Occupied Territories and the International Law." 4 *Plilim* (1994) 39.

Lustick, I. "Israel and the West Bank After Elon Moreh: The Mechanics of De Facto Annexation." 35 *Middle East Journal* (1981) 557.

———. *Unsettled States, Disputed Lands: Britain and Ireland, France and Algeria, Israel and the West Bank-Gaza.* Ithaca: Cornell University Press, 1993.

McDougal, M. S., and Feliciano, F. P. *The International Law of War.* Dordrecht: Martinus Nijhoff, 1994.

McDowall, D. *Palestine and Israel: The Uprising and Beyond.* Berkeley: University of California Press, 1989.

Meron, T. *Human Rights and Humanitarian Norms as Customary Law.* Oxford: Clarendon Press, 1989.

———. "West Bank and Gaza: Human Rights and Humanitarian Law in the Period of Transition." 9 *Isr YHR* (1979) 106.

Mishler, W., and Sheehan, R. S. "The Supreme Court as a Countermajoritarian Institution? The Impact of Public Opinion on Supreme Court Decisions." 87 *American Political Science Review* (1993) 87.

Nathan, E. "The Power of Supervision of the High Court of Justice over Military Government." In *Military Government in the Territories,* edited by M. Shamgar, 109. Jerusalem: Harry Sacher Institute for Legislative Research and Comparative Law, 1982.

Negbi, M. *Justice Under Occupation: The Israeli Supreme Court versus the Military Administration in the Occupied Territories.* Jerusalem: Cana Publishing House, 1981.

Nisan, M. *Israel and the Territories: A Study in Control.* Jerusalem: Turtledove, 1978.

Pacheco, A. "Occupying an Uprising: The Geneva Law and Israeli Administrative Detention Policy During the First Year of the Palestinian General Uprising." 21 *Columbia HRL Rev* (1990) 515.

Parker, R. B., ed. *The Six-Day War: A Retrospective.* Gainesville: University Press of Florida, 1996.

Pedatzur, R. *The Triumph of Embarrassment, Israel and the Territories After the Six-Day War.* Tel Aviv: Bitan, 1996.

Peleg, I. *Human Rights in the West Bank and Gaza: Legacy and Politics.* Syracuse: Syracuse University Press, 1995.

Peretz, D. *The West Bank, History, Politics, Society and Economy.* Boulder: Westview, 1986.

Playfair, E. *Demolition and Sealing of Houses as a Punitive Measure in the Israeli-Occupied West Bank.* Ramallah: Al-Haq/Law in the Service of Man, 1987.

———. "Playing on Principle? Israel's Justification for its Administrative Acts in the Occupied West Bank." In *International Law and the Administration of the Occupied Territories,* edited by E. Playfair, 205. Oxford: Clarendon Press, 1992.

Reicin, C. V. "Preventive Detention, Curfews, Demolitions of Houses, and Deportations: An Analysis of Measures Employed by Israel in the Administered Territories." 8 *Cardozo LR* (1987) 515.

Rishmawi, M. "Administrative Detention in International Law: The Case of the Israeli Occupied West Bank and Gaza." 5 *Palestine Y Int L* (1989) 83.

Ritov, L., and Baron, J. "Reluctance to Vaccinate—Omission Bias and Ambiguity." 3 *J of Behavioral Decision Making* (1990) 263.

———. "Status-Quo and Omission Biases." 5 *J of Risk and Uncertainty* (1992) 49.

Roberts, A. "Prolonged Military Occupation: The Israeli-Occupied Territories Since 1967." 84 *Am J of Int L* (1990) 44.

———. "What is a military occupation?" 54 *Brit Y Int L* (1984) 249.

Rubin, B. "Adoption of International Treaties in Domestic Law by the Courts." 13 *Mishpatim* (1984) 210.

Rubinstein, A. "The Changing Status of the 'Territories' (West Bank and Gaza): From Escrow to Legal Mongrel." 8 *Tel Aviv Studies in Law* (1988) 59.

Salzberger, E., and Oz-Salzberger, F. "The German Tradition of the Israeli Supreme Court." 21 *Tel Aviv U L Rev* (1998) 259.

Schindler, D. "The different types of armed conflicts according to the Geneva Conventions and Protocols." II *Recueil des Cours* (1979) 121.

———, and Toman, J. eds. *The Laws of Armed Conflicts—A Collection of Conventions, Resolutions and Other Documents.* Leiden: Sijthoff, 1973.

Schwenk, E. H. "Legislative Power of the Military Occupant under Article 43 Hague Regulations." 54 *Yale L J* (1945) 393.

Shalev, A. *The Intifada, Causes and Effects.* Tel Aviv: Papyrus, 1990.

Shamgar, M. "Legal Concepts and Problems of the Israeli Military Government—the Initial Stage." In *Military Government in the Territories,* edited by M. Shamgar, 13. Jerusalem: Harry Sacher Institute for Legislative Research and Comparative Law, 1982.

———. "The Observance of International Law in the Administered Territories." 1 *Isr YHR* (1971) 262.

Shamir, R. "'Landmark Cases' and the Reproduction of Legitimacy: The Case of Israel's High Court of Justice." 24 *Law and Soc Rev* (1990) 781.

Shefi, D. "The Reports of the U.N. Special Committees on Israeli Practices in the Territories—A Survey and Evaluation." In *Military Government in the Territories Administered by Israel, 1967–1980, The Legal Aspects,* edited by M. Shamgar, 294. Jerusalem: Harry Sacher Institute for Legislative Research and Comparative Law, 1982.

Shehadeh, R. *Occupier's Law: Israel and the West Bank.* 2nd ed. Washington: Institute for Palestine Studies, 1988.

———. *The West Bank and the Rule of Law.* Geneva: International Commission of Jurists, 1980.

Shelef, L. "The Green Line Is the Border of Judicial Activism: Queries about the Supreme Court Judgments in the Territories." 17 *Tel Aviv U L Rev* (1993) 757.

———. *The Rule of Law and the Nature of Politics.* Tel Aviv: Papirus, 1996.

Shetreet, S. "A Contemporary Model of Emergency Detention Law: An Assessment of the Israeli Law." 14 *Isr YHR* (1984) 182.

———. "The Scope of Judicial Review of National Security Considerations in Free Speech and Other Areas: The Israeli Perspective." 18 *Isr YHR* (1988) 35.

Simon, D. "The Demolition of Homes in the Israeli Occupied Territories." 19 *Yale J of Int L* (1994) 1.

Sommer, H. "Eppur si applica—The Geneva Convention (IV) and Israeli Law." 11 *Tel Aviv U L Rev* (1986) 263.

Stone, J. "Behind the Cease-Fire Lines: Israel's Administration in Gaza and the West Bank." In *Of Law and Man: Essays in Honor of Haim H. Cohn,* edited by S. Shoham. Tel Aviv: Sabra Books, 1997.

———. *No Peace, No Law in the Middle East.* Sidney: Maitland Publications PTY, 1969.

Straschnov, A. *Justice Under Fire.* Tel Aviv: Yedioth Ahronoth, 1994.

The Rule of Law in the Areas Administered by Israel. Tel Aviv: Israel National Section of the International Commission of Jurists, 1981.

Townshend, C. *The British Campaign in Ireland, 1919–1921.* London: Oxford University Press, 1975.

Von Glahn, G. *Law Among Nations.* 6th ed. New York: Macmillan, 1992.

———. "Taxation under Belligerent Occupation." In *International Law and the Administration of Occupied Territories,* edited by E. Playfair, 341. Oxford: Clarendon Press, 1992.

———. "The Protection of Human Rights in Time of Armed Conflicts." 1 *Isr YHR* (1971) 208.

Yingling, R. T., and Ginnane, R. W. "The Geneva Conventions of 1949." 46 *Am J of Int L* (1952) 393.

Zamir, E. *State Lands in Judea and Samaria—Legal Survey.* Jerusalem: Jerusalem Institute for Israel Studies, 1985.

Zamir, I. "On Justice in the High Court of Justice." 26 *HaPraklit* (1970) 212.

———. "Human Rights and National Security." 19 *Mishpatim* (1989) 19.

Zemach, Y. S. *Political Questions in the Courts: A Judicial Function in Democracies in Israel and the United States.* Detroit: Wayne University Press, 1976.

REPORTS AND PLANS

Drobles, M. *Settlement in Judea and Samaria: Strategy, Policy and Planning.* Jerusalem: WZO Settlement Division, 1980.

Interrogation of Palestinians During the Intifada: Ill-treatment, "Moderate Physical Pressure" or Torture? Jerusalem: *B'Tselem*, The Israeli Information Center for Human Rights in the Occupied Territories, 1991.

Master Plan for Settlement in Judea and Samaria and Development Plan for the Area for the years 1983–1986. WZO and the Ministry of Agriculture, 1983.

"Memorandum of the State Department Legal Advisor Concerning Legality of Israeli Settlements in the Occupied Territories." 17 (1) *International Legal Materials* (1978) 777.

Prisoners of Peace: Administrative Detention during the Oslo Process. Jerusalem: *B'Tselem*, The Israeli Information Center for Human Rights in the Occupied Territories, 1997.

Report of Commission of Inquiry into the Methods of Investigation of the GSS Regarding Hostile Terrorist Activities (Landau Report). 23 *Isr L Rev* (1989) 146.

Report of the UN Special Rapporteur on Torture. E/CN.4/1999/61.

Report on the Work of the Conference of Government Experts for the Study of the Conventions for the Protection of War Victims. Geneva: ICRC, 1947.

Report on the Work of the Preliminary Conference of National Red Cross Societies for the Study of the Conventions and of Various Problems relative to the Red Cross. Geneva: ICRC, 1946.

Routine Torture: Interrogation Methods of the General Security Service. Jerusalem: *B'Tselem*, The Israeli Information Center for Human Rights in the Occupied Territories, 1998.

Violations of Human Rights in the Territories 1990/1991. Jerusalem: *B'Tselem*, The Israeli Information Center for Human Rights in the Occupied Territories, 1990.

INDEX

acts of state. *See* justiciability: acts of state

administrative detention. *See* detention, administrative

administrative law, Israeli
 applicability of, 25–27
 duty of hearing under, 26, 156 (*see also* house demolitions: hearing requirement)
 principle of reasonableness under, 69
 principles of, 25–26
 review of military commanders' decisions under, 28, 86, 154, 169

Afu case, 47–48, 51–54, 167, 179, 180

Bach, Justice, 41, 48, 49, 51, 52, 53, 54, 179

bar association, establishment of, 61

Barak, Justice, 10, 14, 39, 68–71, 95, 98, 120, 140, 154, 160, 184

Basic Law: Human Dignity and Liberty. *See* Basic Laws on human rights

Basic Laws on human rights, 13, 15, 141, 142, 155, 188

Begin, Menachem, 8, 9, 81, 82

belligerent occupation, international law of
 applicability, 25, 32, 35–40, 98, 111, 197
 as convenient system of control, 197
 domestic enforceability, 35–36, 39
 principles of governing occupying power, 68–69
 See also Geneva Convention IV; international law, public; Hague Regulations

Beth El case, 22, 36, 43, 81–89, 95

Blum, Yehuda, 33, 38

Camp David Accords, 40, 81, 82, 85

Cheshin, Justice, 22, 150, 160, 192

Christian Society case, 20, 35, 36, 58, 59, 62, 64, 65, 67, 72

civilian settlements, Israeli, 75–94
 Alon plan, 75, 94
 Drobles plan, 76, 90
 establishment of, 1, 7–9
 and highway construction, 94
 justiciability of, 22–24, 43–44, 78
 legality in international law, 8, 77, 89, 99, 187, 218 n.7
 as military need, 80–89, 115, 187, 195